EUROPEAN
PHILOSOPHY
AND
THE
AMERICAN
ACADEMY

THE MONIST LIBRARY OF PHILOSOPHY

EUROPEAN PHILOSOPHY AND THE AMERICAN ACADEMY

Dallas Willard
Pascal Engel
Jorge Gracia
David Detmer
Walter Ward Parks
J. Claude Evans
Herman Philipse
Newton Garver
Christopher Norris
Joseph Margolis

Edited by Barry Smith

The Hegeler Institute
Monist Library of Philosophy
La Salle, Illinois
1994

First printing 1994

Printed and bound in the United States of America.

Library of Congress Cataloging-in-Publication Data

European philosophy and the American Academy / edited by Barry Smith.
—1st ed.
     p. cm.— (Monist library of philosophy)
     Includes index.
     ISBN 0-914417-07-X (pbk.)
     1. Education, Higher—United States—Philosophy. 2. Philosophy,
European. 3. Philosophy, French—20th century. 4. Derrida, Jacques.
5. Deconstruction. I. Smith, Barry, Ph. D. II. Series.
LA228.E87 1994
378.73—dc20   94-32595
                                            CIP

CONTENTS

Foreword

89854

FOREWORD

Many current developments in American academic life—multiculturalism, "political correctness", the growth of critical theory, rhetoric and hermeneutics, the crisis of scholarship in many humanities departments—have been closely associated with, and indeed inspired by, the work of European philosophers such as Foucault, Derrida, Lyotard and others. In Europe itself, in contrast, the influence of these philosophers is restricted to a small coterie, and their ideas have certainly contributed to none of the wide-ranging social and institutional changes we are currently witnessing in some corners of American academia.

The present volume contains the principal papers from the second Monist Colloquium, which was held to address the work of the so-called "advanced continental philosophers" from a critical, scholarly perspective, paying special attention to their influence in the United States. Participants in the meeting included, besides those represented here, Geoffrey Bannister, Myles Brand, Don Crawford, Gerald Graff, Elaine Marks, Kevin Mulligan, Tomas Pavel, Hugh Petrie, Hendrickje E.J. Spoor, and David Ramsay Steele.

The colloquium was held at the magnificent Wingspread site of the Johnson Foundation in Racine, Wisconsin, and I should like, on behalf of all participants, to thank Jon Vondracek and his staff, and also Todd Volker, for their excellent organisation. Thanks are due also the Lynde and Harry Bradley Foundation (Milwaukee), who once more supported the Monist Colloquium series with a generous grant, and to the Hegeler Institute and the Carus family, for providing the framework which made this series possible.

Barry Smith

State University of New York,
Buffalo

Part One

THE UNHINGING OF THE AMERICAN MIND: DERRIDA AS PRETEXT

This conference calls upon us to say something illuminating about the causes of the current condition of the university system in the United States. Social causation is a notoriously slippery topic. It is difficult to say anything with much confidence or even precision about it. But it is also too important to leave unexamined. So I shall simply state what considerable hard thinking and experience has brought me to believe about the matters at hand.

ON THE NATURE OF THE CRISIS

Almost everyone—left or right, up or down—who takes an interest in education agrees that the American university system is in some sort of crisis—and not just financially, or in the sense that it turns out multitudes of people who are uneducated. The heart of the university crisis is, in my view, the simple fact that its institutional structures and processes are no longer organized around knowledge. The life of knowledge is no longer their *telos* and substance. Knowledge and knowing is not what is had in view or consciously supported by them. The people in charge are *in fact* only very rarely thinking about knowledge. It is not what the place "is about" in the mental processes of those who determine, or think they determine, curriculum, program and personnel, what is to count as "good work" or "bad", and who is to be rewarded in various ways or not.

At the other end of university life, the Freshmen are not, on the whole, leaping with joyful anticipation at the prospect of learning, of coming to know. Epistemic hunger and joy are not displacing social and athletic activities or TV watching in their heart. They have many other things on their mind and are only set to go through a process at the university which they believe, for often quite obscure reasons, to be necessary for their present or future well-being. And that is just as well, for they are invariably faced with a set of choices, in progressing toward their degree, which have no unity of substance, content, or form, and at most is supposed to guarantee a certain "spread". (It is amazing the degree to which curriculum committees and administrators are devoted to "spread".)

The absolute disarray of the undergraduate curriculum—outside of the major and pre-professional subsections at least, and even within some of these—conclusively demonstrates that the university is not about knowledge. It is, of course, about granting degrees or certificates, but this is conditioned upon the accumulation of units, and has no necessary connection with the grantees becoming knowledge-able persons, which by and large they dutifully do not.

I am used to the reply that what I am describing has always been the case, that students and faculty have never been more serious about the life of knowledge than now, but that now they are just more *honest*, hence more virtuous. Here I can only say that such replies seem to me completely lacking in comprehension of the world of higher education in the pre-World War I era, for example, and for some time thereafter. The mere words written on the walls of college, university and even high school buildings then simply could not be written now. Imagine now writing on the walls of a new building at any educational institution the words: "Let only the eager, thoughtful and reverent enter here". This is written on the entrance to Pomona College, one of the better private colleges in the country. Written when they were, these words are now excusable because quaint. Written now they would be a joke. Of course they simply could not be written now.

The point I have been making about knowledge cannot be stated by responsible university leaders, nor can it be happily received by them when made by others. Nevertheless, it makes its presence felt in various ways, and that frequently results in statements from university administrators about how knowledge has changed, e.g. as a result of computers, or the ethnic mix of populations, or the way research is arranged and funded, etc. etc. The *Conseil des Universités* of the government of Quebec, for example, even took the quite reasonable step of asking Jean-Francois Lyotard to write a report on the state of knowledge in the Western world. There is a general recognition among higher-level administrators that *something* fundamental has changed.

Lyotard (*The Postmodern Condition,* p. 3) began his report with the statement—or "working hypothesis", as he calls it—that "the status of knowledge is altered as societies enter what is known as the postindustrial age and culture enters what is known as the postmodern age". To the surprise of no one, he reports that "scientific knowledge is a kind of discourse"—a metaphysical truism of the late Twentieth Century which silently crouches at the heart of our situation—and he proceeds progressively to characterise the kind of social ferment that makes up the "knowledge" interchange or condition within this discourse: always involving *social acceptance*, properly understood. (Lyotard, *The Postmodern Condition,* pp. 18-19, 35, 43)

To the surprise of some, perhaps, it emerges at the end of the report that "consensus has become an outmoded and suspect value". (Lyotard, *The Postmodern Condition,* p. 66) Consensus is not the form that epistemic social acceptance now takes. What marks "good work" at present is fruitful antagonisms within the discourse group. Not stability, but instability, is valued, where the best players in the game of "knowledge" are always requesting that *new* rules be introduced to govern the use of descriptive (denotative) language games, and "[t]he only legitimation that can make this kind of request admissible is that it will generate ideas, in other words, new statements." (Lyotard, *The Postmodern Condition*, p. 65)[1]

It is very easy to recognize current university reality in Lyotard's report, and especially in its conclusion, where good work and "the best minds" are understood in terms of novelty and antagonism. There is almost no limit to how far cleverness, careful arranging and chutzpah can take one "career wise". And, if we are prepared to adjust our use of the term 'knowledge' to conform to his implicit recommendation, we could then say that the university is after all concerned with knowledge and knowing, for it *is* concerned to be a place where "discourse" of the type discussed by Lyotard goes on.

But we could not say that the university is now concerned with knowledge "as always". For knowledge in *this* sense of a sub-species of social ferment is not traditionally what has been the focus of university life. In fact, what Lyotard describes is simply the social side of the life of research or inquiry as manifested today, largely in a university setting. He does a quite adequate job of stating what goes on. Many, perhaps most, do now accept the view that research is the function of the university, not knowing of the preservation, extension and communication of knowledge. We have "research universities", but no "universities of knowledge". This latter phrase is not just quaint or strange, but is strongly repugnant. Knowledge talk leaves university people with a vague but powerful uneasiness nowadays. Knowledge finds itself dismissed with various platitudes, such as that what you learn in school is obsolete by the time you graduate. Knowledge is suspect, slightly delusional. In any case it is conditional, transitory, temporal. But research is eternal. In the way things have developed it often seems you could have research going on—possibly by "top" researchers—without involving knowledge at all, except under a Lyotardian definition.

This only confirms what I have just said, that university life is no longer organized around knowing and knowledge. If it were, and if, in particular, research were subordinated to that, the academic scene would be very different from what it now is. Among other things, teaching would have a completely different value and position from what it has. But Lessing's statement, that if God stood before him and offered truth in one hand and the pursuit of truth in the other, he would take the pursuit, expresses an attitude that has simply *won* in the university context. It has won with such force that it no longer requires expression, and perhaps cannot be expressed. Truth sounds like dogmatism. It threatens self-expression, which is perhaps *the* primary right and value in contemporary America.

(At dog races the dogs chase a device which simulates game to them, and which they never catch. They are judged successful by their place in the pack, and by a finish line that has nothing to do with what they are chasing. They are unable to tell that what they are chasing is not what they think it is, and that this makes no difference to the masters of the game—or to them. All that matters to the masters is how fast they are running in relation to the others, or in seconds if they are running against a clock.)

Now what *is* the knowing and knowledge around which, I am claiming, the university system is no longer organized? We shall not try to put too fine a point on this matter here, where, indeed, we step into an area fraught with genuine philosophical difficulties. But the idea of knowledge that guided the universities for almost a millennium—the same idea which inspired both classical thought and the rise and development of modern science—is one according to which to know is to be able to think of things as they are, as distinct from how they only seem or are taken to be, and to be able to do so on an appropriate basis of experience or thought. To learn is to pass from a state of inability so to think of things to a corresponding state of ability. To inquire—or "do research", when it is subordinate to knowing—is to try to learn or find out how things are in some determinate respect.

Now, all hairsplitting and hare-starting aside, anyone who has read the literature of epistemology from Plato to Bertrand Russell will surely recognize that it is concerned with knowledge in the sense just delineated, even where sceptical conclusions are reached. Moreover, if you speak to the ordinary person about knowledge, and explain it in this manner, you will nearly always elicit immediate recognition—at least if they are far enough removed from the university classes that taught them that "No one knows nothin' nohow". In their lives they are constantly dealing with people who know and those who don't— sometimes it is themselves—and they have a fair understanding of what this distinction is. (Of course university people do too, when not defending a position or when they are dealing with their fringe benefits.)

Associated with this view of knowledge is the idea that there are *bodies* of knowledge, which are made up of a content and a method and which impose a discipline upon those who would master them, learn them, and thus become knowledge-able in the respective fields. Geography, for example, while expressing itself in a social and historical group of human beings and their cognitive products, is a body of knowledge about the earth and sundry processes near its surface. To master geography is not to master this social group, but to master the body of knowledge for the sake of which and in subjection to which the group exists. The body of knowledge is a human achievement to be sure. All of the true propositions, the truths, that go into geography (or whatever field) do not constitute it as a body of *knowledge*. They (or some significant subsection of them) must become known, and be in the possession of social institutions, along with the methods of knowing relevant to them, before they constitute a body of knowledge or a discipline. But there is a level of content and methodology for any field, which remains the same and provides the field's continuity through often wide-ranging changes, extensions and transformations that occur, e.g. from Aristotelian to Einsteinian physics, or from Euclid to analytic geometry and beyond. This in turn is anchored in the fact that knowledge, on the model here suggested, is knowledge of how things really are, as contrasted with how they seem or are taken to be.

Thus, as indicated by the very term, a discipline imposes norms as to what good work in its domain must be. Good work must significantly conform—dread word!—to the discipline. For if it does not, it departs (on the traditional view) from the reality that is presented and dealt with through the respective body of knowledge; and the consequences for human life, which depends upon successful accommodation to how things really stand, will be unpredictable at least, and at worst disastrous. Such, I submit, is the picture of knowledge and reality that gave rise to "higher" education and nourished it through the millennia.[2]

And this brings us to the point where the sense of crisis that many feel when looking at the current university scene can perhaps be understood. For the felt attack on the university at present takes the form of the claim that

> there is something pervasively and totally wrong with the disciplines, the bodies of knowledge, which collectively make up the intellectual/artistic, and hence the academic, world.

This claim or attitude rests upon two sub-claims: *First,* that these bodies of knowledge, and the practices based thereon, do not, never did, and in the nature of the case cannot, represent or present what they purport to deal with as it is, in distinction from how it seems or is taken to be. Knowledge, and hence the knowledge business, is not governed by an independent reality; and "good work" and who gets the university (and resultant social) rewards is not measured or dictated by something outside the assignment process or distinct from the persons who manage the process.[3] *Second,* that the process of reward assignment is on the whole controlled, not even by the conscious self-interest or other motivations of individual administrators, publishers, colleagues, etc., though these may on occasion play some part. What such people think they are doing is not necessarily what is happening at all, and in any case does not much matter. For they, and we all, are but the playthings of more encompassing powers, such as transcendental historicity, the dominant *episteme,* or some other pervasive and impersonal structure—class structure and dialectics have been big in the recent past, but less so now—that can only be discerned by something called 'theory'.

And this, of course, is where "those Frenchmen" come in. For they present themselves as, and are widely taken to be, masters of theory. They hold that, *for reasons revealed by their theory,* there is something pervasively and totally wrong with the traditional disciplines—as currently practised, not necessarily in the past, but certainly in the present—and with how they have been conceptualized as the basis for institutions of higher education (and human existence) in the Western world.

This was the Marxist view, but it survives on the Rousseauism that has always been powerfully attractive to Americans—whether they know his name or not—and also was central to the Marxist vision.[4]

The main point where this all forcefully comes home in the current university setting is in the treatment of texts. The undermining of the normative power of the disciplines seems at the popular level to open the way to saying that *any* reading of a text by anybody has a certain legitimacy to it—and this can be rationalized in various ways—or to saying that the reading of the text that is socially sustainable at present is the right one, as long as it *is* socially sustainable. I do not attribute such views to any of our Gallic theorists, but they certainly are held by people who claim to be influenced by them. And the intellectual atmosphere at the teacher/student nexus is thick with such views, coming from both of its sides. This goes along with the view, commonly defended or assumed, that all texts are as good, or can be as good, as any other, since there is no objective ordering of texts as to their value, and no canon other than what is politically enforced.

Now texts and the instrumentalities of their interpretation are the primary means through which humanity in its developed forms passes on its ideas and learnings about life and preserves its identity through time. Concern about how texts and the disciplines in which they are interwoven are treated in the university thus becomes a concern for those concrete forms of humanity (e.g. American society now) in which the university stands as the authority center: that is, the center of *right* to say how things are, and indirectly to determine what may or shall be done.

If these centers come under the control of those who hold such "open" views of the meanings of texts, what limits would there be to what, in the Lyotardian ferment, might present itself as knowledge? And knowledge always presents itself in human life as what ought to be conformed to, or at least may be conformed to, in action. It is determinative of the boundaries of the obligatory and the permissible. If the texts are "open", what standards could then be sustained against desire and will, either at the level of the individual, or in social institutions and practices? Will not, as Plato feared, the belly capture the heart and break its subordination to the head? Will not brute force—call it "reason" in society or history if you will—become what determines law and propriety, as social processes come to be managed by people who simply know how to get their way among a mass of those who no longer believe that they can, with the aid of their culture's texts and the traditional disciplines, determine how things are in nature, art or morality, regardless of how anyone wishes them to be or how people with social authority present them? Will not knowledge itself, as traditionally understood and looked to as the guide to life, simply be lost—or at least be degraded and devalued as a bulwark against desire embodied in political and social objectives? Is this not happening now?

BASIC CAUSES OF THE DISPLACEMENT OF KNOWLEDGE AS *TELOS* OF THE AMERICAN UNIVERSITY

What are the main causal factors back of the current crisis in higher education in the United States? I shall briefly consider the three which I regard as most influential, though several others will be mentioned in the process.

First there is egalitarianism, than which nothing is more dear to the American heart. As the idea that all people should receive equal treatment before the law, it is a moral ideal necessary for a good society and state. However, such equality is not what is commonly understood in the American context where "equality" is exalted. What is understood is that one person is just as good as another. In particular, *I* am just as good as *you* are—whoever you may be.

This deep set of American personality wells up spontaneously in the arts. James Dickey's epic poem, "Sermon", now in stage production, tells the females in its audience: "We should feel as free and correct as the animals feel. They may be penned up, but they strain toward sex wherever they are. You're entitled to sex, to freedom—freedom from male and religious dominance. We are whole and should treat ourselves accordingly."[5] The basic point here is not really about women or "women's issues", but about what people are just in virtue of being human. They are all equal and all wonderful and therefore entitled to do what they want. The drive to be thought in no way deficient often takes amazing forms, such as a recent insistence that deafness be regarded "not as a deprivation of sound, but an enhancement of vision".[6]

But how does this affect the situation in American universities? In particular, how does it deflect away from knowing and knowledge as the *telos* of the institutions of higher learning? Very simply: by filling them with people to whom knowledge and knowing in themselves mean little or nothing, and who think of themselves as just as good as anyone else and having a perfect right to occupy a university position nonetheless.

If we take the education system as a whole, from the early grades on, the most obvious thing about it is that most of the students and much of the staff are not there to learn or teach the disciplines, and in any case are not really engaged in doing so during most of their time. This then carries over to the system of higher education, which has passed from being an opportunity for those who love and revere knowledge, art and scholarship to live in their element, to an obligation which people who care nothing for such things must endure in order to achieve security, respectability and a pleasant life. The overwhelming percentage of those who are present in the university are people who do not feel diminished by an almost total ignorance of mathematics, the history and nature of the sciences, literature or art and its function in life, the ideas which have governed the great civilizations, or...you name it. This is because they do not regard knowledge as a fundamental value in its own right. They would never miss it but for extrinsic reasons.

Now equality in this vague but powerful social sense was "on paper" in America long before it had any significant impact on the university situation. This was mainly because university training was seen, generally, as having little connection with money or success, and usually—as in my own childhood—was actually regarded as a move in the opposite direction. It had a vague superiority about it, which was a kind of consolation prize for having lost in the race for the things that *really* matter in life. But this all begin to change rapidly when hundreds of thousands of GI's begin to flood into academia, after the Second World War, on "The GI Bill of Rights" (more precisely, The Servicemen's Readjustment Act of 1944).

Then the government began to pour money into university research, in response to needs of the economy, industry and the military, and also into the construction of university property. The university became associated with vast amounts of money. In the 50s and 60s huge, totally new universities sprouted in empty spaces previously frequented by rabbits. As space became available for masses of students for whom there previously was just no place available in higher education, government and government supported scholarships were abundantly provided. The challenges of the 60s to the university itself, as anti-egalitarian, was predicated upon the presence in the universities of a huge mass of people who were not there for knowledge but for "opportunity". The effects of these challenges have been widely studied by now. College and university education was simply forced to become something of which all with a right to admittance were capable, given their interests and talents.

To say that "the mass"—as Ortega y Gasset has studied it in his crucial book, *The Revolt of the Masses*—has now occupied the universities, and that this is a major causal factor in the crisis described above, is *not* to say that the students or faculty of the current university are either malicious, lazy, or stupid. In fact, I believe them with very few exceptions to be just the opposite—though some of my acquaintances who are university administrators find this laughable. It is to say that they do not live for knowledge, knowing, learning, and teaching.

We have to add that there is no reason why all people should live for these. Probably a relatively small percentage of humanity should. But American society tells its citizens that the way to security, respect and pleasure lies through higher education, and cites statistics that tie potential employment and income to the level of schooling attained. This forces masses of people into a system that makes little of knowing, but everything of research and getting credits. Then the call to displace knowledge and make other objectives—top-flight research, efficiency in the work place ("competing in world markets"), rectification of social structures, service to society, getting a good job or position, etc. etc.—the *telos* of higher education takes firm root in the minds of those for whom knowledge and knowing has little or no intrinsic value anyway.

A second major factor leading to the current state of the university in this country is empiricism. By this term I refer to the tendency to limit reality, knowledge and value to the sense-perceptible, including the "feelable". Here, as with egalitarianism, we are not dealing with a philosophical conclusion so much as with a social reality, historically developed and developing. Pitirim Sorokin's book *The Crisis of Our Age* is an indispensable resource for understanding empiricism as a cultural reality.

Knowledge itself, and most of the things worth knowing, are not sense-perceptible. This is well illustrated by the field of literature—or, more generally, by reference to texts of all sorts. Literature is not sense-perceptible—though of course one can see and touch books and pages. Nor is the experience of literature or the powers and values interwoven with it, which is what literature as a field of knowledge really deals with. (It is hardly the physics of pages.) But if empiricism is correct, then what you feel when you read a book or poem is the limit of its value. Admittedly, some theorists have toyed with such an idea. I. A. Richard's seems to me to come close to it, at least. But literature as a discipline, creative or interpretative, simply can't survive on such an approach, any more than logic as a discipline can survive if you try to treat validity or implication in terms of the feelings arguments give to people, or try to turn it into the physics of sentences.[7] There is just nothing left that will permit logic to be a field of knowledge, and a similar point must be made for literary studies and all of the humanities and social sciences.[8] Very few of the things in which human life has a knowledge interest, and very few of the things studied in the university, can be sensuously comprehended, though most involve some element of the sense-perceptible. And least of all, perhaps, are knowledge and knowing themselves sense-perceptible.

So how can knowledge justify itself in the face of a society that is dominated by empiricism? It cannot. Thus we see once again why knowledge has had to be displaced as the *telos* of the American university.

Empiricism has also adversely effected the status of knowledge in American culture by giving rise to a version of representationalism in the theory of knowledge—though it is not the only way in which such a theory of knowledge can arise. This version is also sometimes called "epistemological dualism".[9] It is mainly responsible for the view that, in consciousness of objects, we never contact *them* but only our images or representations of them. Thus Hume in his way, and Kant in his, held that all of the identities dealt with cognitively and practically in the world around us are products of our mind (plus "something" in Kant's case). Stated in this general form, their philosophies come out with exactly the same *result* as Derrida's, though the arguments and explanations are different. From the middle of the 20th Century on, "representations" became linguistic, on the Carnapian or the later Wittgensteinian model, and consciousness itself became a linguistic activity. The fact that two thousand years of close scrutiny of consciousness by some pretty bright people had not revealed that consciousness is linguistic suggests to me that the linguisticization of consciousness was not driven by a deeper insight into consciousness, but by the need to make consciousness a part of the physical, sense-perceptible world, which words, sentences, and utterances arguably are. So today, as is well known, what stands between us and a world as it is, apart from us, is not inner representations—ideas, images, impressions—but the language(s) we speak as a part of the culture that defines us. And this is a crucial move for the current university situation. It allows a new dimension of attack upon knowledge as traditionally conceived. The most austere of theories now become language, and this enables us to say such things as "Theory, you know, is just another practice", which means just another manifestation of culture. And there is thought to be no meta- or super-culture or language from which all other cultures can be comparatively judged. It is a later dictate of egalitarianism—and a university dogma today—that no culture can be judged superior to another. Here we see how empiricism supports that position.

The final major causal factor which I shall mention here as leading to the current state of the university is the absolutizing of freedom. There are now only two unquestioned values or justifications for action in American culture. One is pleasure (which gets in under the empiricist wire) and the other is freedom or doing what you want (which is also commonly regarded as feelable). That something "feels good" or is "what you want to do" are unquestioned and strong *prima facie* reasons for action. People are regarded as right and rational if they act upon them, unless there is some strongly countervailing reason, which in turn will have to be spelled out ultimately in terms of longer-run pleasure or freedom. So-called "natural" rights—which Bentham, with genuine hedonistic insight, called "nonsense on stilts"—from time to time threaten this neat arrangement, but with little prospect of setting it aside in American culture, where natural and other rights are most commonly invoked *only* to shore up the pursuit of pleasure and freedom.

Freedom absolutized exists culturally in a sort of free-floating equation with individualism ("doing your own thing", "being your own person") and therethrough with egalitarianism. This complex of ideation and motivation arranges itself in opposition to authority, and opens the way to an automatic and painless triumph for the rebel and the sceptic. To question authority is a sign of intelligence and a sceptical pose can be made to pass for brilliance. Scepticism does not have to be *earned* through the attainment of knowledge.

Now knowledge, by contrast, is essentially the sort of thing that cannot be just any way you please. If you are to know you must painstakingly and even servilely submit yourself to the relevant subject matter and methodologies. The recent popularity of books written against method, or of books with titles such as *Truth and Method*—where truth is opposed, in a certain subtle but fundamental sense, to method—or of theories according to which the major scientific advances occur in certain cataclysmic leaps between incommensurable states of research history, is to be understood as a part of the drive to replace the traditional view of knowledge and knowing with an anti-realist, social process view of knowledge. The attacks on positivistic and falsely objectivistic interpretations of science have important points to make. But the widespread acceptance of the anti-method tendency is not, I think, based upon widespread insight into the nature of knowledge and reality, but upon "Representational" theories of knowledge plus that drive to absolutize will and freedom which constitutes romantic revolutionism, arising out of the eighteenth century, and which harmfully extends individualism, deriving from the late Middle Ages.

Refusal to accept servitude to painful method is a reason why one of the most dismal aspects of university life in America is its pervasive incompetence in mathematics and in languages. And just think of what vast possibilities in the way of knowledge and knowing is lost to the individual because of this. Most everything worth doing is painful and undesirable in its early stages. On the bedrock foundation of egalitarianism, empiricism and freedom, getting through to the "fun" part of languages and mathematics is more than most can manage.

Now, if I am right, egalitarianism, empiricism, and absolutized freedom, understood not as mere philosophical views, but as ideational and motivational complexes developing historically and concretized in American society, are the three main factors leading to the displacement of knowledge and knowing as the spirit, substance or *telos* of the university system. Other things that currently play an important role in university life could be mentioned, but they are of secondary importance when compared to these three. For example, the influence of Pop Culture and "Art". Or the removal of logic from the liberal arts curriculum, often replaced by a strange amalgam called 'critical thinking'. Logic, of course, has something to say about what is essential to knowledge. How could one even know what knowledge is without an understanding of logic? Yet you often find logic spoken of as in instrument of oppression today. And, in any case, it is a field of exact knowledge, where, as in mathematics, you either measure up or you don't. On the other hand, the talk of "many logics" that is now so common, inside technical philosophical circles and out, both has the effect of making logic seem arbitrary (which fits right into the scene, of course), and of inviting people to find or invent "logics" of their own, if they don't like the conclusions that are coming down on them. This makes it very easy to judge work in terms of the "suitability" of its conclusion to social demands rather than in terms of the validity and soundness of the process itself. ("Judged by whom?" we hear in the background, as if this question were *deep*.)

The flight from logic leaves little recourse but to submit to the best professional practice in whatever academic field may be concerned, and opens the way to the faddishness that characterizes the social sciences and the humanities in particular, as this or that powerful personality or trend occupies the ground. Once logic as an objective discipline is set aside, the no doubt necessary pattern of inference to the best explanation too easily allows the "best explanation" to be determined socially or within the politics of the profession. Indeed, explanation itself may be given a socio-historical interpretation.

WHAT ARE DERRIDA *ET AL.* TO ALL OF THIS?

So we and our universities exist in a society where what is widely taken to be best is cause of some of our worst problems. Our dearest social and personal ideals create a dominant mind-set in which a rich and socially powerful institution such as the university can hardly fail to be deflected from its historic mission of knowledge, and therefore is seen by many observers as threatened with the lost of its integrity. Now we turn to the question of whether the deconstruction phenomenon, as we might call it, is responsible for the threat. What I have said thus far surely makes it clear that I can accept no such simple account. But that is not the end of the story. Deconstructionism does exercise an influence, and it really is, in my opinion, in the direction feared by those who resist it. However, it is more reasonable to think of the university crisis and the deconstruction phenomenon as joint effects of a common cause than to think of one as, simply, the cause of the other—though, once established, they may each significantly influence the other. To suppose that deconstructionism and associated thought currents are *the* cause of our problems in academia would be a severe misdiagnosis. They may exacerbate a pre-existing bad situation. But the problem was here before them, and if you got rid of them you would still have the problem.

Why should we not hold Derrida *et al.* more responsible than this? There are, I believe, grounds other than the streams of social causation which far preceded them. Looking at the specifically philosophical interpretations of thought (language) and reality that occupied the American scene before or independently of Heidegger, Habermas, Derrida, *et al.*, we find that Quine and Wilfrid Sellars alone are enough to make Derrida's announcements of "no transcendental signifieds", no "original" data or conceptualizations, no access to the "real stuff" apart from the shapings imparted by language, a little late, to say the least. Anglo-American philosophy has had no first rate philosopher who was a coherent realist since C. S. Peirce. Russell is the closest we have come to it, but he could never shake the idea that metaphysics (ontology) can only be a shadow cast by logic—which with other confusions (especially those about sense data) prevented him from working out a view of the mind/object nexus that would accommodate knowledge in the sense explained above. In any case, from Dewey, through C. I. Lewis, and on through Quine and Sellars, the views of knowledge arrived at really differ very little—especially in outcome—from what the deconstructionists hold, though the role of history, power, and mystical factors such as Derrida's "living present", are of less significance in the continuing American tradition. And the ride of Logical Positivism and Ordinary Language Philosophy through American thought certainly did nothing to blunt its basically anti-realist thrust.

So, in fact, the deconstructionist phenomenon adds little to American thought at the more austerely philosophical level of analysis. But another reason why we should not hold Derrida and company heavily responsible for the current academic tempest that often swirls around their names is that few of those highly visible American figures, in literature and other fields, who claim to be under their influence really do understand the basic elements of deconstructionist thought. They simply use Derrida and others as authorities within professional circles where their names carry weight.

Paul A. Bové, for example, has written a book called *Destructive Poetics: Heidegger and Modern American Poetry*. Armed with Heidegger's attack on or interpretation of the "present to hand", and the metaphysics of presence, Bové relentlessly goes after "reification", opposing it to the "openness" of language (and life and reality, of course). The closed structures of "the reifying West" once set aside, he then provides an interesting and sophisticated reading of openness and free play in the poetry of Whitman, Stevens and Charles Olson. His is a book well worth reading. But it simply starts from a kind of extreme process philosophy that is not grounded in Heidegger's *work* or much of anything else, and it does not take account of the fact, which Derrida recognizes, that Heidegger is much more of an essence philosopher than many of his hang-ers-on would like. I really doubt that "the ongoing process of uncovering, of disclosing the new which occurs in Heidegger's philosophical destruction" (Bové, *Destructive Poetics* p. 161) has much in common with the "openness" that Bové emphasizes and reads out of his poets.

A similar point is to be made with reference to Barbara Herrnstein Smith's widely influential book *Contingencies of Value* already referred to. Basically, she has rediscovered variability in experiences of the same objects, and draws extreme relativist conclusions (especially about valuations of aesthetic objects), which she quite consistently declines to prove. But then she admits that she *does* "attempt to point the way quite energetically" only "because, since she cannot herself live any other way, she's glad for a bit of company". (Smith, *Contingencies of Value* pp. 183-184) That is the last sentence of her book. She's kidding! Of course no publisher would have published the book to help her get some company, nor would she be appointed, paid or promoted just to help her in that regard. In fact, her career moves on the power of the deconstructionist phenomenon in her profession, where it—and therefore her book—is regarded by influential people as correct and justified in how it presents experience and its objects. But she herself does not detail the logic by which discovered relativ-ities have the implications she claims, and she does not explicate the fundamen-tal arguments and analyses of Derrida and others concerning language, con-sciousness and the world. He, along with the deconstructive tendency in modern and contemporary thought, simply serves as a pretext by virtue of a system of authority that functions in her professional setting.

Bové and Smith are among the more careful workers who take Heidegger and Derrida as authority figures. Christopher Norris refers scathingly to "the Derridian camp followers", and rejects the idea that "'deconstruction' is syn-onymous with a handful of overworked catch-words ('textuality', 'freeplay', 'dissemination' and the rest) whose promiscuous usage at the hands of literary critics bears no relation to the role they play in Derrida's work." (Norris, *What's Wrong with Deconstruction,* pp. 137, 139) He insists that "deconstruction dif-fers so markedly from the work of neo-pragmatist adepts like Richard Rorty and Stanley Fish" precisely because of Derrida's concern with the coherence of ideas and his "refusal to accommodate 'current beliefs and practices'". (*Ibid,* p. 139) Deconstruction properly understood respects and follows all legitimate canons of rigor in logic and methodology. So says Norris, whom I have chosen to quote because he represents the most mature and thoughtful development of the Derrida–Searle interchange.

Now I agree with the need to distance deconstruction from the excesses of the camp followers. That is a right which every creative thinker and every seri-ous tendency of thought must reserve to itself. But Norris does not do justice to the extent in which Derrida, intentionally or not, both licenses the excesses of his devotees (though he might never commit them) and justifies the continuing attacks of people like John Searle and John Ellis upon himself as one who is not rigorous and logical in his own analyses and writings. Norris can insist all he wishes on Derrida's allegiance to rigor, but, in fact, anything like standard logic, and the determinacy of concept and proposition which it presupposes, is indelibly tarred with the brush of logocentrism by Derrida. And if there is anything that you learn from Derrida (and Heidegger) it is that logocentrism just doesn't "get it." Logocentrism is precisely what is wrong with knowledge as traditionally conceived in the Western world. And if this is so, then as long as Derrida stays within logocentric boundaries he too isn't "getting it". Since we can, to the contrary, assume that he *is* "getting it", we can assume that he is not operating within the confines of logic by any common conception.

And in fact he isn't. The many stylistic and personal devices he uses in his writing and speaking to cause the logocentric boundaries and hierarchies and orders to shudder and to establish movements and connections associated with terms such as "differance" and "trace" and so forth: all of these are extra-logo-centric or at least mainly so. If they are warranted (or not) in any epistemic sense, it is a sense that falls beyond logic. Norris speaks of how Derrida, in tearing Searle apart in their well-known encounter, was "activating latent or unlooked-for possibilities of sense which thus become the basis for a scrupulously *literal* reading which none the less goes clean against the intentional or manifest drift of Searle's argument." (Norris, *What's Wrong with Deconstruction*, p. 143; cf. p. 151)—Well of course, "latent or [?] unlooked-for possibilities of sense" which are then made the "basis" (?) for "a scrupulously *literal* reading" that flatly contradicts the "manifest drift" of an author's argument! Neither Derrida nor Norris nor any other rigorous deconstructionists have ever made any sense of this contrast between manifest and latent sense. And no wonder, for some of the deepest of metaphysical issues are involved. (What is it to be or not be part of or necessary adjunct to a sense—manifest or otherwise? What kinds of entities are senses? Etc.) Yet this is precisely the boundary between logocentrism and whatever else there is to thought and its objectivities. You begin to "deconstruct" when you move across the boundary and out of "mere" logocentric analysis. Derrida has never tamed this area in such a way that his admirers could be held responsible in it and his critics could be satisfied that what he is doing is anything other than what the loosest "reader response" theory of texts and their meanings would allow.

What this all really comes down to, I think, is that "deconstruction" is not a *method* of thought. It is at best a set of *claims about* thought and discourse and their meanings. If you look at the most fundamental "result" in Derrida's *corpus*, the "demonstration" (if that is a proper term) in *Speech and Phenomena* "that nonpresence and otherness are internal to presence",[10] you will find many claims (about the "primordial structure of repetition" for example), stipulative definitions ("ideality"), plays on words ("re-presentation"), and stories, e.g. about how the experience of voice gives an illusion of presence. But you will not find a sound argument, or even anything put forward as such, for Derrida's earth-shaking conclusion. And this in what Norris insists is "one of the finest achievements of modern analytical philosophy, taking that description to extend well beyond its current, strangely narrowed professional scope". (Norris, *What's Wrong with Deconstruction,* p. 150)

Derrida is a brilliant and fascinating individual who has been able to make a personal style look like cognitive substance in a professional context where knowledge in the traditional sense has already been socially displaced. But deconstruction is no method, any more than was the "ordinary language analysis" that arose and dominated philosophical thought in the Anglo-American countries for a few decades. The latter sustained itself on the personal style of Wittgenstein, with Ryle and Austin as lesser lights. Recall the lengthy interchanges on the nature of logic between Strawson or Ryle, on the one hand, and Carnap or Quine on the other. It sustained itself on personalities for a time. Long enough to weed out or permanently disqualify a large number of graduate students and faculty who didn't get "it", and to professionally lionize others who did. These latter went on to careers as ordinary language philosophers or Wittgensteinians. Then suddenly everyone realized that there was just nothing there to get. A large number of people had to spend the last decade or so of their careers being tolerated while they kept getting what was not there to get. Wittgenstein himself was buried, and later resurrected as an outstanding "Continental" philosopher, where he is probably much happier.

Something similar will happen with Derrida, though I predict a less substantial afterlife in his case. Wittgenstein was after all, I think, one of the two or three greatest philosophical minds of this century. But Derrida only stepped into a pre-existing situation in the American academy that gave him an influence which his creative powers would otherwise not have produced. We need to keep his effects distinct from the deeper-lying causes of the current crisis in the American university, and not try to rectify the latter by attacking him. We also need to try to keep younger scholars from tying their career to him and the deconstruction phenomenon, and to prevent colleagues and students from being black-balled because they do not get his "it" that in truth is not there to get—no small task at present.

*

I should add in closing: I am very happy to be a member of a university faculty, and I treasure my colleagues, students and administrators. I think it is a wonderful place to be, and can not readily come up with something I would like better or think of greater value.

Secondly, I have not tried to go deeply into particular points of philosophical analysis (especially of the mind/language – object nexus), and therefore have begged many crucial philosophical questions. This is regrettable, but otherwise it would have been impossible to cover the topics that I thought would be most relevant to the conference for which these remarks were prepared.

Thirdly, I have spoken of the "unhinging" of the American mind in purposive contrast to Alan Bloom's idea of the "closing" of the American mind. I might as well have chosen "disarray". Such language seems more appropriate because the "closing" which Bloom discusses is seen by him as the result of a resolute "openness" that he regards as the only accepted intellectual or artistic virtue of our age. Frankly, my experience leads me to think of the American mind as disabled, floundering, and incapable of such resolution as he suggests.

Dallas Willard

School of Philosophy
University of Southern California
3709 Trousdale Parkway
Los Angeles, CA 90089–0451

NOTES

1.   The contrast between traditional and critical theory drawn by Horkheimer, "Traditional and Critical Theory", is absolutely essential to understanding the crisis in the university today. Contrast Husserl's account of theory, and his careful specification of its relationships to psychological and social realities, in Volume I of his *Logical Investigations*.

2.   See Plato, *The Republic*, Book 7, and J. H. Newman, *University Subjects*,.

3.   See, for example, Barbara Herrnstein Smith, *Contingencies of Value*.

4.   Conspiracy theories and views of the pervasive wrongness of society are frequent in the Enlightenment period. Recall Mandeville's famous saying that "the moral virtues are the political offspring which flattery begot upon pride". (Selby-Bigge, *British Moralists* vol. II, p. 353.) On this whole issue of pervasive distortion see Selby-Bigge's preface in volume I.

20   DALLAS WILLARD

5. *Los Angeles Times*, Calendar section p. F2, Jan 2 1993. See also Robert J.
Samuelson, "The Trophy Syndrome", *Newsweek* 21 Dec 1992, p. 45.
6. Reported on the CBS program *Sixty Minutes*, November 6 1992.
7. See my paper "Space, Color, Sense Perception and the Epistemology of Logic",
8. See Husserl's penetrating comment, "On certain basic defects of empiricism", an
appendix to subsection 26 of Volume I of his *Logical Investigations*.
9. Lovejoy, *The Revolt Against Dualism*, Lecture I.
10. Derrida, *Speech and Phenomena*, p. 66.

REFERENCES

Jacques Derrida, *Speech and Phenomena*, tr. David B. Allison, Evanston, IL:
    Northwestern University Press, 1973.
Paul A. Bové, *Destructive Poetics: Heidegger and Modern American Poetry*,
    New York: Columbia University Press, 1980.
Max Horkheimer, "Traditional and Critical Theory", in *Critical Theory:
    Selected Essays,* tr. Matthew J. O'Connell *et al.*, New York: Seabury Press,
    1972.
Arthur O. Lovejoy, *The Revolt Against Dualism*, La Salle, IL: Open Court,
    1960.
Jean-Francois Lyotard, *The Postmodern Condition: A Report on Knowledge*, tr.
    Geoff Bennington and Brian Massumi, Minneapolis: University of
    Minnesota Press, 1984,
J. H. Newman, *University Subjects*, New York: Houghton Mifflin, 1913
Christopher Norris, *What's Wrong with Postmodernism: Critical Theory and
    the Ends of Philosophy*, Baltimore: Johns Hopkins Press, 1990.
L.A. Selby-Bigge (ed.), *British Moralists*, edited by , Indianapolis, IN: Bobbs-
    Merrill, 1964.
Pitirim Sorokin, *The Crisis of Our Age*, New York: Dutton 1957.
Barbara Herrnstein Smith, *Contingencies of Value: Alternative Perspectives for
    Critical Theory*, Cambridge, MA: Harvard University Press, 1988
Dallas Willard, "Space, Color, Sense Perception and the Epistemology of
    Logic", *The Monist* 72 (January 1989), 117-133.

THE DECLINE AND FALL OF FRENCH NIETZSCHEO-STRUCTURALISM

Eternal return

The most impressive achievement of some French philosophers currently classified as "post-structuralists" has been to have exported abroad, mainly to America, a set of doctrines and ideas which, for the most part, can be fully understood only within their French context, and which had already fallen into disrepute or begun to face indifference in the country from which they originated by the time they reached the other side of the Atlantic. Such episodes of *differance* are not uncommon within the history of ideas, especially when communication between continents or countries is slow. For instance Comtean positivism reached Brazil at a time when it was already out of fashion in France, and more recently many German philosophers wondered why their French colleagues seemed to be so concerned by their sudden rediscovery of Heidegger's well-known Nazism. When transferred into a different cultural atmosphere, ideas gain new life, to the surprise of those who thought that they were dead. But are these the *same* ideas? Is the American Derrida the same as the French Derrida that we read as students at the end of the 'sixties? Is the American Foucault the same intellectual hero as the man whom we worshiped during the 'seventies when he was lecturing on *Discipline and Punishment* and was involved in leftist groups? Is the Lyotard who is the subject of a *Lyotard Reader* more readable in English than in French? Like the Ship of Theseus, each of these floating edifices has been built out of various planks distinct from those of which they were constituted at their origin, to the degree that it is even possible that all the planks have been removed and replaced by new ones. And perhaps, as in the case of the Ship of Theseus, the question "Is it the same?" does not make much sense.

I shall not try here to assess the various changes which these ideas have undergone in crossing the Atlantic, for I lack the sociological expertise necessary to understand why such and such a topic can, in the American context, strike one note while it strikes another in France. I suspect that the difficulty that we have in identifying the various meanings of some post-structuralist doctrines in their respective environments has to do with one of their essential features: their extremely *contextual* character, the fact that they do not make sense unless they are variously interpreted by the various groups of readers that they attract, depending on the context and set of interests shared by these readers. Hence also their success: the vaguer and the more contextual an assertion is, the easier it is for people to appropriate for themselves its supposed meanings. The

phenomenon is well known from politics, and in philosophy it is as old as the
Sophists. My main concern, however, will not be the changes in these doctrines,
but with what remains the same. After all, the partisans of post-structuralism
can point out that the very fact that they started a new life outside their ecologi-
cal origin shows that there is something of lasting value in them, precisely that
core of doctrines which remains the same. Unfortunately, however, this very
core of doctrines seems to be of no value at all.

I propose here to focus upon a limited set of doctrines in French post-structuralist thought, namely those which their authors have borrowed from
Nietzsche. Most of the French post-structuralists have claimed to be
Nietzscheans, and it is this marriage of structuralism with Nietzscheanism
which gives its particular tone to much of French contemporary thought.
Nietzsche is what Deleuze, Foucault, Derrida, Lyotard, and many *poetae
minores* of French post-structuralism have in common. It might be said that
there are as many Nietzsches as there are interpretations of him by those writers, and that it is a distortion of their thought to rank them under this single
heading. This is true, and it is in a sense normal, given the Protean character of
Nietzsche's thought. But it is not my intention to consider the various particular
interpretations of Nietzsche given by French Nietzscheans, but only to consider
what I believe to be their common core. Although it is true that Nietzscheanism
amounts rather to a *Zeitgeist* of the whole period from 1960 to 1980 in France
than to a distinctive set of doctrines,[1] still we should resist the suggestion that it
is impossible to abstract a set of basic ideas and theses from different writers
and to discuss them in careful fashion. Of course Nietzscheans dislike their philosophy being reduced to a series of axioms or principles, for this seems to them
to be both cumbersome (the real thinker, we must never forget, *dances*) and
treacherous (there is always more to a philosophy than a set of axioms, and to
think otherwise is to misunderstand deeply what philosophy *is*). But we should
not be impressed by such *a priori* denials of relevance, for it is precisely these
denials which put the Nietzschean in the position of being immune to criticism.

I shall allow myself another distortion, and take as more or less paradig-
matic of what I shall call Nietzscheo-Structuralism (NS for short) the views of
Gilles Deleuze, whose recent book *Qu'est-ce que la philosophie?* happens to
contain many of the views which are here at issue.[2] Deleuze is, it seems to me,
the least well known of NS philosophers. This is an injustice, since he is, in a
sense, the most systematic and the one who tried to articulate the most rigorously—if I may say so—the philosophical views of Nietzscheo-Structuralism and
to push them towards their more extreme consequences, indeed to their utmost
incoherence. So this paper will be, for a large part, an indirect commentary on
Deleuze's book. It is very likely that what I have to say is neither original nor

new, but it seems precisely to be old and *banal* thoughts to which French Nietzscheans are blind.[3]

Meaning Torpedoed

Nietzscheo-structuralism began its career in France in about 1962, when Deleuze published his justly acclaimed *Nietzsche et la philosophie*. Nietzscheanism had already had a long history in France, where it had been appropriated before the Second World War (curiously enough) both by reactionary thinkers of the *Action Française* and by revolutionary anarchists such as Bataille and his group.[4] Bataille's Nietzsche is a mystic, who discovers, through the criticism of all religions and philosophical systems (and especially Hegel's, as interpreted by Kojève) the experience of madness and of nothingness.[5] How could this pure irrationalism be coupled with the *prima facie* pure rationalism of structuralists such as Levi-Strauss? Presumably because both Nietzsche and the structuralists agreed on the fact that in any form of human activity or thought the point of view of the subjects of the activities and thoughts has no authority over its meaning or significance. It is in this sense that Nietzsche's name came to be associated with Marx and Freud, as, in Ricoeur's words, "masters of suspicion", and as critics of the subjective point of view of actors on their own activities. It is a banality that there is a difference between the objective meaning of a given phenomenon (for instance a social phenomenon) and the consciousness which people have of that phenomenon. The structuralist then has to *interpret* this meaning. For instance, myths have a meaning which is different from the meaning that people give them, literary texts have a hidden structure which is distinct from the surface structure that people read in them. The structuralist uncovers this structure. But from this purely positivistic idea the NS philosopher extrapolates the thesis that there is no single, objective, or "correct" interpretation. There are always interpretations, and interpretations of interpretations, and so on. As Michel Foucault expressed it in his seminal paper of 1964 "Marx, Nietzsche, Freud", the three axioms are: 1) interpretation has become an infinite task, 2) if interpretation can never be ended, it is because there is nothing to interpret, 3) interpretation has to interpret itself *ad infinitum*. Structuralism had been presented from the start as a doctrine about meaning and about the discovery of the"true" meaning of structures through structural or linguistic analysis. But the radicalization of structuralist hermeneutics by NS produced the opposite result:

Thesis 1. There is no such thing as meaning.

Now, *prima facie*, this thesis should not be unfamiliar to an analytic philosopher. According to Kripke, this is the "meaning scepticism" for which Wittgenstein argued in his "rule following considerations".[6] It could also be compared to Quine's thesis of the indeterminacy of translation: there is no "fact of the matter" about meaning.[7] But meaning *scepticism,* and meaning *nihilism* are two different things. On Wittgenstein's view (or on Quine's) it does not follow from the fact that meaning is indeterminate that there is no such thing as meaning at all, or that there are no rules to follow. In general it is not the case that, from the fact that a concept is vague, it follows that it does not mean anything or that it cannot be used. But this inference is constantly made by NS philosophers.[8] Ironically enough for Nietzscheans who want to "overcome Platonism" in philosophy, the inference rests upon a very Platonistic view of concepts, according to which concepts must have sharp necessary and sufficient conditions for their application, so that wherever these conditions are not fulfilled (i.e. almost everywhere) the relevant concepts become empty or contentless. This view of concepts has been discredited in most contemporary philosophy of language from Wittgenstein to Kripke and Putnam, and also in psychology.[9] If they wanted to argue that understanding a language is a matter of interpretation, Nietzscheans would have been better inspired to look at Davidson's theory of interpretation, which, to some extent could have given them some justifications for their views (although it does not lead to such nihilism about meaning).[10] Of course the NS is unaware of these developments, and of many other developments in contemporary philosophy of language.[11] In spite of the pretension of NS to produce a critique of meaning, it is surprising how uncritical about the notion of meaning those philosophers have been who pretended to base their basic insights on this very notion.

Being torpedoed

If there is no such thing as meaning, why should we look for meanings, why should we interpret? Because meanings and interpretations are the product of basic *forces*. This leads to :

Thesis 2. Nothing exists but forces.

Thesis 2 is the positive ontological counterpart of Thesis 1. So what is there for Nietzscheo-Structuralists? In one sense, forces can be understood as *instincts*, in a biological sense, according to a traditional reading of Nietzschean naturalism. But this would conflict with the idea that there are no facts, only interpretations. Interpretations, however, have to arise against something which is independent of them. They have to be interpretations of *something* when they are not interpretations of interpretations. But this something cannot be a fact, it cannot be an entity or set of entities which inquiry might isolate. Forces are not simply instincts or affects, which would be at bottom dispositions or habits. Rather they are transformations of an ultimate reality which Deleuze variously calls "pure multiplicity", "pure Difference", "the Diverse" (in *Difference and Repetition*), "body without organs" (in *Anti-Oedipus*), the "plane of immanence" or "nature" or "chaos" (Deleuze, *Qu'est-ce que la philosophie?*, ch. 2). This pure multiplicity pre-exists, it is there before anything can be thought. This is the way Deleuze interprets Nietzsche's *Wille zur Macht*. As Deleuze says, the will to power is not something which the will wants; it is *what* wants in the will. It is a purely affirmative force. But this affirmative original force, which is a pure *quale*, coexists with other forces, which are not active, but reactive. Thus there are two kinds of forces, both active and reactive. The task of philosophy, for the Nietzschean, is to let the active forces triumph against the reactive ones. In morals, in particular, it is to fight against the reactive forces of resentment of the weak and to promote the active forces of innocence and irresponsibility of the strong. At the level of thought, we find a similar dualism. From the pure *apeiron*, pure difference, or field of forces human thought extracts an Order, an Identity, or a Sameness, and thus loses its True Nature. Only a thought which would respect Difference *as* Difference would be an authentic thought about what there is. The history of human thought, and the history of philosophy in particular, is the history of the various attempts to find an order within things which are, in their very essence, chaos, pure difference or "delirium" (indeed Foucault's analysis of *Las Meninas* at the onset of *The Order of Things* carries just this message).

Thus philosophers divide into two camps : those who try to negate pure Difference and to transform it into identity in thought or concept, through the discovery of a transcendent order (Platonism) or through dialectics (Hegelianism); and those who are, according to Deleuze, able to think pure Difference as it is in itself and to let the affirmative forces go, such as Spinoza or Nietzsche. Deleuze, however, believes that most philosophers are able to approach more or less the very essence of Difference itself (a Good Thing), but in one way or another they miss the target, and reinterpret it as an Identity (a Bad Thing). Thus Leibniz comes close to Difference, but interprets it in terms of some form or order in the mind of God, Kant discovers the diverse in intuition, but he "folds" it unto concepts, etc.[12] The scheme, as you will notice, is similar to Heidegger's insistence on the fact that the thought of Being *qua* Being (the Ontological Difference) lies hidden in Onto-Theology and has to be unveiled.

We should not quarrel with this crazy NS ontology as such. In a Carnapian vein, I would be prepared to say that everyone is free to adopt the ontology that pleases him.[13] Thus if Deleuze, or anyone else, wants to say that the ultimate

nature of reality is made of a Something which looks much like Eduard
Hartmann's Unconscious (of which, as Brentano pointed out, nothing can be
said, or, as Ramsey would have said, nothing can be whistled either), then we
can let him say that. But I would say in a Quinean vein that we should care
about the consequences and the cost of these ontological views. One of the
peculiarities of NS in the history of recent philosophy is that its upholders are
prepared to defend this ontology at any cost, even at the cost of the most
implausible of consequences.

Truth torpedoed

First, there are epistemological consequences, the most striking of which is:

Thesis 3. There is no such thing as truth.

What does or could this mean? This thesis is, in a sense, a corollary of
Thesis 1: there is no truth because there are only interpretations. But it is also a
corollary of Thesis 2: truth can only be an *effect* of a certain kind of "discourse", something which a particular interpreter *claims* to have attained or to
be seeking, but which is only the product of his interpretation, and therefore of
the forces which he tends to represent. What is the difference between Thesis 3
and a form of idealism according to which there are no facts, only thoughts and
statements about facts? In a sense there is little difference. The idealist Léon
Brunschwig, whose views were quite influential in France during the first part
of the twentieth century, used to say that Egypt is just the history of Egyptolo-
gy. Some years later, the philosopher of science Gaston Bachelard held that
realism and empiricism are necessarily false doctrines because there are no facts
investigated by science, only theoretical constructions. Indeed the structuralists
of the 'sixties were also prone to adopt the view that the nature of reality is
determined by the structures—social, linguistic, and otherwise—which are,
according to them, all-powerful in our thoughts and activities. Thus philosophers trained within this context would be prepared to accept the idealistic thesis about truth without discussion or argument. Of course idealism is not in
itself an absurd doctrine, but the "argument" which underlies the NS idealism is
fallacious: from the fact that reality is thought by us, or that it is in some sense
"structured" by our thoughts, it does not follow that there is no reality at all
about which our thoughts could be true. The NS philosopher, however, is not
really trying to put forward an idealistic view about truth, although Thesis 3
comes close to it. What he wants to say is that, as Nietzsche himself said, the
very *concept* of truth is mistaken as a philosophical concept ("Truth is a kind of
mistake"). Someone who uses this concept should be suspected of trying to

impose on us a mistaken view of things, indeed his *own* view (*We* are good, *they* are bad). So he has no claim to objectivity. Here the Nietzschean might say either of two things: either the person has no claim to objectivity or truth because there is no such thing as truth, in which case we are led back to the idealist "argument" above, or he wants to speak in the name of a different sense of objectivity, which is given to him by his genealogical method of interpretation, in which case Thesis 3 is just self-defeating, as many have remarked.[14] What the Nietzschean Callicles wants to criticize is the *value* of truth. But, to use one of his favorite jokes, his criticism must have a truth-*value*. Typical logician's maneuver! How cheap! But if it is so cheap, why shouldn't there be a cheap and easy response to this objection? The only response which the NS seems to have is illustrated, for instance, by Deleuze (*Qu'est-ce que la philosophie?*, ch. 6). Asking for truth and coherence, willing our statements to have a truth value, either the true or the false, he says, is the typical logician's move. But logic itself is not normative.[15] Logic, like truth, is something which is willed, like power. Logic is an "effect of truth"; as such it is suspect. So we should not *obey* logic, because the logician wants to be *obeyed*: he wants to be the master, like Humpty Dumpty. He wants to be in power! What a villain! But we Nietzscheans resist! We are the true *résistants*! I caricature only slightly.[16] Once again the NS philosopher is mistaking the value of truth and objectivity, and the normativity of these values and of logic, for a *Wille zur Macht* on the part of the logician or philosopher who invokes these values. The Nietzschean is right: logic imposes certain obligations—the obligation to think logically, according to the canons of correct reasoning—but this obligation and these canons are not at the service of any cause.[17] They are indeed "weapons" that the Nietzschean is free to use or to stop using, but only, in the latter case, at the cost of incoherence. I have here nothing more to say than what Aristotle says against the Sophists in Book G of the *Metaphysics*. The only thing the Nietzschean has to say about logic is just the childish view that logic is as sort of police-force of the mind. Frege is the Torquemada of philosophy. The basic confusion could also be denounced in the name of a different view of logic, namely Wittgenstein's. According to Wittgenstein, the "hardness" of the logical "must" is but the effect of conventions that *we* have chosen. This, it seems, should be grist for the Nietzschean's mill. But it is not. For Wittgenstein never says that, from the fact that logical rules are conventions, it follows that they are *arbitrary*, and that they could be obeyed or disobeyed at will. They are the products of our "form of life". And Wittgenstein was utterly opposed to the idea that we could change our logic. Nietzsche's naturalism *could*, in some respects, be interpreted in that way. But this is not the way the French NS interpret him. Instead they prefer to hold the absurd doctrine that logic does not rule anything except those who are stupid enough to be abused by it.

In his more lucid moments, however, Deleuze does seem prepared to say that the objection he has against truth is not that the *concept* of truth is an illusion, but that the traditional *definition* of truth is mistaken. But this is an entirely different matter from what Thesis 3 asserts. Deleuze seems at times ready to entertain the idea that he could be defending a different concept of truth from the classical one, and that there could be a deeper logic than truth-based logic.[18] But he never defines it: sometimes he alludes to intuitionistic logic, sometimes he seems to recreate an intensional logic, sometimes he just equates truth and utility in a pragmatist vein (see below). In general, the Nietzschean is just not interested in the topic of the definition of truth (why should we try to define truth, if truth is a mistake?). This topic, however, has been the object of much attention in the twentieth century. Philosophers have been discussing, for example, whether truth has to be defined as correspondence, coherence or warranted assertability. They have suggested deflationary theories of truth, according to which truth would be only a redundant concept expressible by such truisms as '"p" is true if and only if p'. But none of the problems the NS philosopher addresses concern these topics. When Richard Rorty suggested his so-called "pragmatist" view of truth, according to which truth is but a "compliment" which we pay to our assertions, he expressed some form of Nietzschean doctrine. But although he broadly approves of the Nietzschean move,[19] Rorty is more conscious of what is at stake than the French Nietzscheans. They just seem to presuppose that truth, if it is to mean anything at all, must mean something like correspondence (cf. Deleuze, *Qu'est-ce que la philosophie?*, ch. 5, "science aims at reference", see below). But as any philosopher working on these topics knows, all the difficult issues about truth turn on its definition, not on the fact that one is "for" it or "against" it.

Knowledge torpedoed

The second epistemological thesis, which follows from (3) is :

Thesis 4. There is no such thing as epistemology.

At least here we find some sort of analysis by implication: an essential component of knowledge is truth, but since (Thesis 3) there is no truth, then (Thesis 4) there is no such thing as (pure) knowledge. The reasoning is parallel to that which leads to Thesis 3: there is only a will to truth, and thus a will to knowledge. So there is no theory of knowledge at all, but only a genealogy of the knowledge instinct. This view is most clearly expressed by Foucault in "Nietzsche, la généalogie et l'histoire". There Foucault proposes his programme of replacing "epistemology" by "a doctrine of the *perspectives of affects*" (perspectivism) and a genealogy of such perspectives, in Nietzsche's sense of a "genealogy of morals". Trace the origins of the instincts and of the affects which lead to the desire for knowledge and you will have said all there is to say about knowledge. To this programme belongs Foucault's notion of an *Archaeology of Knowledge*.[20] If you try to read this book as a kind of method for a new style of history or philosophy of science, then you will not understand anything. Foucault's use of notions like 'statement' or 'discursive formation', although they *seem* to belong to a rather traditional vocabulary, will be misunderstood if read in a classical perspective. If, however, one reads Foucault's work as a treatise about the *effects* of discourse, about what Foucault conceives as the decipherment of attempts to gain power through the appropriation of truth, then it becomes understandable. Foucault's great achievement has been to exploit the epistemology of French historians of science like Canguilhem as a hermeneutic weapon against all knowledge. Canguilhem himself was not completely innocent of this possible reading of his work. For instance in a famous paper called "Qu'est-ce que la psychologie?", which influenced a whole generation of French philosophers, he attacked psychology by articulating the suspicion that this science might be bent to the service of social order.[21] Foucault took up the idea and applied it to medicine, psychiatry, criminology, sociology, etc. "Knowledge is power, power knowledge." Truth is willed. But *of course.* Knowledge is power. *Of course.* But it does not follow that knowledge and truth are *only* that. In his last books on the history of sexuality, Foucault claimed to be criticizing the "desire for truth" which was present, according to him, from the Greek notion of *parrhesia* to the Christian concept of an avowal in such practices as confession.[22] He cleverly cultivates the ambiguity already noticed above, between a criticism of truth as a philosophical concept and a criticism of our *attitude* towards truth. Frege-Torquemada would have a name for this: this is just psychologism, the confusion between truth and the recognition of truth. Such is the genealogist's way. Thus it comes as no surprise that Foucault ended his carrier by calling himself an historian, although he allowed himself the liberty of using hermeneutics, conceived as the unveiling of instincts (sexual instincts of course), an instrument of research which no genuine historian is willing to allow himself.

The traditional task of epistemology is to evaluate our claims to knowledge. For the Nietzschean, this can only mean that knowledge is praised, or desired. This systematic confusion of judgments of truth with evaluative judgments, and in turn of evaluative judgments with the expression of desires, is basic in NS. Once again, the thesis *can* be of interest when properly understood: the American philosopher Richard Rudner once said that "the scientist *qua* scientist makes value judgments", and Hilary Putnam argued, against positivism, that truth and objectivity are relevant not only to fact-stating discourse but also to evaluative and normative judgments. They are epistemic values.[23] But here too the Nietzschean makes a fallacious inference: from the fact that truth and objectivity are values for the scientist, it does not follow that fact-stating discourse reduces to evaluative discourse and that evaluation is only the expression of a desire. To state or to assert that France is hexagonal is not necessarily to praise it for having this shape. The confusion could be illustrated in many ways. For instance, when they discovered (belatedly) the work of J. L. Austin, the French NS retained from it mainly the view that since you can do things with words, every fact-stating assertion is *always* a disguised order, an injunction from the speaker for the hearer to do something. Therefore (*sic*) scientific assertions, which purport to say the truth, are in fact performative utterances enjoining us to obey the orders of the Big Brother of Truth. But of course Austin never said such an absurd thing. He just said that an assertion *can* be an order.[24] "Please, tell me how to derive 'ought' from 'is'. Well, let me tell you first how to derive 'all' from 'some'."

At least it could be said of NS philosophers like Foucault that they have been "new archivists", in Deleuze's words:[25] they have produced new approaches in the history of science by linking it to the sociology of science and by drawing attention to unnoticed connections between fields which the traditional philosophers of science had kept apart. But, with many others, I fail to see what's so new about the succession of separate *epistemai* and the pure relativism which follows therefrom. The fact that Kuhn's work (*The Copernican Revolution* dates back to 1960, six years before *The Order of Things*) may lend itself to such a relativistic interpretation is no proof of its value.[26] More importantly, if we look at what the NS really has to say about science, we will be surprised to discover that it comes down to pure positivism and operationalism. This is explicitly argued (for once!) by Deleuze in chapter 5 of *Qu'est-ce que la philosophie?* There he tells us that science, unlike philosophy, produces no concepts, but only mathematical *functions* ("fonctifs"). In a Comtean spirit, Deleuze claims that science produces laws, through an ideography whose model is the differential calculus and whose aim is to hook a symbolism to phenomena without trying to find real properties in things. In doing this, science does not move away from the basic nature of being which for NS is, let us remind ourselves, chaos. Scientific functions are "partial observers" on chaos. Thus the true science is a form of "chaology". (Deleuze, *Qu'est-ce que la philosophie?*, pp. 122-127) It should not be surprising that the contemporary scientific interest in chaos is in this way recruited to the service of a purely irrationalistic world view. What *is* surprising is that the apology for chaos, indeterminism, etc. comes along with a positivistic view of scientific theories according to which such theories do not try to elucidate the nature of reality but are only instruments to produce "effects". I am happy to emphasize the fact that NS, in the end, in this way pays homage to vulgar pragmatism, positivism and instrumentalism, for analytic philosophers in France have so often been accused of being just poor dull positivists and pragmatists. Ironically enough, these accusations are made in the name of a disinterested search for truth, which the positivist or pragmatist is supposed to reduce to usefulness and interest. But as we have seen, the NS is not afraid of being incoherent. He is just afraid of not having the last word.

Consciousness explained away

I come now to what is perhaps the most well-known of NS doctrines, the criticism of consciousness and subjectivity, which, because it is so well-known, I shall comment upon only briefly. It is closely linked with Thesis 1: the conscious subject has no authority over his own thoughts, and to Thesis 2, which leads to:

Thesis 5. Consciousness and subjectivity are just effects (of affects)

As I have said already, this thesis is one of the basic structuralist theses, and the NS can claim no originality in this regard: Althusser, Lacan, Levi-Strauss and other avowedly non Nietzschean thinkers have all proclaimed the "death of the subject".[27] The trouble, as many have remarked,[28] is that the obituary covers many dead. It's rather a family vault. 'Consciousness' sometimes means the Cartesian *cogito* or the Thinking Substance, sometimes the personal subject which lies behind all representations, sometimes it means representation itself, sometimes moral conscience (from the *Genealogy of Morals*), the subject of rights, etc. Although the popular and newspaper versions of Nietzscheanism, and sometimes even the more sophisticated ones, confused all these, Deleuze has been careful to distinguish the "classical age" of "representation" as the reign of the individual, the romantic age as the reign of the personal subject (the Self), and modernity as the age of the democratic individual.[29] Post-modernity, as is well known, will be the happy age of the dissolution of the subject. Structuralism also pervades the history of philosophy. But whereas structuralist historians of philosophy like Guéroult confined their objects of study to particular philosophical systems, Deleuze cross-analyses them by multiplying the various figures which are going to act as structures of thought and which are exemplified in many systems (*Qu'est-ce que la philosophie?*, ch. 3). Never mind if some thinkers or sets of ideas do not fit these classifications. The exceptions are there to confirm the rules. Strangely enough, Deleuze's reconstructions of the history of philosophy have an Hegelian character: he wants to make everything fit into his scheme, and does not allow any contingency in the history of ideas.

And why, in spite of all his attempts to find layers in the realm of subjectivity, do we have the impression that his criticism of consciousness and subjectivity is so massive that it often amounts just to some sort of handwaving in a critical direction? After twenty years of criticism of subjectivity we still do not know exactly what was being criticized all along. In fact the criticism has been so ineffectual that it has been easy to promote various "revivals" of subjectivity, of persons, and so on. Lacan already warned us: the subject is like the joker in a game: it cropped up here, it will come back there. Well, one might say that just the same thing happened within contemporary analytic philosophy: after a period where logical behaviourism, functionalism, materialism and "no-ownership" theories of the self in various forms have dominated the scene, philosophers are now "rediscovering" consciousness, the self, subjectivity. There is, however, a slight difference: those philosophers are dealing with difficult problems: of the nature of *qualia*, intentionality, the part played by the individual and by the environment in the nature of thought. Some analytic philosophers have held the thesis that an individual has no authority over his thought. But when an analytic philosopher like Dennett tries to build a theory of consciousness which would get rid of the various traditional characteristics of subjectivity, *qualia* or mental substance, he actually tries to construct such a theory, not only as a philosophical, but also as an empirical, scientifically informed, theory.[30] For the analytic philosopher, there is no "deconstruction" without construction. There is all the difference in the world between doing something (or trying to do something) and saying that one does it.

Th(s)inking Philosophy

I have mainly presented negative themes, for NS presents itself mainly as a critical enterprise. Deleuze presents Nietzsche's philosophy as a kind of continuation of Kant's critique of metaphysics, a hyper–critique.[31] But is there anything positive in these views, any happy message? Yes, there is. Once philosophy has escaped the various obnoxious attempts to reduce it to science, logic, religion, metaphysics, marketing,[32] it can finally espouse its true essence, which is art. This is a classic Nietzschean theme which, more than any other, defines the NS enterprise, and which indeed is one of the basic beliefs of French philosophers during the second half of this century: philosophy is closer to art —to literature in particular—than to science. Nietzsche wanted "philosopher-artists'', who are able to dance ("A big ass is a sin against the Holy Spirit'', says *Ecce Homo*) and to *affirm* the positive forces against the deadly systems of reason. Thus Deleuze's heroes are more often writers than philosophers: Kafka, Kleist, Mallarmé, Proust, Beckett, Malcolm Lowry, Antonin Artaud, Lewis Carroll (the author of *Sylvie and Bruno*, not of a *Logic*, but of *funny* logical examples), etc.[33]

All are treated as authors of *philosophical* ideas and concepts. I myself learnt a lot about contemporary literature by reading Deleuze. Now Deleuze is careful *not* to propose the overly simple thesis that philosophy and literature are *identical*. On the contrary he insists on the specificity of philosophy with respect both to science and to art: science creates *functions*, art creates *conceptual personae* (e.g. Don Juan; Deleuze, *Qu'est-ce que la philosophie?*, ch. 3) and (in painting) *blocks of sensation* based on *percepts* and *affects* (*Qu'est-ce que la philosophie?* ch. 7). Philosophy does something different:

Thesis 6. Philosophy creates concepts.

At last this seems to be an acceptable thesis! But it all depends upon what it is taken to mean. Deleuze rejects all traditional conceptions of concepts (*Qu'est-ce que la philosophie?*, ch. 2, *et passim*). Concepts are not to be defined by their extensions, but they are not intensions in the Carnapian sense of rules determining extensions either. They are "intensions" but in the sense of *intensities*, "centres of vibration" (p. 2), "forms or forces", but not functions (p. 137), made up of percepts and affects, "blocks" (ch. 7), "chaoïd states" of the brain. Concepts are Protean entities: they are but reflexions of the original chaos. In other terms they are anything but representations, meanings, extensions, intensions, criteria, stereotypes, paradigms, or whatever. Needless to say, you can do anything with a concept. Even a bird can come close to doing something with concepts.[34] I have already noted above how Platonistic this supposedly anti-Platonistic view of concepts can be. The NS believes that once he has rejected the view that a concept might represent, within a unity, a class of entities which fall under it, and that once he has assimilated concepts to variations of affects, which have no stable meaning—thus being close to metaphors (a Derridean theme)—he has thereby undermined all classical theories of representation. Let us agree with him that the classical view of concepts is false. But he is mistaken on the proper strategy to show this. The correct thing to do is not to assert the *opposite* view according to which concepts are pure multiplicities and diversities, but *to deny the premise* on which the classical view rests, namely the idea that concepts must have strict necessary and sufficient conditions of application.[35] Now I admit that, in a sense, this is what the deconstructionist does: for instance, by asserting that concepts are closer to metaphors than is usually thought, Derrida "undermines" the classical view of concepts. But Derrida also asserts that concepts *are*, in their essence, metaphorical.[36] On the contrary, on the view of concepts alluded to here (concepts as stereotypes), it does not follow from the fact that concepts and metaphors share, so to speak, a common core of vagueness, that they are both "metaphorical".[37] From the fact that wheat bread and rye bread come from a cereal which has similar genetic roots, it does not follow that they are the same bread.

Although he insists on the difference between philosophy and art, Deleuze is faithful to Nietzsche in considering philosophy as a kind of artistic enterprise. At the basis of value judgments are aesthetic judgments. Philosophers *create* concepts, just as artists create works. Philosophical concepts are supposed to have the same sort of singularity as works of art. Indeed they are objects not of discussion but of admiration. When faced with a beautiful philosophical concept (say, Kant's notion of a *noumenon*) you should just sit back and admire it. You should not question it. Although, for the NS, philosophy is a critique, it has nothing to do with discussion or dialogue (Deleuze, *Qu'est-ce que la philosophie?*, pp. 15, 138), and it has nothing to do with conversation, either (thus Deleuze disagrees with Rorty). Discussion is just a narcissistic practice where one reaffirms the opinions of everybody, of the majority. The philosopher, on the contrary, belongs necessarily to a *minority*.[38] The philosopher is always *alone*. Nietzsche used to say "Why should I care about refutations?" and "That which needs to be demonstrated is of little value". The NS does not care about arguments, reasons, intersubjectivity, objectivity. Nevertheless, the Nietzschean does not doubt that his concepts are genuine creations. If someone comes along and attempts to show him that he has not "created" any new concept, or that he is wrong, he will just ignore him. Like the child who plays with time in *Zarathustra*, he is right *because he said it*. He is forever vaccinated against any kind of criticism.

I don't want to break the child's toy. I shall not spend time trying to show how absurd and self-defeating such views are. This has been done by many others.[39] But we should follow the Nietzschean's advice, and look at the effects and consequences. I shall only point to two of them. First, the view that philosophy stands alone, against all knowledge and forms of speech, in splendid isolation, has produced within the French intellectuals what Musil called a "professional ideology" according to which *any* criticism directed against philosophers (and especially against NS philosophers) is necessarily the effect of some sort of malevolence, an attack against a Sacred Object. It is just (like the present piece, I presume) a form of nasty polemics. It never occurs to the NS that he might be criticized for good reasons, because there are for him no reasons, no truths (and therefore no falsehoods) to partake, only affects. (At least we have settled a basic philosophical issue: reasons *are* causes, only causes!) Schizophrenia and paranoia are the only alternatives, as Deleuze's *Anti-Oedipus* amply shows, and as Derrida's reactions to Searle and others also shows.

Second, the systematic denial of what Kant called *Öffentlichkeit* leads to catastrophic consequences in political philosophy. The French Nietzscheans have, from the start, been careful to separate Nietzsche's views from their

embarrassing association with Nazism and Fascism. Although the ghost is difficult to hide in the closet, and resurfaces sometimes,[40] it would be unfair to
charge them with this too easy accusation. I do not doubt for one second that
people like Deleuze, Derrida, Lyotard or Foucault, had never had *anything* to do
with such doctrines. On the contrary they have in many ways been in the fore-
front of the defense of the oppressed and have often taken courageous positions
in political and in civic matters. But, to say the least, they did not have the theory of their practice. Deleuze's reading of Nietzsche's doctrine of the "strong" as
promoting irresponsibility, of culture as a form of drill,[41] has done little to distinguish the apology for the complete autonomy of the individual from an apology for tyranny,[42] the politics of systematically sustaining minorities as minorities, such as homosexuals, victims of psychiatry, prisoners,[43] dissociated from a
defence of democracy, became quite often indistinguishable from the defence of
private interests and desires.[44] The politics of neo–Nietzscheanism is but one
episode in a long story of political failures of French intellectuals since the
Second World War, one which has been commented upon so many times that it
is not necessary to insist upon it here.

Back to Zero

Foucault once said "*Le siècle sera deleuzien*". And indeed it has been, to a large
extent. It is not an exaggeration to say that, since Nietzscheo-Structuralism has
been influential in France for more than twenty years, at least twenty years have
been lost, a time during which the most elementary ideals of philosophy, and
indeed philosophy as a professional academic enterprise, have been systematically downgraded and made the object of contempt and suspicion. I have not
talked here of the deep crisis of the university during the same period. The NS
cannot, of course, be held responsible for that. But the best defence of academic
ideals is not to attack them, as the NS did. I anticipate the reactions: who
defended philosophy, the freedom of speech and thought more than those writers? Again, their sincerity is not to be doubted. But the least that we might
expect from a philosopher is some form of responsibility for what he says. The
NS have expounded the absurd doctrines outlined above without batting an eye-
lid. Have I myself indulged in polemics and caricature against thinkers who are
painstakingly trying seriously to think through the basic issues of modern philosophy? But who is serious? Thieves are the first to shout "Stop thief!" Did I
beg the question against them by presupposing that meaning, truth, being or
knowledge are secure and firm notions which are in no need of being questioned? Not at all. Indeed those notions have constantly to be called into question. But what the NS "experience" has taught us is that the proper way to question them is not by turning the tables, by overthrowing the idols. I have

suggested that there are much more effective ways of criticizing traditional philosophical ideals than by emptying space. But the NS philosophy leaves everything as it is. The wheels of its criticism turn in the void.[45]

From the start, Nietzscheo–structuralism has failed on its own terms, like the House of Usher. But its decline has been slow. *Français, encore un effort?*[48]

Pascal Engel

Université de Caen
and
CREA,Ecole Polytechnique, Paris
1 rue Descartes
F-75005 Paris

NOTES

1.   I have been much helped in characterizing this atmosphere by the papers in Ferry and Renaut (eds), *Pourquoi nous ne sommes pas nietzschéens*, with which I fully agree, and especially Descombes' paper, "Le moment français de Nietzsche", pp. 101-128. See also Ferry and Renaut, *La pensée 68*, Paris: Gallimard, 1986. Eng. trans. *French Philosophy of the Sixties*, Amherst: The University of Massachussetts Press, 1990.

2.   I have reviewed this book in *Lettres philosophiques*.

3.   It might be said, therefore, that I am here guilty of misusing a form of "paradigm case argument" that so many French thinkers themselves use: taking one author as representative of a whole trend of thought (e.g. Rousseau as the paradigm of "logocentrism") and extending some doctrines from one writer to other writers. I am well aware, for instance, that most of what I attribute here to Deleuze cannot readily be attributed to, say, Derrida. It is obvious, in particular, as Prof. Gracia remarked in his comments on this paper at the Wingspread Conference, that Derrida would never accept the dogmatic "theses" (1)-(6) below *as I formulate them*, and that he has probably never accepted them. So I am quite ready to accept that what I describe here does not apply to Derrida in general, although I put forward some connections between the Nietzschean theses (1)-(6) and some of Derrida's views. The Nietzscheanism characterized here would better be called "vulgar Nietzscheanism". But it is not obvious, in spite of many denials, that "sophisticated Nietzscheans" such as many French philosophers of the period 1960-80, *including Derrida*, do not come close to the vulgar form of the doctrine. Be that as it may, Deleuze, in the book examined here, fosters his own sophisticated form of vulgar Nietzscheanism in a quite "metaphysical" tone, and most of the time he puts forward just the doctrines (1)-(6) that are here listed. Much of this exegetical problem comes down to the distinction which one must make between Heideggero-Nietzscheanism (Derrida) and

what one might call Metaphysical Nietzscheanism (Deleuze). The fact that there are big differences between the two does not mean that there is no connection between the two.

4. Cf. Taguieff, "Nietzsche dans la rhétorique réactionnaire". On Bataille and his group, Le Collège de Sociologie, see D. Hollier, *Le collège de sociologie*, J. M. Besnier, *La politique de l'impossible*, and Bataille, *Oeuvres Complètes*, tome 1, Paris, Gallimard, 1971. Some French Nietzscheans, like Blanchot, come from both the reactionary and the revolutionary tradition.

5. Bataille, *L'expérience interieure* and *Sur Nietzsche*. On Kojève, see Descombes, *Modern French Philosophy*, ch. 1.

6. Kripke, *Wittgenstein on Rules and Private Language*.

7. See Wheeler, "The Indeterminacy of French Interpretation", where Quine is compared to Derrida. See my comments on this paper in "Interpretation without Hermeneutics: A Plea against Ecumenism".

8. In particular by Derrida: cf. Searle, "The World Turned Upside Down".

9. Cf. Smith and Medin, *Categories and Concepts*. On the confusion made by the Nietzschean between understanding and interpreting see in particular Descombes, "Le moment franáais de Nietzsche".

10. I have analyzed some similarities between Davidson's theory of interpretation and hermeneutics in "Interpretation Without Hermeneutics".

11. See Pavel, *The Feud of Language*.

12, See in particular Deleuze, *Leibniz, le pli*.

13. We could even formulate another principle of tolerance: the crazier an ontology is, the more tolerant you should be about it.

14. See for instance A. Comte-Sponville, "La brute, le sophiste et l'esthète", p. 69, and also A. Boyer, "Hiérarchie et vérité", p. 24.

15. Deleuze, *Qu'est-ce que la philosophie?*, p. 132. Here my impression is that Deleuze is attacking the views put forward in my book *La norme du vrai* (see his quotation on p. 134.) But I may be slightly paranoid about this, which of course only confirms his views.

16. "C'est une véritable haine qui anime la logique, dans sa rivalité ou volonté de supplanter la philosophie" (Deleuze, *Qu'est-ce que la philosophie?*, p. 133). On pp. 136-139 Deleuze assimilates the "image of thought" which is proposed, according to him, by logic, to a model of opinion or *doxa*, an "orthodoxy". I am quite happy to be considered as a representative of common sense. "Critical commonsensism", as Peirce called it, is not an option Deleuze considers.

17. See the epilogue of my book *La norme du vrai*.

18. See Deleuze, *Différence et répétition*, ch. IV, and *Qu'est-ce que la philosophie?*, p. 123.

19. Rorty accepts, for instance, Foucault's idea that truth is but an "effect of power"; see his "Réponse à Jacques Bouveresse".

20. Foucault, *L'archeologie du savoir*. Deleuze approves. See his *Foucault*.

21. Canguilhem, "Qu'est-ce que la psychologie?". The influence of this paper on Foucault, and in turn on historians of science such as Ian Hacking, has been enormous.

22. Foucault, *La volonté de savoir* and *L'usage des plaisirs*.

23. H. Putnam, *Reason, Truth, and History*.

24. See Deleuze, *Rhyzome*. The confusion is also present in Derrida's commentaries on Austin. I do not insist on this, since it has been dealt with at length in Searle's well known polemics against Derrida.

25. Deleuze, *Foucault*.

26. Thomas Pavel drew my attention to Larry Laudan's note on Foucault, in *Progress and its Problems*, p. 241.

27. See in particular Deleuze's most interesting paper of 1967, "Qu'est-ce que le structuralisme?", where Deleuze ties together within his own ontology most of the themes of structuralist thought.

28. See A. Renaut, *L'ère de l'individu*.

29. See in particular Deleuze, *Différence et répétition* and *Logique du sens*.

30. Dennett, *Consciousness Explained*.

31. See Deleuze, *Nietzsche et la philosophie*, and also *La philosophie critique de Kant*, together with a curious text, "Sur quatre formules qui pourraient résumer la philosophie kantienne", where Kant is presented as the forerunner of some of the NS themes: the formal nature of time, the dissolution of the self, the assimilation of the Good to the Moral Law, the discordance between the faculties of the mind in the Third *Critique*.

32. According to Deleuze, the last "rival" and enemy of philosophy is the marketing and technology of communication: it not only pretends to have *concepts*, but also to *sell* them (*Qu'est-ce que la philosophie?*, p. 15). *Simony!*

33. See especially Deleuze, *Proust et les signes*, and Deleuze and Guattari, *Kafka, pour une littérature mineure*, Deleuze, *Présentation de Sacher Masoch*.

34. "The *Scenopoietes Dentirostris*, a bird from the rain-forests of Australia, throws from the tree the leaves that it cuts every morning, puts them on its back so that their internal face contrasts with the earth, and thus constructs for itself a scenery like a ready-made, and it sings just above it, with a complex song composed of its own notes which it imitates within intervals, while it extracts the yellow root of feathers under its beak : he is a true artist." (Deleuze, *Qu'est-ce que la philosophie?* p. 174; my translation)

35. Thus Deleuze criticizes (1991, p. 135) the idea that their might be a "logic of vagueness" (e.g. Zadeh's fuzzy set theory) because it would reduce vagueness to another form of precision (for instance by introducing degrees of truth). One might agree with that. But it does not follow that there cannot be a logic of vague predicates. For instance if the view that there is a second–order (or third order, etc.) of vagueness is correct, then there is a logic of this kind of vagueness (see my paper "Les concepts vagues sont–ils des concepts sans frontières?").

36. See Derrida, "White Mythology".

37. For a theory where concepts and metaphors share this core, see, for instance, Sperber and Wilson, *Relevance*.

38. See for instance, Deleuze, "Philosophie et minorité", and Deleuze and Guattari, *Kafka*.

39. See in particular the papers by Boyer, Ferry and Renaut in Ferry and Renaut (eds), *Pourquoi nous ne sommes pas nietzschéens*, and also Bouveresse, "Sur quelques

conséquences indésirables du pragmatisme", pp. 48–49.

40.   See Comte–Sponville, "La brute, le sophiste et l'esthète" and Taguieff "Nietzsche dans la rhétorique réactionnaire".

41.   Deleuze, *Nietzsche et la philosophie*, p. 157.

42.   Descombes, WHICH WORK?? pp. 125–126.

43.   See for instance, Deleuze and Foucault's *Entretien* in the issue of *L'Arc* on Deleuze (1972).

44.   See for instance René Schérer's defence of paedophilia in *L'emile perverti*, and the manifesto signed by Foucault and others in 1970, "Cent mille milliards de pervers" (censored by the state censorship authorities).

45.   I agree here with Sosa's excellent paper, "Serious Philosophy and the Freedom of Spirit".

46.   I thank the participants in the Wingspread Colloquium, and in particular my commentator Jorge Gracia, for his excellent comments. I thank also Mark Anspach, whose numerous philosophical and stylistic remarks did a lot to improve this paper. A last, cautionary note: I did not pretend to attack French philosophers *tout court*, but only those French philosophers who have taken more or less the front of the stage in recent years. I am confident that in the country of Descartes, Condillac, Laplace, Cournot, Poincaré, Duhem, Cavaillès, Herbrand, Granger, Vuillemin and Bouveresse, the resources exist to overcome the unfortunate parenthesis that I have here painted in broad strokes.

REFERENCES

G. Bataille, *L'expérience interieure*, Paris: Gallimard, 1941

——, *Oeuvres Complètes* tome 1, Paris: Gallimard, 1971

——, *Sur Nietzsche*, Paris: Gallimard, 1944.

J. Bouveresse, "Sur quelques conséquences indésirables du pragmatisme", in J.P. Cometti (ed.), *Lire Rorty*.

A. Boyer, "Hiérarchie et vérité" in L. Ferry and A. Renaut (eds), *Pourquoi nous ne sommes pas nietzschéens*.

J. M. Besnier, *La politique de l'impossible*, La Découverte, Paris, 1989

George Canguilhem, "Qu'est-ce que la psychologie?", *Cahiers pour l'analyse* 1, (1966).

J. P. Cometti (ed.), *Lire Rorty*, Combas: L'Eclat 1992,

A. Comte-Sponville, "La brute, le sophiste et l'esthète", in L. Ferry and A. Renaut (eds.), *Pourquoi nous ne sommes pas nietzschéens*.

Gilles Deleuze, *Différence et répétition*, Paris: PUF 1968.

——, *Foucault*, Paris: Minuit 1986. English translation *Foucault*, Minneapolis: University of Minnesota Press 1988.

——, *Leibniz, le pli*, Paris: Minuit, 1990.

Gilles Deleuze, *Logique du sens*. Paris: Minuit 1969. English translation *The Logic of Sense*, New York: Columbia University Press 1990.

——, *Nietzsche et la philosophie*, Paris: PUF 1962. English translation *Nietzsche and Philosophy*, Athlone 1983.

——, *La philosophie critique de Kant*, Paris: PUF 1963.

——, "Philosophie et minorité", *Critique* XXXV, (1978), pp. 154–155,

——, *Présentation de Sacher Masoch*, Paris: Minuit, 1967.

——, *Proust et les signes*, Paris: PUF 1964.

——, Sur quatre formules qui pourraient résumer la philosophie kantienne", *Philosophie* 9, 1986, 29–34

——, *Qu'est-ce que la philosophie?*, Paris: Minuit, 1991.

——, "Qu'est-ce que le structuralisme?", in F. Châtelet (ed.), *Histoire de la philosophie* VIII, Paris: Hachette 1973, pp. 299-335,

——, *Rhyzome*, Paris: Minuit 1976.

Gilles Deleuze and F. Guattari, *Kafka, pour une littérature mineure*, Paris: Minuit, 1975.

D. Dennett, *Consciousness Explained*, New York: Little Brown 1991.

J. Derrida, "White Mythology", in Derrida, *La dissemination,* Paris: Seuil 1972. English translation in Derrida, *Dissemination*, Chicago: University of Chicago Press 1983.

V. Descombes, *Modern French Philosophy*, Cambridge: Cambridge University Press 1980.

——, "Le moment français de Nietzsche", in L. Ferry and A. Renaut (eds.), *Pourquoi nous ne sommes pas nietzschéens*, 101-128.

Pascal Engel (ed.), "The Analytic-Continental Divide", *Stanford French Review* (forthcoming).

Pascal Engel, "Les concepts vagues sont–ils des concepts sans frontières?", *Revue Internationale de Philosophie* (1993).

——, "Interpretation without Hermeneutics: A Plea against Ecumenism", *Topoi* 10, (1991), 137-146.

——, *La norme du vrai,* Paris: Gallimard, 1989, Engl. trans. *The Norm of Truth*, Hemel Hempstead: Harvester Wheatsheaf, 1991., Paris: Gallimard, 1989; English translation *The Norm of Truth*, Hemel Hempstead: Harvester Wheatsheaf, 1991.

——, Review of Gilles Deleuze, *Qu'est-ce que la Philosophie?*, *Lettres Philosophiques* 4, (1992).

L. Ferry and A. Renaut, *La pensée 68*, Paris: Gallimard, 1986. English Translation *French Philosophy of the Sixties*, Amherst: The University of Massachusetts Press, 1990.

L. Ferry and A. Renaut (eds), *Pourquoi nous ne sommes pas nietzschéens*, Paris: Grasset, 1991

M. Foucault, *L'archéologie du savoir*, Paris: Gallimard 1970.

——, "Marx, Nietzsche, Freud", in *Nietzsche, Colloque de Royaumont*, Paris: Minuit, 1964.

——, "Nietzsche, la généalogie et l'histoire", in *Homage à Jean Hyppolite*, Paris: PUF 1971.

——, *L'usage des plaisirs*, Paris: Gallimard, 1984.

——, *La volonté de savoir*, Paris: Gallimard, 1976,

D. Hollier, *Le collège de sociologie*, Paris: Gallimard, 1979.

S. Kripke, *Wittgenstein on Rules and Private Language*, Oxford: Blackwell, 1981.

Larry Laudan, *Progress and its Problems*Berkeley: University of California Press 1977.

F. Nietzsche, *Volonté de Puissance* tr. Bianquis, Paris: Gallimard.

T. Pavel, *The Feud of Language*, French translation *Le mirage linguistique*, Paris: Minuit, 1990.

H. Putnam, *Reason, Truth, and History*, Cambridge: Cambridge University Press 1979.

A. Renaut, *L'ère de l'individu*, Paris: Gallimard 1989.

R. Rorty, "Réponse à Jacques Bouveresse" in J. P. Cometti, ed., *Lire Rorty*; English version in P. Engel (ed.) "The Analytic-Continental Divide".

R. Schérer, *L'Emile perverti*, Paris 1970.

J. Searle, "The World Turned Upside Down", *New York Review of Books* (1980).

E.E. Smith and D.L. Medin, *Categories and Concepts*, Cambridge, MA: Harvard University Press, 1981.

E. Sosa, "Serious Philosophy and the Freedom of Spirit", *Journal of Philosophy* 84, (1987), 707–726.

D. Sperber and D. Wilson, *Relevance*, Oxford: Blackwell 1986.

P. A. Taguieff, "Nietzsche dans la rhétorique réactionnaire", in Luc Ferry et Alain Renaut (eds.), *Pourquoi nous ne sommes pas nietzschéens*, pp. 217-305.

S. Wheeler III, "The Indeterminacy of French Interpretation", in E. LePore (ed.), *Truth and Interpretation: Perspectives on the Philosophy of Donald Davidson*, Oxford: Blackwell, Oxford, 1986.

CAN THERE BE DEFINITIVE INTERPRETATIONS?
An Interpretation of Foucault in Response to Engel

In "The Decline and Fall of French Nietzscheo-Structuralism" Prof. Engel has zeroed on what is, without a doubt, the centerpiece among the European ideas which have recently influenced the American Academy. This is the idea, in short, that there can be no definitive interpretations. In Foucault's notorious formulation as reported by Prof. Engel: "1) interpretation has become an infinite task, 2) if interpretation can never be ended, it is because there is nothing to interpret, [and] 3) interpretation has to interpret itself *ad infinitum*."[1] Prof. Engel then proceeds to discuss six theses which he considers to be at the heart of this position. I do not have the space to examine these theses in detail here, nor Prof. Engel's enlightening and often provocative analyses of them. Rather than trying to accomplish the impossible, then, I shall instead concentrate on the core idea concerning the impossibility of definitive interpretations expressed by the first of Foucault's points. My aim will be to show that both those who adopt this idea and those who are shocked by it fail to understand two important distinctions concerning interpretations.[2] I shall argue that if one understands those distinctions, the claim that there can be no definitive interpretations loses its shocking character, and thus can find a place within a sensible and comprehensive hermeneutic theory. This will serve, moreover, to illustrate indirectly what I believe is true of much of the philosophical literature coming out of what Prof. Engel calls Nietzscheo-Structuralism. I am referring to the fact that it often contains rather obvious truisms which appear shocking and paradoxical only because of the lack of clarity with which they are presented. Sometimes these truisms are banalities, as Prof. Engel has pointed out, but at other times they signal important principles that need to be incorporated into any sound hermeneutic theory. Thus my remarks, in contrast with those of Prof. Engel, can be construed as a defence of the Nietzscheo-Structuralists, but only as a half-hearted and ambiguous defence at best. In this my remarks contrast also with the apology presented on behalf of the French by other contributors to this volume of *The Monist Library of Philosophy*.[3]

Let me turn, then, to the two distinctions in question: First, a distinction among three different functions of textual interpretations and, second, a distinction between textual and nontextual interpretations.

Before I turn to these, however, I should make clear two things. The first is what I mean by an interpretation. The term 'interpretation' is used in various ways in the literature.[4] Very often an interpretation is simply an understanding. At other times an interpretation is the process or activity whereby an understanding is developed, and still at other times it is conceived as an explanation.[5] Because of the limitations under which I have to work here, however, I will limit the notion of interpretation to that of a text T_3 composed of a text T_2 which is added to another text T_1 in order to produce acts of understanding in an audience in relation to T_1.[6] In this sense an interpretation includes both the *interpretandum* and the *interpretans*, just as a definition includes the *definiendum* and the *definiens*.[7]

The second thing I need to make clear is that, in order to get the discussion started, I assume that, if there can be definitive interpretations of texts, there can be only one definitive interpretation per text. This applies, regardless of what one conceives definitive interpretations or texts to be. Now let me turn to the first of the three specific functions of textual interpretations I wish to distinguish.

This function, which I shall call the Historical Function, aims to recreate in the contemporary audience the acts of understanding of the historical author and the historical audience of the text under interpretation. The aim of the interpreter in this case is to try to have an audience understand a text as its historical author and historical audience understood it. This is obviously a purely historical aim, whose purpose is not to go beyond the parameters of understanding experienced by the historical author and the historical audience. Indeed, if the effect of the interpretation is to create in the contemporary audience acts of understanding which neither the historical author nor the historical audience experienced, then the interpretation is a bad one. For those acts of understanding would imply a meaning which is essentially different from the meaning implied by the acts of understanding the historical author and the historical audience had. And in such a case the interpretation fails to produce understanding and produces misunderstanding instead. Taken in this sense, the task of the interpreter is to add a text to the text under interpretation in order to make up for the differences in culture, circumstances, and so on between the historical author and the historical audience of a text on the one hand and its contemporary audience on the other.

A second specific function of interpretations, also concordant with their overall generic function, I shall call the Meaning Function. This function is to produce in contemporary audiences acts of understanding which may go beyond the acts of understanding of the historical author and the historical audience of the text, revealing aspects of the meaning of the text with which their historical authors and historical audiences were not acquainted.[8] Obviously, the aim of this kind of interpretation is not the recreation of the understandings of the historical author and the historical audience, and the measure of the success or failure of the interpretation has nothing to do with such understandings. Moreover, it assumes that the text in question has a meaning which is broader, and perhaps deeper, than the meaning the historical author and historical audience of the text thought it had.[9]

Finally, a third specific function of interpretations, which I shall call Implicative Function, is to produce in contemporary audiences acts of understanding whereby those audiences understand the implications of the meaning of texts, regardless of whether the historical author and the historical audiences were or were not aware of those implications.[10] Again, the aim of the interpreter in this case is not historical in the sense implied by the first function, and the success or failure of the interpretation cannot be measured by how close it reproduces in a contemporary audience the acts of understanding which the historical author and historical audience of the text had.

Two points follow from what has been said. The first is that the three functions mentioned are not mutually exclusive. An interpretation may have all these functions simultaneously, although in practice interpretations that try to do so usually create more confusion than understanding. Indeed, the unconscious mixing of these functions by interpreters is the main flaw of most interpretations of texts. Interpreters who are not aware of the differences among these functions mix them in such a way that they leave their audiences thoroughly confused as to what they understand the historical author and historical audience understood, what the meaning of the text is, or what the implications of that meaning are. It is essential to the production of successful textual interpretations to distinguish among these functions, although the functions are not incompatible in principle.

The second point is that the pre-eminence of one of these functions with respect to a particular text depends very much on the type of text in question as determined by the cultural function it is supposed to carry out. In a divinely revealed text, where the author's understanding determines its meaning and the aim of the audience is to find out that meaning, the first function is most important even if unlikely to be carried out successfully.[11] But in a legal text, where the aim is to serve as a guide for action, the second and third functions may be more important.

The different functions of interpretations explain also the fact that there may be different, but equally effective, interpretations of a text, a point most relevant to the question of definitive interpretation. Consider the following text:

1. Loosely wrapped in a newspaper he carried a book.

And consider the following interpretations of it:

2. 'Loosely wrapped in a newspaper he carried a book' means that he carried a book which was loosely wrapped in a newspaper.

3. 'Loosely wrapped in a newspaper he carried a book' means that he was loosely wrapped in a newspaper while carrying a book.

4. 'Loosely wrapped in a newspaper he carried a book' means either that he carried a book which was loosely wrapped in a newspaper or that he was loosely wrapped in a newspaper while carrying a book.

If the function of one interpretation is to reproduce the acts of understanding of the historical author with respect to (1) and the historical author understood (1) as (3), and the function of another interpretation is to produce an understanding of the meaning of (1), regardless of what the historical author thought it meant, then both (3) and (4) are effective, even though they conflict, as long as one keeps in mind their different specific functions. (For present purposes I am assuming, of course, that (4) correctly expresses the meaning of (1).) Likewise, it may turn out that the same interpretation carries out more than one function. Consider the case in which the historical author of (1) understood it as (4). In this case (4) would fulfill two functions: the recreation in the contemporary audience of the acts of understanding the historical author had and also the production in that audience of acts of understanding which made it understand the meaning of (1).

Many of the puzzles raised in the contemporary literature concerned with the identity of texts and the possibility of conflicting interpretations which agitate those Prof. Engel has called Nietzscheo-Structuralists vanish when one considers the nature of interpretations and their functions.[12] In this way we can resolve the vexing issue of whether interpretations involve construction or discovery, for example.[13] From what has been said it follows that all interpretations involve construction, namely, the production of a text which will produce acts of understanding in an audience. And they involve discovery to the degree that interpreters must search for the best means to produce those acts of understanding. But interpretations do not directly involve the construction or discovery of meaning. That task falls to understanding, although interpretations presuppose understanding of meaning.[14]

If what I have argued concerning the nature and function of interpretations makes sense, then it is not possible to think that there can be one definitive interpretation of a text, even in the narrow case in which its function is to reproduce the acts of understanding of the historical author and historical audience of the text in a contemporary audience (let alone the other two). This is so as long as there are cultural and conceptual differences between the historical author and the historical audience of the historical text on the one hand and the audience contemporary with the interpreter on the other.[15] For each new audience will require a new interpretation that will bridge the gaps between it and the historical author and the historical audience of the historical text if there are cultural, social, and other differences which separate it from the historical author, the historical audience, and the audiences for which other interpretations were produced. The only way in which there could be one definitive interpretation of a text would be if its audiences always had the same cultural and conceptual framework, but that, although not logically impossible, is not a realistic option.

Of course, there is no reason why there could not be a definitive interpretation of a text for a particular time and place, that is, an interpretation that best helps to bridge the gaps between the text and the audience of that time and place. And there is no reason either why there cannot be interpretations that are more enduring than others. Indeed, some interpretations may be such that they can bridge the gap between the historical text and several subsequent audiences rather than just one.

If the function of an interpretation is not understood narrowly, as referring only to the Historical Function, but broadly, as referring to the Meaning and Implicative Functions as well, then it is even more clear that there cannot be one definitive interpretation of a text. For in that case the function of an interpretation is not the recreation in a contemporary audience of the acts of understanding of the historical author and the historical audience in relation to a text. Its function is rather (1) the production of acts of understanding which reveal the meaning of the text, even if the historical author and the historical audience did not have those acts, and (2) the production of acts which reveal the implications of that meaning. For the number of interpretations will depend on the breadth and implications of the meaning of the text. Moreover, in some cases the meaning of texts is open ended, as determined by their cultural function, leaving open also the number of interpretations that may be given to them. In these cases it is not possible to speak of one definitive interpretation of a text.

But this is not all. The picture we have of interpretations is too incomplete to serve our purpose. To complete the picture we must turn to the second distinction mentioned at the beginning. This is a distinction between textual and nontextual interpretations. This distinction is based on the cultural function of interpretations. An interpretation as I have presented it here is, first and foremost, an attempt to produce acts of understanding in an audience in relation to a text. In some cases, such acts of understanding are intended to be closely related to the meaning of the text, but in others they are not. Indeed we often seek to produce acts of understanding in an audience vis-à-vis a text not simply to grasp its meaning or the implications of its meaning, but for other reasons as well, such as making known the historical significance of past events, the character of other persons, and so on. These various purposes give rise to different sorts of interpretations.

Interpretations whose main or only purpose is to produce understandings of the meanings of texts (whether those meanings are determined by the acts of understanding of the historical author and the historical audience or not) and of the implications of those meanings, may be distinguished from a second sort. This second sort consists of interpretations whose primary aim is not to produce such understandings, even when such understandings are necessary for the fulfilment of the primary aim of the interpretations. I call the first textual interpretations and the second nontextual interpretations.[16] A textual interpretation is precisely the sort of interpretation we have been discussing so far. It is an interpretation of a text that adds to the text whatever is thought by the interpreter to be necessary in order to get certain results in contemporary minds in relation to the text, when those results are taken in one of three ways: first, as the recreation of the acts of understanding of the historical author and the historical audience, that is, as the understanding of the meaning the historical author and the historical audience had; second, as the production of acts of understanding whereby the meaning of the text, regardless of what the historical author and the historical audience thought, are understood by the contemporary audience; and, third, as the production of acts of understanding whereby the implications of the meaning of the text are understood by the contemporary audience. A nontextual interpretation is one that, although it may be based on a textual interpretation, has something else as its primary aim, even if such an aim involves or is a kind of understanding. In short, the functions of nontextual interpretations are different from the three functions textual interpretations have and are not primarily directed toward the meaning of the text or its implications.

The distinction between textual and nontextual interpretations may be easily illustrated by contrasting a textual interpretation with a historical interpretation, for historical interpretations constitute one type of nontextual interpretation. The significance of this example derives from the fact that the role of the interpreter who seeks to produce a textual interpretation is also usually a historical one; she wants to produce understandings in a contemporary audience, either understandings which also the historical author and the historical audience had or which they did not have but nonetheless are legitimate understandings of the meaning of the text, or she wants to produce understandings of the implications of the meaning of the text. And this is achieved by finding out something about the past. The task of the historian who wishes to provide a historical interpretation, however, goes beyond that of the interpreter; her primary task is not to produce a textual interpretation, but over and above that to provide a historical account of the past, and this account involves much more than a textual interpretation.

A historical interpretation is more than a textual interpretation because it seeks to reconstruct the intricate weave of thoughts and ideas and relations which were not recorded in the historical text and which are neither part of its meaning nor of the implications of that meaning.[17] This is, indeed, what makes history appear more than just a series of atomically discrete events.[18] The ultimate aim of the historian is to produce an account of the past and that account includes not only textual interpretations, but also the reconstruction of the larger context in which the text was produced, the ideas that the historical author did not put down in writing or express in speech, the relations among various texts from the same author and from other authors, the causal connections among texts, and so on. The aim of the historian is more than the creation of an instrument that would cause the reproduction of the acts of understanding of the author and the contemporaneous audience when they were confronted with the text, or that would help the contemporary audience understand the meaning of the text in new ways, or to grasp better the implications of that meaning. The historian also wants to produce other acts of understanding in her audience which neither the historical author nor the audience had or could have had precisely because of their historical (e.g., temporal, cultural, and spatial) limitations and which are possible for the historian and his contemporary audience owing to their different historical location and perspective. These acts are not acts of understanding of just the meaning of the text or of the implications of that meaning, but go beyond them in significant ways.

In short, a textual interpretation is only the beginning and only one element of a historical interpretation. The task of historians is much larger than simply to offer textual interpretations of texts, although if they are going to get anywhere in their task they must begin with those types of interpretations. *Qua* textual interpreters, they need (1) to reproduce in the minds of their audience acts of understanding similar to those present in the minds of the authors and their historical audiences, (2) to produce in those audiences a better understanding of the texts in question by helping them understand parts of the meaning of the texts not understood by its historical authors and audiences, and (3) to help those audiences grasp some of the implications of that meaning. But this is not all they do. *Qua* historians their job is to go beyond this and provide an account of history that goes beyond the text. Historical interpretations, like other nontextual interpretations aim to produce acts of understanding which involve more than the text, its meaning and the implications of that meaning; they involve the relation of the text to other things.

Historical interpretations are just one sort of nontextual interpretations. There are many others, depending on the cultural functions interpretations may have. For example, there can be philosophical, inspirational, legal, political, scientific, and literary interpretations, among others. And within these there may be various subcategories as well. There are also psychological interpretations in which a text is seen as revealing something about the person who produced it in

addition to whatever other meaning it has. This is a very popular type of interpretation among those literary critics who have bought into the Freudian scheme
and are trying to apply it, sometimes indiscriminately, to every text they confront.

For our limited purposes the most significant aspect of the distinction
between textual and nontextual interpretations is that it makes clear, as did the
distinction among the three functions of textual interpretations, that there can
never be one and only one definitive interpretation of a text. For the number of
nontextual interpretations of a text are as many as the nontextual functions
members of a society and culture can device for them. Whether there can be
definitive interpretations of a certain type, for example, psychological ones,
depends very much on the rules which apply to that particular type of interpretation as devised by a particular society. In some cases it may be so, but in others
it may not.

CONCLUSION

Now let me summarize what I have been saying by going back to the point
made by Foucault: "Interpretation has become an endless task." Placed in the
context of the two distinctions I have introduced, we can see both that he was
right and that what he says is not as puzzling as it first appears. Interpretation is
an endless task because the number of interpretations is potentially infinite. And
the number of interpretations is potentially infinite because there can be as
many interpretations as audiences that require them and as functions which
societies devise for them. The problem of those in the American Academy who
emulate the Nietzscheo-Structuralists is that often they miss the real thrust of
the Nietzscheo-Structuralist's views. Indeed, it may be that, as Prof. Engel suggested, it is the noncontextual reading of their sources which leads to the absur-
dities sometimes found in their own writings. Or it may be that it is the cryptic
and noncontextual formulation of their views by their critics that does so. But,
then, I should not preach, for my reading of Foucault's statement is hardly contextual. The difference between those in the American Academy who emulate
the Nietzscheo-Structuralists and those who criticize them on the one hand and
me on the other is that I am fully aware of the liberties I take when I read them,
for I am conscious of the type of interpretation to which I subject their texts.[19] J

Jorge J.E. Gracia

State University of New York at Buffalo

NOTES

1.   For the text of Foucault, see Michel Foucault, "Nietzsche, Freud, Marx", p. 63. The standard translation of Foucault's text reads "interpretation has become an *endless task*". My emphasis.

2.   Apart from Foucault, there are many others who favor the view that there cannot be definitive interpretations. For example, Miller, "Tradition and Difference" p. 12; Bloom, *The Anxiety of Influence,* p. 95; Gadamer, *Truth and Method,* p. 264. For opposite views, see Hirsch, *Validity in Interpretation,* p. 5, and *The Aims of Interpretation,* pp. 90-91 and P. D. Juhl, *Interpretation,* pp. 7-8.

3.   Particularly the articles by Newton Garver and Christopher Norris.

4.   Apart from the senses of 'interpretation' I mention, there are others which are not so obvious or clear, but which are nevertheless frequently present in hermeneutical discussions. For example, the expression 'there is still room for interpretation' suggests that an interpretation is a certain type of understanding different from one expected or canonical. Cf. Ricoeur, "Creativity in Language: Word, Polysemy, Metaphor". Along somewhat similar lines, an interpretation may be taken as an understanding which goes beyond what is warranted by directly observable phenomena. See my *Philosophy and Its History,* p. 48. Sometimes 'interpretation' is used as a synonym of 'meaning'; see J.W. Meiland, "Interpretation as a Cognitive Discipline", p. 25.

5.   See Morris Weitz, *Hamlet and the Philosophy of Literary Criticism,* ch. 15.

6.   The texts make other texts understandable. A version of the distinction between understanding and making understandable is found in Schleiermacher, *Hermeneutics,* p. 96. This distinction is rejected by Gadamer in *Truth and Method,* pp. 274 ff. See Brice Wachterhauser's discussion of this issue in "Interpreting Texts: Objectivity of Participation?" p. 443.

7.   See my "Texts and Their Interpretation". Some postmodernists reject the idea of a text that antecedes, is the referent of, or is separate from an interpretation, just as they reject the view of such a text anteceding, being the referent of, or being separate from an understanding. The notion that an interpretation involves an addition to an original text, modifying it in some ways, is suggested by Abrams in "The Deconstructive Angel", p. 426, but he does not distinguish clearly between interpretation as understanding and interpretation as I have taken it here.

8.   Some postmodernists would have to reject this function because they do not see interpretations as capturing meaning at all. See Barthes, *S/Z,* pp. 11-12.

9.   That the historical authors of texts and their historical audiences may not understand all that a text means is widely accepted by philosophers of very different persuasions and frequently illustrated in our everyday experience. For we often say something which is understood by our immediate audience in the way we understand it, but which later is shown by others to mean much more or much less than what we and our immediate audience thought it meant. See, for example, Kant, *Critique of Pure Reason,* ch. 1, sec. 1, p. 310. Miguel de Unamuno, with his characteristic wit, asks, "Since when is the author of a book the person to understand it best?"; "On the Reading and Interpretation of *Don Quijote*", p. 974.

10. Those authors who reject a distinction between the meaning of a text and the implications of that meaning would have to reject the distinction between the Meaning and Implicative Functions. For an author who follows this line, see Jones, *Philosophy and the Novel*, p. 182. Wachterhauser attributes to Gadamer the view that the logical implications of what authors say are included in the meaning of what they say: "Interpreting Texts" p. 448.

11. In some cases it would be impossible. For example, if the divinity in question is infinite, it would be impossible for a finite being to have acts of understanding in relation to a text which are of the same sort as those the divinity has.

12. For some of the puzzles, see, for example, Currie, "Work and Text".

13. There has been much discussion of this issue in the literature. See, for example, Stern, "Factual Constraints on Interpreting".

14. The issue of whether there can be definitive understandings of a text is a different, although related issue. I discuss this and other issues related to understanding in Chapter 9 of a book I have under preparation, *A Theory of Textuality*.

15. This point has been well understood by deconstructionists, although for different reasons than I give here. See J. Hillis Miller, "Steven's Rock", p. 331.

16. M.H. Abram's notion of "linguistic interpretation", which he contrasts with "historical interpretation", may appear to be similar to my notion of "textual interpretation" I give here. They cannot be taken as equivalent, however, because his view of interpretation is closer to understanding than to my view. "The Deconstructive Angel", p. 426.

17. For a different view of historical and nonhistorical interpretations, see Jones, *Philosophy and the Novel*, p. 184.

18. Gracia, *Philosophy and Its History*, pp. 42ff.

19. I am grateful to the participants of the conference "European Philosophy and the American Academy" for their many comments and criticisms of this paper which helped me rethink some of the issues it addresses. I am particularly grateful to Barry Smith, Kevin Mulligan, Newton Garver, Dallas Willard, Myles Brand, and Thomas Pavel. I am also grateful to Jeremy Fantl for a careful reading of the text which revealed some weaknesses in it.

REFERENCES

M.H. Abrams, "The Deconstructive Angel", *Critical Inquiry* 3 (1977).

Roland Barthes, *S/Z*, Paris: Editions du Seuil 1970.

Harold Bloom, *The Anxiety of Influence: A Theory of Poetry*, New York: Oxford University Press 1973.

Gregory Currie, "Work and Text", *Mind* 100 (1991).

Michel Foucault, "Nietzsche, Freud, Marx", in Gayle L. Orminston and Alan D. Schrift (eds.), *Transforming the Hermeneutic Context: From Nietzsche to Nancy*, Albany, NY: SUNY Press 1990; English translation of "Nietzsche", *Cahiers de Royaumont, Philosophie* 6 (1967), 183-97.

Hans-Georg Gadamer, *Truth and Method,* 2nd ed., tr. Garrett Barden and Robert Cummings, New York: Crossroad, 1975.

Jorge J.E. Gracia, *Philosophy and Its History: Issues in Philosophical Historiography,* Albany, NY: SUNY Press 1992.

——, "Texts and Their Interpretation", *The Review of Metaphysics* 43 (1988).

E. D. Hirsch, Jr., *The Aims of Interpretation,* Chicago: Chicago University Press 1976.

——, *Validity in Interpretation,* New Haven, CT: Yale University Press 1967.

Peter Jones, *Philosophy and the Novel,* Oxford: Clarendon Press 1975.

P. D. Juhl, *Interpretation: An Essay in the Philosophy of Literary Criticism,* Princeton, NJ: Princeton University Press 1980.

Immanuel Kant, *Critique of Pure Reason,* tr. Norman Kemp Smith, London: Macmillan 1973.

J.W. Meiland, "Interpretation as a Cognitive Discipline", *Philosophy and Literature* 2 (1978).

J. Hillis Miller, "Steven's Rock and Criticism as Cure II", *Georgia Review* 30 (1976).

J. Hillis Miller, "Tradition and Difference", *Diacritics* 2 (1972).

Paul Ricoeur, "Creativity in Language: Word, Polysemy, Metaphor", in Charles E. Regan and David Stewart (eds.), *The Philosophy of Paul Ricoeur: An Anthology of His Work,* Boston: Beacon Press 1978

F.D.E. Schleiermacher, *Hermeneutics: The Handwritten Manuscripts,* ed. Heinz Kimmerle, tr. James Duke and Jack Forstman, Missoula, MT: Scholars Press 1977.

Laurent Stern "Factual Constraints on Interpreting", *The Monist* 73 (1990).

Miguel de Unamuno, "On the Reading and Interpretation of *Don Quijote*", in J. R. Jones and K. Douglas (eds.), *Miguel de Cervantes, Don Quijote,* New York: W. W. Norton 1981,

Brice Wachterhauser, "Interpreting Texts: Objectivity of Participation?", *Man and World* 19 (1986).

Morris Weitz, *Hamlet and the Philosophy of Literary Criticism,* Chicago: University of Chicago Press 1964.

OBSTACLES TO FRUITFUL DISCUSSION IN THE AMERICAN ACADEMY:
THE CASE OF DECONSTRUCTION

My purpose in this paper is to address two interrelated issues. On the one hand, I want to discuss some of the obstacles to the fruitful discussion of deconstruction in the American academy. On the other hand, I intend to consider some of the ways in which the acceptance of deconstruction, in at least some of its forms, tends in general to stand in the way of constructive dialogue, on whatever topic, in American colleges and universities. In pursuing these aims I will draw inspiration from Herman Philipse's analysis of Heidegger's "rhetorical stratagems."[1] For I notice that many of the stratagems that Philipse identifies in connection with Heidegger apply, with appropriate adjustments, just as well to Derrida, and/or to some popular conceptions of deconstruction, as to Heidegger, and, moreover, that what all of these stratagems have in common is that they serve to block off meaningful discussion. Thus, by applying Philipse's insights, or variations on them, directly to deconstruction and to the issue of discussion in the American academy, I hope to provide a useful bridge between his discussion of Heidegger and the principal concerns of the present conference.

Before taking up the stratagems, however, let me offer a few preliminary remarks which might help to prevent misunderstandings of my project. First, while I will be focusing on, and criticizing, primarily the rhetorical stratagems used by the defenders of deconstruction, I do not want to suggest that the critics of deconstruction are blameless in connection with the current low quality of debate over deconstruction. To the contrary, I find that many critics of deconstruction do not even bother to become acquainted first-hand with deconstructionist texts before issuing their objections, but rather dismiss deconstruction sweepingly because, for example, it is a specimen of continental philosophy (a move made by some analytic philosophers), or because it is vaguely associated with feminism, multiculturalism, "political correctness", and kindred phenomena (a move made by many cultural and political conservatives). Finally, even among those who harbor no such ideological predisposition to reject deconstruction, but who suffer, perhaps, from an undue respect for contemporary journalism, many conclude solely on the basis of the numerous sensationalist-sic, ill-informed newspaper and popular magazine accounts of deconstruction that it is obvious nonsense, unworthy of serious consideration.

Unfortunately, however, it has been my experience that very many of the defenders of deconstruction, when faced with criticisms of a more serious, responsible, and well-informed nature, such as those presented in J. Claude

Evans's *Strategies of Deconstruction*, tend in their responses to descend to depths of anti-intellectualism almost equal to those described in the preceding paragraph. I will attempt to show this in detail by describing several specific rhetorical stratagems, commonly used by some deconstructionists, which have the effect, whether intended or not, of blocking all meaningful discussion of deconstruction, and, in some cases, of everything else as well. I should make it clear, however, that not all of these stratagems are to be found in the works of Derrida, let alone in those of all defenders of deconstruction. On the other hand, however, I have encountered all of them on numerous occasions, and I will document some of them. Those which I do not document are ones I have encountered only, though repeatedly, in oral discussions. Thus, I will have to rely on the experience of the reader in his or her own discussions of deconstruction to verify or falsify my claim that these stratagems are indeed real and ubiquitous. My largest aim in all of this is not the utterly quixotic one of attempting to refute every form of deconstruction once and for all, but rather, and I hope both more plausibly and more modestly, simply to make clearer and more vivid some of the main obstacles to fruitful discussion about deconstruction, or about other things because of deconstruction, so that people of good will and intellectual integrity, no matter what their views on deconstruction, might be better able to help remove some of these obstacles and thus to facilitate the beginning of productive dialogue.

Finally, let me also make it clear that Professor Philipse is not to be blamed for what follows. For, while I have been inspired by his list of rhetorical stratagems, I am the one who is responsible for applying them to deconstruction. Moreover, I have modified some of his stratagems, added many others of my own, and given all of them new names. I might also mention that, while the first two stratagems undermine only the discussion specifically of deconstruction, the remaining eight have much wider application (though I sometimes do not bother to point this out).

The stratagem of the global/local flip-flop.

Defenders of deconstruction frequently object, and rightly so, to attempts at global, sweeping denunciations of deconstruction. They admonish critics of deconstruction to proceed more slowly and carefully, and to produce instead *specific* criticisms of *specific* points in *specific* deconstructionist texts. However, when one does so—and again, I would cite Evans as a good example of one who indeed does so—the response by some of these same defenders of deconstruction is that the critic has missed the point, namely, that the value of deconstruction is to be found elsewhere, and consists of something larger, more global, than the particular point taken up by the critic. Thus, one is told that the point and value of deconstruction is that it inspires people to read, and, in particular, to read closely and carefully, or that it opens up philosophy to those, such as women, blacks, and non-westerners, who have previously been marginalized, or again, that it leads to a healthy, and ethically and politically desirable, kind of skepticism. In this way, deconstruction is rendered immune from criticism, because the critic, always and in principle, misses the point. When the critic's point is global, the defense shifts to the local; when the criticism is local, the defense is global.

The stratagem of the radical/banal flip-flop.

Part of the attraction of deconstruction lies in its seemingly radical quality. Derrida, in particular, often issues utterances which, if taken at face value, appear to be in wild opposition to the clearest givens of experience and to the most obvious dicta of common sense. His famous assertion that "there is nothing outside the text"[2] is perhaps the most prominent example of this. Now, what deconstruction gains in the excitement generated by its radicalness it tends to lose in plausibility. However, since Derrida's claims readily lend themselves to diverse interpretations—whether this be due to Derrida's obscurity or, as some deconstructionists would have it, because all language is similarly ambiguous, I will not address at present—they can easily be understood in a manner which renders them far more plausible then they would be on their radical construal, though at the cost of thereby reducing their novelty and excitement value. Thus, "there is nothing outside the text" might be taken as meaning either something like the assertion that nothing exists but language (a provocative but implausible thesis), or else something like the claim that there is a linguistic component to our understanding of anything whatsoever, or, tamer still, that it is a useful heuristic device to think of everything in terms of its linguistic aspect (plausible theses, but ones with which the world had already been quite familiar prior to the advent of Derrida). Some defenders of Derrida try to have the best of both worlds—that is, to uphold both the radicalness and the plausibility of Derrida's claims—through a flip-flop maneuver. That is, to deflect the criticism that Derrida's claims are improbable, his defenders stress the banal interpretation of his utterances; but to deflect the criticism that naturally arises next, namely, that these utterances are, then, unoriginal commonplaces, the defenders resurrect the radical interpretation. The obscurity of Derrida's language—or else of language itself—makes it possible for the defenders of Derrida to glide back and forth between these different interpretations quite easily within the framework of a single short conversation.

The stratagem of the all-embracing abstraction.

Another way to deflect criticisms is to employ an abstract concept that is so general as to be able to encompass just about everything, so that all of the criticisms can be reduced to this general concept and thereby rejected in one fell swoop, eliminating the need to answer them one at a time. Some deconstructionists use the term 'logocentrism' in this way. This stratagem is also often used to terminate discussion of topics other than deconstruction, for if one can wipe away a large cluster of distinct theories at once through the claim that they are all logocentric, there is no need to attend to the different theories carefully, to evaluate them, and to choose among them. Consequently, there is no need for the discussion which would normally serve as a preliminary to, and indeed as a part of, these activities.

The stratagem of homogenization.

The reduction of (nearly) everything to logocentrism sometimes seems to be merely one part of a general program of reduction and homogenization. Indeed, many readers of deconstructionist texts have complained that such texts are characterized by a remarkable degree of sameness—a paradoxical finding given that deconstruction is intended to be a philosophy of difference. Such texts are homogeneous precisely in that they all find the same things, such as difference, wherever they look. They are reductionistic, moreover, in that they all find nothing but these same things. As James M. Edie laments, in connection with the deconstructive literature:

> all too often what one first begins to read hopefully as a critical philosophical argument...ends with the simple conclusion that what other philosophers, or 'the tradition', or some text—taken for purposes of illustration—just lacks is the notion of *la Différance*, and *that* both ends the argument and the paper.[3]

Or again, from the pro-deconstruction standpoint, consider the autobiographical reflections of Barry W. Sarchett:

> I had been taught that only certain select texts were full of the 'complexity' and 'ambiguity' which mark the truly worthwhile literary work. But then I realized that an insightful and probing reader can make any text dance with possibility...At this point, all sorts of barriers and boundaries began breaking down in my thinking. Formerly self-evident distinctions between good and bad, high and low began to look more and more suspicious.[4]

So the effect of Sarchett's form of deconstruction is to render everything the same—nothing is more or less complex or ambiguous, or better or worse, than anything else. The one positive quality that Sarchett does identify in all texts, he identifies equally in all of them: the reading of any of them generates, always and of necessity, an "endless proliferation of difference".[5]

While it is tempting to challenge Sarchett's views directly, that would be outside of the scope of this paper. So I will point out here only that such an a priori commitment to uniformity of result stands as a substantial obstacle to the fruitful discussion of anything, for it tends to make such discussion both pointless (since nearly every discussion has as its aim the drawing of a conclusion at odds with Sarchett's homogenized view—e.g. it attempts to show that one thing is better than another, or more complex than another, or more *something* than another) and impossible (because nearly every such discussion has to rely on the admissibility of premises similarly at odds with the view that everything is the same as everything else).

The stratagem of indiscriminate analogy.

Because everything, in some way or another, and at some level of abstraction, is similar to everything else, one can, by means of a careless or unprincipled use of analogies, say just about anything. This stratagem is often found in deconstructionist arguments, and is especially favored as a means by which to fend off criticisms. For example, consider this statement of Derrida's, from his article responding to the revelations that the deconstructionist Paul de Man had, as a young man, written anti-Semitic, pro-Nazi articles, and had concealed this fact—indeed, lying about it on several occasions—for the rest of his life:

> To judge, to condemn the work or the man on the basis of what was a brief episode, to call for closing, that is to say, at least figuratively, for censuring or burning his books is to reproduce the exterminating gesture against which one accuses de Man of not having armed himself sooner with the necessary vigilance.[6]

Leaving aside the many other issues one might address in response to this remarkable passage (e.g. the attack on a straw man, in that no one, to my knowledge, had called for the burning of de Man's books, and the euphemism entailed by the reference to de Man's merely "not having armed himself against" anti-Semitism and Nazism "sooner and with the necessary vigilance"), one is struck by Derrida's indiscriminate use of analogies. Yes, I suppose there are some similarities between the acts of criticizing a person's works and calling for their destruction by fire, but surely the radical differences between these acts are even more significant, and are such as to render Derrida's facile comparison unconvincing. The same point applies even more clearly to Derrida's equation of the burning of de Man's books (which, remember, no one really did, though some "at least figuratively" did so by criticizing them) with the extermination of the Jews (and others) in the Nazi death camps.

Another way to make this point about indiscriminate analogies is to point out how frequently one can reply to an analogy offered by a defender of deconstruction by constructing an equally plausible analogy on the same issue which supports the opposite conclusion. For example, defenders of deconstruction sometimes claim that deconstruction's emphasis on what had previously been regarded as marginal in texts shows that it is a pro-feminist philosophy since women, too, have previously been marginalized in most cultures, including that of western philosophy. Leaving aside other problems with this analogy (e.g. that while it seems quite plausible to suppose that some parts of a text really essentially are, and therefore should remain, marginal—consider, for example, the issue of which footnote convention happens to be used in a particular scholarly work—it seems even more clear that there is no justification for marginalizing people, let alone one half of all people), notice how easy it is to use such analogical thinking to support the opposite conclusion, namely, that deconstruction is an essentially sexist instrument of male domination and violence. "Yes, let's deconstruct your text—we'll take the sections you thought were marginal, elevate them to a status that is contrary to that of your own intentions, and make you say the opposite of what you meant. We'll make your text explode from within, under the weight of its own contradictions." This sort of unsympathetic reading, this ripping apart of texts, this deconstruction—*this* is pro-feminist?

In any case, and as the quotation from Derrida graphically illustrates, the widespread use of arguments from analogy, when not coupled with a scrupulous attention to the question of what is and is not a legitimate analogy, and to the issue of the limits and dangers of analogical arguments, constitutes an obstacle to fruitful discussion, since it makes it possible indiscriminately to affirm absolutely anything whatsoever.

The stratagem of principled opposition to criticism.

Some defenders of deconstruction claim that criticism itself should be avoided in favor of a policy of always respecting another's perspective, and of attempting to appreciate, share in, and learn from his or her point of view. Such a position immunizes deconstruction from refutation, and acts as an obstacle to fruitful discussion insofar as such discussion is intended, in part, as a vehicle by means of which some views might eventually be shown to be mistaken and in need of being replaced by others. (Incidentally, it is clear, both from his example and by his explicit statements on the matter,[7] that Derrida does not share this principled opposition to criticism. Still, as we have seen in the passage on de Man quoted above, and in other places as well,[8] he does have a tendency to confuse criticism of ideas with an attempt to censor them. One way of seeing the difference is to recognize that the former is an important, perhaps an essential, element of productive dialogue, while the latter inhibits it).

The stratagem of obscurity.

Obscurity immunizes against refutation. If one does not know what a given claim means, one cannot show that the claim is mistaken.

Does Derrida employ this stratagem? Here I want to be careful, for two reasons. First, it is impossible to prove that someone's writings are unreasonably or objectionably obscure. I could quote some impenetrable passages, but that would be unfair, since the passages would be removed from their contexts. Thus, I can only ask my readers to decide for themselves, based on their own careful reading of Derrida's works, whether or not they agree with my judgment that they are excessively obscure. Secondly, I do not wish to advance a philistine position on this matter. I acknowledge that a certain amount of obscurity may be necessary when a writer is attempting to communicate especially new and radical, or otherwise inherently difficult, ideas. I acknowledge, moreover, that obscurity is somewhat relative to audience, so that a work intended for readers in possession of a certain amount of technical knowledge in some specific area might be judged clear by its intended audience, but obscure by others lacking the relevant background knowledge. Thus, in light of these considerations, and because of my resulting uncertainty on this issue, I will offer only a conditional judgment: *if* it is the case that Derrida's works are, in context, and relative to the intrinsic difficulty of their ideas and to the background knowledge of their intended audience, objectionably obscure, *then*, in the light of the undeniable immunizing power of obscurity, it is legitimate to speak of a "stratagem of obscurity" in connection with those works.

The ad hominem stratagem.

I find that criticisms of deconstruction are often, though certainly not always nor even usually, met with ad hominem rejoinders. Thus, the claim that, for example, Derrida badly misreads Husserl at a specific point in a particular text, elicits the reply that the critic is an analytic philosopher, or a conservative, or logocentric, or closed-minded, or, paradoxically, unwilling to have a discussion. Such claims are frequently untrue and are often advanced without a shred of supporting evidence. More to the point, however, such ad hominem replies do not join the point made by the critic, and in fact amount to a complete change of subject, from Derrida's ideas to the convictions and personality of the critic. In this way the goal of rational discussion of Derrida is frustrated.

The stratagem of opposition to logic.

G. B. Madison states, approvingly, that

> [p]ostmodern philosophical discourse...often deliberately ignores the requirements
> of logic (e.g., the principle of non-contradiction), because what it wishes to say nec-
> essarily cannot be said by logic (in the eyes of many postmodernists it is no objec-
> tion to an utterance that it be 'inconsistent' or 'improbable').[9]

Such a position is often, though I think mistakenly,[10] attributed to Derrida,
even by his admirers.[11]

In order to explain why such a move precludes fruitful discussion of anything, including, of course, deconstruction, I cannot improve upon Patrick Colm
Hogan's formulation:

> [T]hose who deny the Principle of Non-Contradiction quite literally allow no con-
> tradiction. There simply is no way of disputing their claim[s]...To controvert their
> claims one would need, for example, to present evidence in contradiction with their
> generalizations, or isolate fallacious inferences in their reasonings, but the claims
> themselves disallow this. A denial of the Principle of Non-Contradiction makes all
> of one's claims into dogma, brooking no dispute."[12]

The stratagem of relativism.

I will approach this strategem indirectly. Professor Gerald Graff, if I have taken
accurate notes on his remarks during the present conference, holds the position
that "present problems in higher education have nothing to do with dumb ideas
by professors." His point, if I understand him aright, is that the American academy is a place in which so many interesting and worthwhile ideas are already
available for study and debate that we need not fear the presence of some
"dumb" ones. Rather, what is needed in higher education is simply for a rigorous, challenging, coherent, well-organized program of consideration of this
array of positions to be made accessible to students. Such a program of "teaching the conflicts" among the ideas and theories presently advocated in the
academy should be capable of serving as the foundation of a sound education.
Thus, even if relativism is widespread in American higher education, and even
if, further, relativism is a "dumb idea," there is no cause for alarm.[13]

If the objection to relativism were only that relativism is a dumb idea—like
astrology, for example—I would find this reasoning convincing. After all, there
are other ideas out there besides the bad ones, and perhaps the good ones are
capable of driving out the bad. Such a result would seem especially likely if students were to learn critical thinking skills, as well as substantially to increase
their store of background knowledge, results which we might expect to come
about from their serious consideration of current debates in the academy. Such

improvements in the students' knowledge and skills should indeed render them increasingly capable of distinguishing competently between better and worse ideas.

However, the worry over relativism is of a different sort. It is that relativism, insofar as it suggests that there are no real distinctions of better and worse among ideas, tends to undermine the motivation to learn the skills necessary for discerning such distinctions, or for exercising such discernment once the capacity for it has been acquired. The objection to relativism, in short, is not that relativism deserves no consideration, nor even that it would be a bad thing should many people eventually arrive at a relativist position at the conclusion of a process of serious inquiry, competently conducted; rather, the worry is that the premature adoption of such a worldview acts as a barrier to the acquisition of such competence and as a disincentive to the undertaking of such inquiry. For after all, if what I believe is "true for me", and if what you believe is "true for you", I need not concern myself with the possibility that I might be wrong and you might be right, and thus, I lose one very powerful potential motive for wanting to investigate your views—or any other views than my own, for that matter. The same point applies, with even greater urgency, to the issue of disagreements between cultures. For that reason, I do not understand why relativism is often thought of as a philosophy consistent with, let alone supportive of, multiculturalism in education.

But is Derrida a relativist? I do not think so.[15] Still, a good many deconstructionists are relativists, and see their relativism as flowing directly from their support of deconstruction. In any case, the issue of the impact of relativism on fruitful inquiry and discussion in the American academy is sufficiently important, and sufficiently related to the concerns of this paper, to merit this brief discussion.

Let me conclude by addressing briefly some possible reactions to my remarks. Some readers, I would guess, might take the position that the deconstructive stratagems I have described do not really function so as to cut off productive dialogue, or, alternatively, that deconstruction should be defended in spite of the fact that it entails this (perhaps) unfortunate consequence. At this point, I have nothing left to say to such readers.

Other readers, however, might suspect that I have provided only a caricature of deconstruction. After all, I have already admitted that not all of these stratagems are to be found in the works of all, or, in some cases, even most, defenders of deconstruction. Perhaps, then, none of the stratagems are necessarily (or essentially or by nature) connected to deconstruction. If that is indeed the case, moreover, it might after all be possible to construct a version of deconstruction which would indeed be faithful to the best and most challenging ideas of Derrida, but which, at the same time, would not lead to the breakdowns in communication which seem to flow from the already existing varieties. If, unlikely though it admittedly would be, my remarks here were to serve, in some small way, to stimulate, inspire, or provoke the clear formulation and defense of such a version of deconstruction—a version which would refute my contention that deconstruction undermines the fruitful discussion both of itself and of everything else—I would be pleased.

David Detmer

Purdue University–Calumet

NOTES

1.   Philipse, "Heidegger's Question of Being". See especially Section 4, "Stratagems".
2.   Derrida, *Of Grammatology*, p. 163.
3.   Edie, "Husserl vs. Derrida", p. 103.
4.   Sarchett, "What's All the Fuss About This Postmodernist Stuff?", pp. 383-384.
5.   Sarchett, "What's All the Fuss About This Postmodernist Stuff?", p. 388.
6.   Derrida, "Like the Sound of the Sea Deep Within a Shell: Paul de Man's War," trans. Peggy Kamuf, in Werner Hamacher, Neil Hertz, and Thomas Keenan, eds., *On Paul de Man's Wartime Journalism* (Lincoln: University of Nebraska Press, 1989), p. 157.
7.   I have in mind primarily Derrida's "Afterword: Toward an Ethic of Discussion".
8.   See, for example, Derrida's "Like the Sound of the Sea Deep Within a Shell", p. 155, and his "Biodegradables: Seven Diary Fragments".
9.   G. B. Madison, "Merleau-Ponty's Destruction of Logocentrism", p. 135.
10. See, for example, Derrida, "Afterword".
11. See, for example, Barbara Johnson's Translator's Introduction to in Derrida, *Dissemination*, p. xvii; and Gasché, *The Tain of the Mirror,* p. 104.
12. Hogan, *The Politics of Interpretation*, p. 35.
13. For a much better explanation of Graff's views, see his fine *Beyond the Culture Wars*.
14. Once again, see Derrida's "Afterword".

REFERENCES

Jacques Derrida, "Afterword: Toward an Ethic of Discussion", tr. Samuel Weber, in Derrida, *Limited Inc.*

Jacques Derrida, "Biodegradables: Seven Diary Fragments," tr. Peggy Kamuf, *Critical Inquiry* 15 (1989).

——, *Dissemination,* Chicago: University of Chicago Press 1981.

——, "Like the Sound of the Sea Deep Within a Shell: Paul de Man's War", tr. Peggy Kamuf, in Werner Hamacher, Neil Hertz, and Thomas Keenan (eds.), *On Paul de Man's Wartime Journalism,* Lincoln: University of Nebraska Press 1989.

——, *Limited Inc,* Evanston, Illinois: Northwestern University Press 1988.

——, *Of Grammatology,* tr. Gayatri Chakravorty Spivak, (Baltimore: Johns Hopkins University Press 1976.

James M. Edie, "Husserl vs. Derrida", *Human Studies* 13 (1990).

J. Claude Evans, *Strategies of Deconstruction,* Minneapolis: University of Minnesota Press 1991.

Rodolphe Gasché, *The Tain of the Mirror: Derrida and the Philosophy of Reflection*, Cambridge, MA: Harvard University Press 1986.

Gerald Graff, *Beyond the Culture Wars*, New York: Norton 1992.

Patrick Colm Hogan, *The Politics of Interpretation*, New York: Oxford University Press 1990.

G. B. Madison, "Merleau-Ponty's Destruction of Logocentrism", in M. C. Dillon (ed.), *Merleau-Ponty Vivant,* Albany: State University of New York Press 1991.

Herman Philipse, "Heidegger's Question of Being: A Critical Interpretation", this volume.

Barry W. Sarchett, "What's All the Fuss About This Postmodernist Stuff?" in John Arthur (ed.), *Morality and Moral Controversies*, Englewood Cliffs, New Jersey: Prentice Hall 1993.

TEXTUAL IMPERIALISM

One of the oddities of deconstruction lies in the epistemological privilege it has accorded to writing. While speech, presence, consciousness, perception, the human subject, and other realities in the world of human subjective experience have been targets of a relentless attack, writing has prospered; indeed, writing emerges as a kind of anti-foundational first possibility in a new deconstructive Genesis. While it might seem like a rather bizarre species of anti-humanism that takes the liberation and celebration of writing as worthy recompense for the abolition of man, this deconstructive doctrine can be rationalized, I believe, when we recollect how deconstructors themselves make a living. For most scholars in the humanities in Western institutions of higher learning, employment, promotion, and fame are secured primarily through publication. By reducing the world to discourse and discourse to textuality and writing, deconstructors are able to redefine reality in terms of that activity in which they are most adept and over which they can best exercise their control. In short, the deconstructive celebration of writing is a disguised assertion of superiority on the part of a particular scholarly class.

In recent theory, writing's place of pride was not secured through a fully articulated and reasoned demonstration. Rather, it was engineered through a kind of rhetorical coup. Jacques Derrida, the man most responsible for the dramatic revaluation of writing, developed a specialized critical vocabulary—featuring such terms as *écriture*, trace, inscription, marginalization, and supplementarity—in which metaphors involving the concept of writing were the central organizing structure. But since Derrida seldom defines his terms, the extent to which the acceptance of his theoretical insights depends on a self-surrender to this system of metaphors has rarely been made explicit. Of course, an insight or theory is not discredited merely by the fact that it is constituted on the ground of a linguistic figure. Yet one may legitimately ask why one system of metaphors has been favored over reasonable alternatives. When one begins seriously to interrogate the privileging of writing in deconstructive discourse, the effect, I believe, is seriously to call into question the value of the deconstructive contribution to the study of language.

The point at which writing as a revolutionary subversive force made its way most decisively into deconstructive theory was in the course of the deconstruction of signification. And this deconstruction was accomplished through elaborating and accentuating the role of linguistic *difference*. According to Ferdinand de Saussure, difference is inextricably implicated in the signification process in that signifier and signified can exist only as differential constructs.[1] Thus the signifier, which Saussure defined as a sound image, depends on the exclusion—and the cognition of the exclusion—of what it is not. The voiced bilabial stop *b*, for example, is constituted as a phoneme partly by virtue of the fact that it is not the voiceless bilabial stop *p*; and so the signifier *lab* articulates itself partly through its distinctiveness from the signifier *lap*. It is through noting distinctions and differences such as this that we are able to identify signifiers amid the masses of chaotic sound. In the same way a concept acquires its identity partly through those distinctive features that differentiate it from other concepts. Though an oak is indeed a tree, it is a specific kind of tree, and thus 'oak' and 'tree' are non-identical; similarly, oak and willow differ from each other, although both are members of a common genus. Nothing in the mind exists apart from difference; inevitably, then, difference is built into the structure of signifiers and signifieds at all levels.

Further, difference is crucial not only to the structure of signifiers and signifieds individually but to the relation between them. Saussure described this relationship as an arbitrary one, in the sense that the signifier and signified are joined by no natural link.[2] Nothing in the sound structure of the spoken word 'tree' requires that it refer to that concept that we commonly agree to be 'tree'; thus a Frenchman will use an entirely different signifier ('arbre') to designate this concept, and he will understand the meaning of the spoken English word 'tree' only if he has learned the English language. Even though the relationship between the signifier and signified is unmotivated, however, it is, according to Saussure, not haphazard. Convention regulates it; and even the most defiant of revolutionaries operate within the confines of linguistic convention, else they could not communicate at all. Although it is perfectly possible for any of us to use the spoken word 'tree' to refer in our own minds to such concepts as 'watermelon' or 'the Pythagorean theorem', in our daily interactions no one (apart from Humpty Dumpty) chooses to do this, since such practice would waste everyone's time, annoy our interlocutors, and accomplish nothing. All of this is fairly obvious and has long been understood by students of language.

The deconstructive critique of signification proceeds by radicalizing certain elements in the Saussurean formulation. A central term in this project is the Derridean neologism, *différance*.[3] *Différance*, to Derrida, means both to differ and defer; by conjoining these concepts, Derrida means to amplify on Saussure's observation that "in language there are only differences *without positive terms*"; that is, "language has neither ideas nor sounds that existed before the linguistic system, but only conceptual and phonic differences that have issued from this system."[4] To Derrida, this implies that a signifier or signified is non-identical with itself, that its self-presence is deferred through its reliance on that from which it differs. A signifier (to take this instance) cannot simply be, any more than the phoneme designated by the letter 't' can simply exist in itself; its very possibility depends on its positioning in a chain of differences. *Dif-*

férance is thus the *play* of difference, or the "movement of the play that 'produces'...these differences."[5] It is the contextuality of any element within the
linguistic system, the possibility that is presupposed when any element within
that system comes into view.

Derrida construes this critique of the relationship between the signifier and
the signified as an attack on the metaphysics of presence. The idea of presence
is undermined by the fact that the "present" element, whatever this may be,
always presupposes the absent other. Language, according to what deconstruction represents as the "logocentric" fallacy, appears to bring into consciousness what is original; that is, the meaning of an utterance seems to consist
in the relationship between that utterance and some prior reality, the truth concerning which that utterance brings before the mind. But in fact that origin or
reality is always designated through a token, and the structure of the token
always depends on the radical absence of that which is betokened. The moment
of the "present reality" never arrives, because its reality is always undermined
by its dependence on what it excludes, marginalizes, casts out from its being.
There is no origin or originary reality, because the very possibility of an origin
is itself made possible by the play of difference. Nor can *différance* itself be
characterized as an origin, because it has no substance and does not act; it is
rather that which is presupposed by anything phenomenologically evident.
Différance is not even a negation or vacuum, for it cannot be distinguished from
the language whose possibility it provides.

Writing figures in this program in that it is the enunciation of *différance*,
the marking and the inscription through which the differentiated surface of multiple meanings and presences is enabled to stand forth.[6] Derrida's argument
here, particularly as developed in *Of Grammatology*, works through the subversion of the usual hierarchical relationship between writing and speech, according to which speech is language in its original and primary condition whereas
writing is the integument, the imitation, the representation of speech. But writing, counters Derrida, has been glossed over and its disruptive potential suppressed by this the dominant "phonocentrism" of Western civilization. That
phonocentrism—which is particularly identified with speech and the illusion of
self-presence in voice and vocalizing—is thus implicated in a metaphysics of
presence, which is in turn linked with notions of consciousness, being, and transcendence. Thus Derrida characterizes that "logocentrism which is also a
phonocentrism" as "absolute proximity of voice and being, of voice and the
meaning of being, of voice and the ideality of meaning".[7] Writing, which is the
"disruption of presence in a mark",[8] represents "*la brisure*", the hinge and the
discontinuity, the reversal and the doubling which make "enigmatic what one
thinks one understands by the words 'proximity', 'immediacy', 'presence'..."[9]
Writing as the representation of speech seems to be external to language, like

clothing; yet this very externality marks supplementarity as that which always already precedes and subverts the autonomy and self-sufficiency of being and presence. The externality, the superfluousness, the secondariness of writing turns out to be the mark of the possibility of that to which it is external and superfluous and "second".

The question that I wish to ask is: even if we grant Derrida's view of the supplementarity of the originary and the linguistic constructedness of the apparently real—and I wish it to be understood that I do *not* grant this—but even if we do, why is 'writing' a good name for this putatively primal division in the structure of being? Why writing and not something else? Indeed, why writing rather than oral speech?[10]

Let us consider Derrida's rationalization of the grammatological character of *différance*. As a neologism *différance* is intended to bring into view the subversive role which writing plays with respect to speech. *Différance* with an 'a' is indistinguishable in pronunciation from the standard French word *différence* with an 'e'; the "difference" between the two words, inaudible and thus imperceptible within the world of speech, is displayed only in writing. The " 'a' of differance", Derrida tells us, "is not heard; it remains silent, secret, and discreet, like a tomb."[11] But does it? When *I* use the word, I mark my pronunciation of *différance* by accenting and lengthening the final syllable and lowering its nasalized vowel: 'dif-fér-*aahnce*'. In my experience, interlocutors familiar with the subject and Derrida's coinage can indeed "hear the difference" and, if the point was initially in question, often register the successful communication by nodding, saying "hmmmmm", or in other ways. This particular difference is easily expressible through speech. Others might not be; but so what? The mere fact that there are differences which writing brings to consciousness more readily than speech cannot legitimately serve as a basis for the generalization that difference is itself a thing of writing or that writing is the enunciation of difference.

For examples can easily be adduced in which speech effortlessly enunciates differences that writing obscures. Take the following patch of hypothetical dialogue:

> Student: "Do you think that Derrida's discussion of *différance* has made a significant contribution to the philosophy of language?"
> Professor: "Sure."

Now the professor's one-word answer, 'sure', could convey radically different meanings, depending on its intonation. If I were the professor and I wished to communicate that I did indeed believe in the value of Derrida's contribution, I would say 'sure' at a moderate speed, beginning at a low pitch, rising, and falling off slightly at the end. If, on the other hand, I wished to convey my recognition that other people regard Derrida's contribution as a significant one, that I myself was not much interested in Derrida one way or the other, that I had no wish to quarrel over the matter but would like to get on with whatever we were discussing before, I would say 'sure' at a somewhat higher pitch in a clipped-off manner. Then again, if I wanted to communicate sarcasm and scorn for Derrida's views on *différance*, I would draw out the word 'sure', beginning on an exaggeratedly low pitch, rising to a markedly high pitch, and then falling off drastically at the end. None of these distinctive oral enunciations could be communicated anything like as effectively and economically in writing as they could in speech. And while I might not successfully convey my intended meanings through these intonational expedients, then again, interlocutors who knew me well might catch my sense at once and respond in a way that registers this. After all, most speakers of a language become quite adept in exploiting its phonological resources and can use the distinctively phonic possibilities in vocalization with great effect.

Here, then, is an example of a difference that speech enunciates and writing obscures. "The 'sure' difference", I might say, mimicking—or echoing—Derrida, "is not seen or read; it remains invisible, entombed within the text, yet resonating still from the living speech of men." If speech can express differences that writing cannot—or that writing can only approximate with great labor—why should we accept difference as something that is written more than it is spoken? Indeed, in my readings of Derrida's work I have not yet found a convincing argument or demonstration for the special association between writing and difference that deals with obvious objections such as the one that I have just raised. Rather, his "argument" on this point—in *Of Grammatology*, *Writing and Difference*, *Positions*, and other places—is accomplished through sudden rhetorical assertion. Speech is subverted through "writing", meaning through "trace": thus Derrida deploys metaphors that reconceive linguistic processes in terms of writing, and he infers from this that language—and the reality which language negotiates—is fundamentally written. But it is always possible to create metaphors whereby one domain is construed in terms of another;[12] and if one uncritically accepts these metaphors, it is easy to slip into the assumption that these domains are intrinsically related rather than related through the choice of the one who has opted for metaphors of this kind. Certainly reality is a "text" if one chooses to bring into the foreground of one's awareness the similarly between reflecting on reality and reading a book. Yet to a sportsman, the claim that reality is a "game" might have an immediacy of appeal that the "text" model lacks. Then again, a biologist might regard reality as an evolutionary process dominated by the struggle and interplay of "organic" entities; a businessman might conceive it as the background for a venture of capital with prospective profits or losses; a dramatist might think of it as a scene for dialogue between actors; a mathematician might see it in terms of numerology or set theory. Why should the "text" metaphors be privileged above these—or innumerable other—metaphoric systems? Why is language or reality more textual than it is something else?

I believe that there is a simple and elegant explanation for the virtually uncontested triumph of "writing" and "text" metaphors under the regime of deconstruction. Since we are, in the end, human beings, and since the word 'writing' designates an activity that all scholars are familiar with, the textualiztion of the world" is a pitch to scholarly vocational biases. The "scene of writing", if I may reliteralize the phrase Derrida used in his essay on Freud,[13] is centered around the activity of the writer, and the writer, in discourse of this type, is almost certain to be a scholar. Let us imagine a particular scholar—Derrida— seated at his desk, writing. Since his most influential treatises on writing and grammatology were composed in the late 1960s, he probably wrote with pen or pencil, or at most on a typewriter; word processors had not been invented yet, and few authors rely on dictation anymore. Derrida's theme was difference. Confronted with a blank page, the line—the pencilled trace—breaks the illusion of wholeness, as gestalt therapists could explain to us in detail. Yet the object of his meditation is the world of philosophy, which has traditionally been the discourse in which fundamental questions of ontology and epistemology have been posed. Nothing would be more natural than for such a scholar to conceive these broader issues in terms of the immediate, concrete activity in which he is engaged. And for other scholars of the same type—philosophy professors and literary critics, for example—such a system of metaphors would exercise a powerful appeal, since it would establish the concrete, creaturely experience that is at the basis of scholarly activity in the humanities as the central, organizing structure for the process of knowing and even knowledge itself.

Indeed, that human act of sitting at a desk and writing is at the heart and center of the humanistic scholar's professional life, and this is particularly so for those scholars who teach the least and publish the most. It would be only natural for such persons to be flattered by a theory that transforms the activity which most distinguishes their professional life from that of other people into that opening, that "om" point, through which the universe of appearances issues forth. Such a conception makes such scholars into God figures, in that they are concentrated on that primal activity itself, whereas other people—who sell cars, say, or run for elections—are already inscribed or written without knowing it. Yet academic etiquette prohibits overt boasting; we scholars lack the candor of a Muhammad Ali, who made no secret of his estimation of himself when he bounded around the boxing ring shouting, "I am the greatest!" To conceal the fact that just such a boast is what deconstruction really makes for textual scholars, the agent of writing has been obscured, mystified, buried under mountains of impenetrable prose. The author, we are told, has died; writing, as preinscription, is performed by no human hand; *différance*, always supplemental, has no cause and resists all characterization. Yet in their observable effects in deconstructive discourse, writing and *différance* have an ideological and philosophical and political profile that corresponds with that of academic deconstructors themselves in a most uncanny manner; and deconstructive authors such as Derrida, though dead, bloom miraculously back to life again the moment they are criticized.

In short, the deconstructive celebration of writing is a disguise, and what lies beneath the disguise is scholarly class snobbery, a veiled assertion that textualist scholars are better and more important than other people in other walks of life. I do not imagine that I will make myself popular among academic theorists for saying this. Nonetheless, it is time to stop beating around the bush. To put it as baldly as possible: when textualist philosophers and critics celebrate writing, they are engaged in a campaign of self-promotion, since the textual field is the scene of their major professional activity and the site of their greatest mastery. By thus defining the world as a text and the quintessential subversive act as writing, in a single bound they catapult themselves to the summit of the pyramid of knowledge. In a textual world, textualists are emperors.

This power grab has not been without its effect. It has rationalized an intellectual grandiosity whereby deconstructors, presuming to have discovered the key that unlocks all doors, have proceeded to deconstruct one field after another; this has exerted immense impact on the politics of criticism, since publishers, hiring committees, and granting agencies, persuaded that the textualization of knowledge is "cutting edge", have helped create professional conditions such that textualists have flourished and their critics have not. Further, over the last decade, as hard leftist politics have increasingly come to prevail in many fields, the textualization of knowledge and reality has created a screened off zone, an elite ideological preserve, in which academic radicals could create rhetorical weapons by means of which a radical political vision could be imposed on the university and, through the university, on society at large. Deconstruction had fashioned a mechanism of self-immunization against empirical testing; so when the ideologies of race, class, and gender were coordinated and locked in with the deconstructive rhetoric of marginalization and subversion, the resulting hybrid was splendidly suited to the purposes of political assertion and advocacy. Whether, for example, in 1993 feminists and Marxists are indeed marginalized in humanities departments, as the politically refurbished deconstructive rhetoric of "exclusion" and "oppression" and "marginalization" would seem to imply, is a question that could be tested empirically through a study of hiring patterns, publication proclivities by major journals, and other suitable measures. But when the world is a text and when the text that we read is fashioned and contoured by ideologues who have mastered the textualist rhetoric prevailing in many departmental arenas, the common reality and common perception that authorize empirical measurement in the first place are dismissed in advance. In this way a textualist political discourse is able to formulate and impose its own distorted and ideologically self-serving reality in place of the common reality that most people experience, negotiate through their conversational inter-changes, and accept as a basis for their community life.

It is this common reality and world of common sense that, in conclusion, I would like to defend, in opposition to the counterintuitive and anti-empirical textualization of reality that is deconstruction's self-defining move. I realize, of course, that common sense is another of the many conceptions that nowadays one is forbidden to approve of. The reason why this is so is that common sense finds its immediate and natural home, from a linguistic standpoint, in the world of oral dialogue and conversation. The textualist assault on speech and orality is animated by a thoroughly elitist desire on the part of textualist scholars to win for their knowledge and their perception supremacy over the knowledge and perception of ordinary people who do not publish in the journals that these tex-tualists do. I would do well to scorn "the human subject" if I want to publish an article in *Critical Inquiry*; on the other hand, after I've deposited that article in the mail, I had better believe in "the human subject" again if I want to have a satisfactory dinner-time conversation with my wife. A Derridean might reply, of course, that this reinvention of the human subject for the purposes of a meal-time conversation illustrates the double gesture, the turn of writing back against itself whereby it reinvents what it previously exposed as impossible, the rein-scription of the apparent in the wake of its deconstruction.[14] But from the stand-point of a skeptical non-textualist, what all this goes to show is that textualists never really believed in their theories in the first place, abandon them the moment something comes up that impacts on their personal lives, and summon the idea of reinscription to cover over the fact that their ideas don't work in the real world.

This non-textualist standpoint is anchored in a perception that, unlike deconstruction, is close to the world of human experience, affirms the legitima-cy of that experience, and insists that textually formulated propositions be tested against that experience. Dialogue and conversation provide models of language use that are superior to those of textualist theory, for the recognition that lan-guage is dialogic creates a place again for the people between whom dialogues spring up.[15] When, at breakfast time, I comment on how nice the coffee smells, my discourse is consummated by surrendering itself, on the one hand, to the response of my interlocutor, and on the other hand, to experience of an olfactory sensory perception that need not be linguistic.[16] Discourse has its ends and lim-its; and it is through those limits that I lead a meaningful human life.

Conversation continuously lives and moves amid these limitations, not because conversation is itself handicapped, but because conversation alludes to shared fields that do not need to be fully articulated within language. Consider the case of sexual love-makers: will their pleasure be enhanced if they try to enunciate in words every physical sensation? Conversation in such settings is immersed in a world of experience that words like 'text' and 'writing' are much too small to contain. The word is a drop in a much larger pool; the terms of human interchange involve many intangibles and inexpressibles which enform and impress themselves upon the awareness of interlocutors as forcibly as linguistic—and textual—constructs do. While Derrida, in his highly textualized utterances, can afford to deny such ideas as presence and proximity to human experience, these subjective human realities cannot be denied in conversation, for such denial would strip one's saying of all sense.

It is easy to make this denial in textualist discourse, however, for textualization occurs at a remove from the immediacy of human life. My hypothetical article for *Critical Inquiry* will probably get published two or three years after I write it, and the multiple scenes of reading that follow its publication will probably never be known to me. I do not mean here to be disparaging textualized communication, which has its very distinctive powers and uses. My argument is simply that dialogue and conversation occur much closer to the site of human interactivity and common (intersubjective) reality than texts and writing do. Textualist theory denies the human subject because textualist discourse transpires so far from where most human beings are. For people in their normal human modality, speech is primary. After all, they learn it first: human societies developed speech long before they developed writing, and babies learn to speak voluntarily, whereas they often have to be forced to learn to read and write in elementary school. Yet speech enjoys precedence further in the sense that most people like it better. Students chat in the halls or watch soap operas on television instead of reading their assignments; even textualist scholars negotiate reputations and assessments of recent books in quiet conversations at bars on the conference circuit. A subterranean orality subtends and, to a degree, controls textualist discourse. For textualists cannot help being human, however hard they try to deny it in their books.

Deconstructive anti-humanism and the deconstructive textualization of the world is an aggressive attempt on the part of a particular scholarly class to overthrow the natural order of language so that textualist discourse may reign supreme among the social discourses of our time and so that the perceptions of ordinary people, who feel no attraction to textualism, may be forced to yield to the perceptions of their scholarly betters. Far from representing an assault on elitism, deconstruction is the epitome of elitism in the worst sense. Textualized discourses fill a need in the economy of human knowledge, to be sure. They pioneer modes of knowledge that can be discovered in no other way and so have contributed enormously to the quality of human existence. At the same time, the coldness and heartlessness to which textualized discourses are prone need to be tempered through a continuing and repeated reaffirmation of the common scene of human life and the non-textualized conversations that ordinary people have about it. The world is *not* a text. Rather, the text exists within the world. If our textualist Napoleons could remember that they are, in the end, little men and women just like the rest of us, the world of the mind could again become a place where human beings can make their home.

Ward Parks

The Heritage Foundation
214 Massachusetts Avenue NE
Washington, DC 20002

NOTES

1.   Saussure, *Course in General Linguistics*. Particularly pertinent to the following discussion are the opening sections of Part One, "General Principles", especially pp. 65-78 and the fourth chapter of Part Two (pp. 111–22).

2.   See Saussure's discussion of "the arbitrary nature of the sign", which he posits as one of the sign's "two primordial characteristics" (*Course in General Linguistics*, pp. 67–70).

3.   Derrida's fullest explication of this idea is his essay "Differance". Derrida's critique of Saussure is developed further in *Of Grammatology;* on *différance* and its relation to Derrida's idea of the trace, see especially pp. 61-65. More informal presentations appear in the interviews in *Positions*; particularly pertinent is the interview with Julia Kristeva entitled "Semiology and Grammatology" (pp. 15–38).

4.   Saussure, *Course in General Linguistics*, p. 120.

5.   Derrida, "Differance", p. 141.

6.   Derrida's major discussions of writing (*écriture*) appear in *Of Grammatology*, *Positions*, and *Writing and Difference*. For an accessible introductory account, see Barbara Johnson, "Writing".

7.   Derrida, *Of Grammatology*, pp. 11–12.

8.   Derrida, "Signature Event Context," in Derrida, *Limited Inc*, p. 19.

9.   Derrida, *Of Grammatology*, p. 70; Derrida's discussion of *la brisure*, translated as "the hinge", appears in pp. 65–73.

10.   For a seminal oralist critique of deconstructive textualism, see Ong, *Orality and Literacy*, pp. 165–70. I have criticized the textualist bias of deconstructive and other contemporary theoretical trends in a number of articles; see particularly "The Textualization of Orality in Modern Literary Criticism".

11. Derrida, "Differance", p. 132.

12. In fact, the metaphoricity of language and thought has all along been a central idea in deconstruction, and particularly in the *oeuvre* of Paul de Man; for an exposition of this point, see "The Epistemology of Metaphor". Essays in de Man's *Allegories of Reading* explore this topic in depth. Deconstructionists were not the first, of course, to recognize the importance of metaphor, nor does the belief that metaphor is integral to cognition make one a deconstructionist. For a valuable critique of Derrida's approach to metaphor, see Christopher Butler, *Interpretation, Deconstruction, and Ideology*, pp. 8–25.

13. Derrida, "Freud and the Scene of Writing". This critique of Freud represents, in effect, a radical textualization of the human psyche.

14. According to Nealon in "The Discipline of Deconstruction", this is precisely the aspect of Derrida's philosophy that was ignored by the Yale school of deconstructionists, including, for example, de Man and Jonathan Culler. Nealon puts himself in the difficult position of having to justify this thesis in face of the fact that Derrida himself seemed to approve their (Culler's and de Man's) deconstructive formulations; further, Culler himself exhibits a clear grasp of the principle of reinscription in his summing up of the deconstructive "grafting" process in *On Deconstruction*, p. 150. Nealon's pietism is typical of the attitude of many deconstructors, who attribute all the failings in deconstruction to Derrida's followers and never to Derrida himself.

15. An important figure in the history of dialogics is Mikhail Bakhtin, although, as I argue in "The Textualization of Orality", Bakhtin's version of dialogics involves significant textualizing movements. Nonetheless, Bakhtin's concern was very much a revalorization of the ordinary. For significant recent statements on this theme, see Morson, "Prosaics: an Approach to the Humanities" and "Bakhtin and the Present Moment".

16. Of course, if one insists that all modalities of human perception and consciousness are linguistic, then the olfactory sense becomes linguistic by definitional fiat. Recent theorists have used this tactic again and again: by such argument the world (according to deconstructionists) becomes a text because it can be conceived textually; thought (according to structuralists) is linguistic because its articulation involves the use of linguistic structures; all assertions (according to academic leftists) are political because they are relatable to political determinants. But these arguments prove nothing. The mere fact that a phenomenon can be examined from a particular perspective or within a particular frame of reference does not prove that particular frame of reference has a special entitlement to the phenomenon. Sense perception is linguistic if it operates in accordance with linguistic principles rather than in some other way. This is a proposition that could be tested empirically; and an excellent field in which to pursue such an inquiry would be that of cognitive psychology. In fact, cognitive psychologists would be far from unanimous in their approbation of this idea; though models vary, many cognitive psychologists recognize both linguistic and essentially non-linguistic modes of cognition. For a summary of research, see Anderson, *Cognitive Psychology and Its Implications*.

REFERENCES

John R. Anderson, *Cognitive Psychology and Its Implications*, New York: W. H. Freeman, 1990.

Christopher Butler, *Interpretation, Deconstruction, and Ideology: An Introduction to Some Current Issues in Literary Theory*, Oxford: Clarendon Press 1984.

Jonathan Culler, *On Deconstruction: Theory and Criticism After Structuralism* Ithaca, New York: Cornell University Press 1982.

Jacques Derrida, "Differance", in Derrida, *Speech and Phenomena*, pp. 129–60.

——, "Freud and the Scene of Writing," in Derrida, *Writing and Difference*, pp. 196–231.

——, *Of Grammatology*, tr. Gayatri Chakravorty Spivak, Baltimore:: The John Hopkins Press 1974.

——, *Limited Inc*, Evanston, Illinois: Northwestern University Press 1988.

——, *Positions*, tr. Alan Bass, Chicago: University of Chicago Press 1981.

——, *Speech and Phenomena and Other Essays on Husserl's Theory of Signs*, tr. David B. Allison; Evanston, Illinois: Northwestern University Press 1973.

——, *Writing and Difference*, tr. by Alan Bass, Chicago: University of Chicago Press, 1978.

Barbara Johnson, "Writing", in Frank Lentricchia and Thomas McLaughlin (eds.), *Critical Terms for Literary Study*, Chicago: University of Chicago Press 1990, pp. 39-49.

Paul de Man, *Allegories of Reading: Figural Language in Rousseau, Nietzsche, Rilke, and Proust*, New Haven: Yale University Press 1979.

——, "The Epistemology of Metaphor", *Critical Inquiry* 5 (1978), 13–30

Gary Saul Morson, "Prosaics: an Approach to the Humanities", *The American Scholar* 57 (1988), 515–28.

——, "Bakhtin and the Present Moment", *The American Scholar* 60 (1991), 201–22

Jeffrey T. Nealon, "The Discipline of Deconstruction", *PMLA* 107 (1992), 1266-1279.

Walter J. Ong, *Orality and Literacy: The Technologizing of the Word*, London: Methuen 1982.

Ward Parks, "The Textualization of Orality in Modern Literary Criticism", in A. N. Doane and Carol Braun Pasternack (eds.), *Vox intexta: Orality and Textuality in the Middle Ages*, Madison: University of Wisconsin Press 1991, pp. 46–61.

Ferdinand de Saussure, *Course in General Linguistics*, ed. Charles Bally and Albert Sechehaye in collaboration with Albert Riedlinger, tr. Wade Baskin, New York: McGraw-Hill 1966.

THE RIGORS OF DECONSTRUCTION

Jacques Derrida had his first, and to date strongest, impact in the field of literary criticism and its theory. From the early 1970s to well into the 1980s, deconstruction was all the rage in literary criticism. Being all the rage is, of course, a mixed phenomenon, since probably more people were enraged by the high-jinks of the "deconstructionists" than were enthralled by the new vistas it opened up. But for the young Turks of a new uprising, that is part of the fun of being the new, rebellious kids on the block. Toward the end of the 1980s, however, it was clear that the highwater of deconstruction as a fashion lay in the past. To note this, however, is not to say anything against deconstruction, since it is true of any new movement of thought that it is only after it ceases to be "the latest thing" that we can in all seriousness begin to see just how important it is, just what its lasting significance may be.

Interestingly, the years that began to see the decline of deconstruction as a fashion in literary criticism witnessed a rising interest in Derrida's work in philosophy. A number of books on Derrida appeared. However, even as more and more is being written both about Derrida and, more importantly, in a Derridean spirit, there are still too few attempts to give Derrida's own *philosophical* texts the kind of close reading that these texts themselves set out to give to texts from the philosophical tradition. So what I want to do today is to give a critical assessment of the philosophical significance of a few of Derrida's philosophical texts.

Now even today, if one wants to speak about deconstruction, it behoves one to make clear just what one takes deconstruction to be, since so much confusion seems to reign about it. But in fact, to attempt to give a definition of "deconstruction" would be to demonstrate a lack of understanding. One of the recurrent themes of Derrida's deconstructive work has been the very question "What is it?", a question that has dominated the philosophical agenda since Socrates. And Derrida has been concerned precisely to exhibit what he claims to be the limits of this question. So it is hardly surprising to find him writing that "All sentences of the type 'deconstruction is X' or 'deconstruction is not X' miss the point, which is to say that they are at least false" ("Letter to a Japanese Friend", p. 4), and that "...each deconstructive 'event' remains singular" ("Letter to a Japanese Friend", p. 3). There *is* no what-it-is of deconstruction.

But this does not mean that nothing can be said about the events of deconstruction that lead to the delimiting of the "what is it?" question.

BACKGROUND: THE METAPHYSICS OF PRESENCE

An important part of the background of Derrida's deconstruction can be found
in Heidegger's project of the "destruction [*Destruktion*]" of the history of ontology. The task of the destruction or, perhaps better, the *de-structuring*
(Bernasconi, "Seeing Double", p. 231) of the history of ontology arises because,
Heidegger claims, Western philosophy since Plato has interpreted Being in
terms of one privileged temporal dimension, namely the present. After all, as
Aristotle notes (at least according to Heidegger and Derrida—see below), the
past and the future are not: the past is not anymore, the future is not yet. It can
thus be only the present that *is*. Since the very terms in which we experience
and think about Being are imbued with this tradition, Heidegger argues that we
cannot simply reject them and start over: there is no pure beginning. Thus in
order to pose the question of the meaning of Being anew, we have to "destruc-
ture" the history of ontology, returning thereby to "the original experiences in
which the first and subsequently guiding determinations were gained" (*Being
and Time*, 22/67). Heidegger also speaks of a "critical unbuilding" or literally
"deconstruction [*Abbau*]" of traditional concepts (*Basic Problems*, 31/22-23), a
term which Heidegger seems to have taken over from his teacher Edmund
Husserl.

Now while Heidegger's "de-structuring" of the history of ontology provides the background of Derridean deconstruction, Derrida is not simply working out the Heideggerian project, or at least he insists that this is not what he is
doing. (Indeed, in the first publication of what became the first part of Derrida's
Of Grammatology, the word he used was "*détruire*", changing it to "*déconstru-
ire*" a year later (Bernasconi, "Seeing Double", p. 235), precisely in order to
distinguish what he was doing from the Heideggerian project while still
announcing the Heideggerian heritage. And, more recently, Derrida has denounced certain French Heideggerians who think that by translating Heidegger's '*Destruktion*' and '*Abbau*' by 'deconstruction', they can show that the
Derridean project is just a continuation of the Heideggerian project.) One can
give an initial approach to Derrida's work by seeing it as a *radicalization* of the
Heideggerian enterprise. Heidegger, Derrida argues, fails to overcome the metaphysics of presence, since in his insistence on continuing to regard the task of
thought as being the thought of Being, he recurs to a kind of presence
[*Anwesenheit*] which he attempts to distinguish from temporal presence
[*Gegenwart, Gegenwärtigkeit*]. Derrida undercuts Heidegger with what I take to
be his claim that there are no "original experiences" which we could uncover by
"destructuring", or that there are no "master words" that can express the very
event of the manifestation of Being.

Now I don't want to get into an extended discussion of the metaphysics of presence here. It should suffice to note that the epistemic dimension of this metaphysics finds, in one way or another, the origin of truth and the foundation of knowledge in presence: the epistemology of the metaphysics of presence is a foundationalism of one sort or another. Knowledge has a foundation, and it will be found in a presence of some kind.

Logocentrism

Painting in very broad strokes, we can say that Derrida's term for this foundationalism is 'logocentrism', a term used a great deal both in Derrida and in deconstructionist literature in general, but which is rarely thematized. The Greek term *'logos'* derives from the verb *'legein'*, meaning first 'to gather, pick up, lay together', and then 'to recount, tell, say, speak' (i.e., to gather in words). *'Logos'* bears a number of related meanings: an utterance, the words spoken, or what is said. In philosophical thought *'logos'* came to take on the meaning of reasonable speech or argument. Socrates often says—let's examine your *logos*, your account or argument. And he warns against *misology*, the scorn of argument, inquiry, and reason. It came to mean 'theory', and is the root of our word 'logic' and of the suffix meaning 'science of', as in soci*ology*, bi*ology*, psychol*ogy*. Briefly, a logocentric position would be one that assumes that *logos* as reason is autonomous and self-grounding. It assumes that the Being of beings can be grasped in our knowledge of things, and that our knowledge itself is firmly grounded. Derrida sets out to undermine this assumption, asking of Husserl's reflections on linguistic expression, for example, "How can we justify the *decision* which subordinates a reflection on the sign to a logic?" (Derrida, *Speech and Phenomena*, p. 6/7) Can this decision itself be justified—justified logically—without begging the question? Husserl spoke of logic as "the *self-explication of pure reason* itself," a "science in which pure theoretical reason accomplishes a complete investigation of its own sense and perfectly objectivates itself in a system of principles" (Husserl, *Formal and Transcendental Logic*, p. 34/30-31). By speaking of a *decision* to subject language to logic, Derrida indicates that he will challenge the ability of reason to ground itself. But rather than offering independent arguments—which would themselves have to be logical, cogent, coherent, and thus subject to the same decision they are to challenge—Derrida turns to those texts in which the logocentric tradition attempts its own self-justification. His claim is that for any logocentric argument, one can show that the more rigorous it is, i.e., the more logical, the more it will turn out that there is a moment of *alogos*, of non-logicality, at work in that very argument, making possible while simultaneously undermining the logocentric claim itself. (In its universality, the preceding sentence is itself

logocentric, and Derrida is generally cautious in making such claims.)
Logocentrism, rigorously developed, *deconstructs itself.*

> Deconstruction takes place, it is an event that does not await the deliberation, con-
> sciousness, or organization of a subject, or even of modernity. *It deconstructs it-self.*
> *It can be deconstructed.* (Derrida, "Letter to a Japanese Friend", p. 4)

Rigor

Now if the traditional ideal of grounded knowledge, the ideal of a theoretical
coherence and rigor that can in principle completely master its object—and in
so doing be master of itself—is to be deconstructed, what is the measure of a
"successful" deconstruction? What would it mean to speak of a "rigorous"
deconstruction? Some partisans of deconstruction reject the very question. For
example, Andrew Parker writes that

> phrases such as "If Derrida is anywhere near the truth on Husserl"…simply have no
> bearing on the practice of deconstruction, for Derrida is interested not in being
> "true" to Husserl but in reinscribing the notion of "truth" as it *deconstructs* the
> Husserlian text. (Parker, "Taking Sides", p. 67)

However, over the years Derrida has repeatedly committed himself to a certain ideal of rigor. He often insists that the texts he is dealing with are themselves rigorous, and this is important, since the deconstruction of a sloppy text
would hardly yield anything of interest beyond the limits of the text in question.
In such a case, deconstruction could not be distinguished from an old-fashioned
critical reading of the text. But Derrida also commits himself to "respect[ing]
the classical norms", namely norms *of interpretation* (Derrida, *Of Grammatology*, p. 8/lxxxix). Deconstruction never reduces to commentary, but rigorous
commentary has its place in a deconstructive reading:

> To recognize and respect all its classical exigencies is not easy and requires all the
> instruments of traditional criticism. Without this recognition and this respect, criti-
> cal production would risk developing in any direction at all and authorize itself to
> say almost anything. (Derrida, *Of Grammatology*, p. 227/158)

In other words, deconstructive reading has to pass *through* traditional rigor
even if the ultimate effect is to show that such rigor is never as absolute and
well-founded as it claims to be.

I think that this presents a fundamental fork in the road for any understanding and appropriation of Derrida. *Either* we take Derrida seriously in his
demand that his own analyses, as well as any reading of his texts, be rigorous,
the alternative being that we then authorize both Derrida and ourselves to say
almost anything, a true nihilism, since saying anything is functionally equivalent to saying nothing, *or* we follow Richard Rorty, who denies that deconstruc-

tion can provide "*both* 'rigorous argument within philosophy and displacement of philosophical categories and philosophical attempts at mastery'" (Rorty, "Is Derrida a Transcendental Philosopher?", p. 207, quoting Culler, *On Deconstruction*, p. 28). Rorty argues (if "argue" is the right word!) that Derrida should never have attempted to provide rigorous arguments:

> I do not think that demonstrations of "internal incoherence" or of "presuppositional relationships" ever do much to disabuse us of bad [NB!] old ideas or institutions. Disabusing gets done, instead, by offering us sparkling new ideas, or utopian visions of glorious new institutions. (Rorty, "Is Derrida a Transcendental Philosopher?", pp. 208-9)

I am simply going to assume that we should take Derrida's demand for rigor in deconstruction seriously. In what follows I want to give a brief critical discussion of Derrida's deconstructive treatment of what he calls the "phonocentrism" of Husserl and Saussure, and of Heidegger's reading of Aristotle and Hegel on time. Each of the texts has been praised by people who are clearly competent to make a critical assessment.

THE DECONSTRUCTION OF THE VOICE

The deconstruction of logocentrism has been one of Derrida's persistent concerns. He claims that logocentrism, which assumes the centrality and well-foundedness of knowledge, necessarily takes the form of phonocentrism, the primacy of the voice as the medium which makes the mastery and self-mastery of knowledge possible. The idea here is that it is only in speech that thought is fully present to itself. When I speak, I both hear and understand myself speak (the French *s'entendre* expresses both hearing and understanding). For phonocentrism, in speech thought is present to itself (one hears/understands oneself speak) and is thus in command of what it means or wants to say; it is thus able to subject meaning to strictly logical and cognitive principles. Writing, by contrast, is derivative. It stands for the spoken word, is a sign of a sign rather than the direct expression of meaning itself. When I read, even if I am reading a text I wrote, the meaning can escape me. Thus Plato could have Socrates argue that writing is the death of thought, whereas speech is the living medium of thought itself. Derrida has pursued the deconstruction of this phonocentrism in texts dealing with Plato, Aristotle, Rousseau, Husserl, and Saussure. I shall deal only with his work on Husserl and Saussure.

Husserl

Derrida has written a number of texts on Husserl. Just two years ago, his early master's thesis on Husserl was published. In 1963 he published a book-length introduction to a late Husserl text entitled "The Origin of Geometry", and he has written several essays devoted to Husserl. The most famous, and by far the most influential, of his texts on Husserl is *Speech and Phenomena*, a book which originally appeared in 1967, devoted to a close reading of several sections in the first of Husserl's *Logical Investigations*. This book has been praised by philosophers as diverse as Richard Rorty, Hans-Georg Gadamer, Emmanuel Levinas, Christopher Norris, and others. However, a careful reading of *Speech and Phenomena*, one which goes back and really reads the Husserlian texts Derrida is dealing with, shows that Derrida's supposed "deconstruction" of Husserl is shot through with errors and distortions. Let me give a few examples from my book, *Strategies of Deconstruction*.

1. At one point in his discussion of Husserl's analyses of time consciousness, Derrida quotes a phrase from Husserl, taking it to deal with perception or presentation. A look at the context shows that Husserl was in fact dealing with re-presentation (Evans, *Strategies of Deconstruction*, p. 101). Now this is the kind of thing that can happen to anyone: one of your note-cards of quotations gets put in the wrong pile. So we shouldn't make too much of this.

2. In one chapter, Derrida uses a number of German terms, especially the word *Vorstellung*, and the way he uses the word presupposes that we know what the term means. However, the term, which plays a crucial if checkered role in the history of German philosophy (Knüfer, *Geschichte des Begriffs 'Vorstellung'*), can express a variety of meanings, and in the Fifth Investigation of the *Logical Investigations* Husserl distinguishes between no fewer than thirteen different senses of *Vorstellung*, a performance that Gustav Bergmann once called "as richly satisfying as a Bach concerto" (Bergmann, "The Ontology of Edmund Husserl", p. 219 n. 28). Derrida never even mentions this section, and when one goes back through Derrida's text, matching his different uses of the word to the meanings distinguished by Husserl, it becomes clear that he jumps from one meaning to another so wildly that his text becomes incoherent. The use of the German term, which at first glance seems to serve the end of technical precision, serves only to cloud the water.

3. One has to keep a very close watch on Derrida's own choice of words. In one chapter he begins with Husserl's claim that in communicative speech two different functions of expressions are "interwoven". A linguistic utter-

ance "expresses" its meaning, but in living speech the sounds uttered also "indicate" the experiences of the speaker to the listener. Now Husserl claims that we can separate these two functions. Thus, although the two functions are interwoven in communication, we can thematize the one without the other.

Derrida wants to challenge just this, and the challenge should arise strictly and only from Husserl's text itself. Here it is instructive to watch the way Derrida talks about the relation between the two functions. He first gives an accurate French translation of Husserl's text, but in his discussion of the passage he shifts from writing "interwoven [*entrelacé*]" to "interwoven or entangled [*s'entrelacer, s'enchevetre*]". He then shifts to using the term "*pris dans*" (one function is "caught up in" the other), and asserts immediately "*Pris, c'est-à-dire contaminé*": "Caught up, that is to say *contaminated*" (Derrida, *Speech and Phenomena*, p. 20/20). So from Husserl's claim that the two functions are *interwoven* in communicative speech, we arrive at the claim that one function is *contaminated by* the other, something that Derrida assumes would disturb Husserl a great deal. But there is no argument here, only the slow and subtle shift from one term to another and on to another. A crucial premise for Derrida's reading is thus insinuated, and it takes a careful reader to note that the issue is being prejudiced, indeed perhaps fatally prejudiced for the uncritical reader (which includes most of the readers of record).

4. Finally, in a section dealing with Husserl's account of essentially occasional or indexical expressions, Derrida gives what might be called a classically deconstructive reading, in that he claims to exhibit Husserl being compelled by the force of his own analysis to draw a conclusion that in fact contradicts the theory he is developing.

    What is at issue here? An occasional expression is an expression whose meaning is a function of the occasion of its use, in contrast to objective expressions, whose meaning is not a function of the circumstances of their utterance. If I write the Pythagorean Theorem on the blackboard and you happen by later, you can understand what is written on the board, though you may not know why it is there. But if I write 'I will be back shortly' and leave, when you happen by you can in one sense understand what the sentence says, but you don't understand the full meaning, since you don't know who 'I' refers to. To understand this meaning, you need to know the circumstances of the writing. You need to know who wrote it. This means that in one sense the word 'I' has the same meaning whoever utters it. But in another sense, Husserl writes,

What its meaning is at the moment can be gleaned only from the living utterance and from the intuitive circumstances which surround it. If we read this word without knowing who wrote it, it is perhaps not meaningless, but it is at least estranged from its normal meaning. (Husserl, *Logical Investigations*, II.1 p.82/I p.315).

But, Derrida notes, Husserl's own theory of meaning draws a strict distinction between the meaning of a word on the one hand, and the concrete reference of the word. Thus, when Husserl writes that the meaning of the word 'I' "can be gleaned only from...the intuitive circumstances which surround it", Derrida draws the noose with a dramatic "Husserl's premises should sanction our saying exactly the contrary". (Derrida, *Speech and Phenomena, p.* 107/96)

But Derrida gives none of the details of Husserl's analysis of occasional expressions, and when the details are brought in, it becomes clear that there is no tension between Husserl's theory and his concrete analyses. Husserl distinguishes between the indicating meaning of the word, the meaning common to every usage of the word 'I', and the indicated meaning, the singular presentation of the person referred to by this particular utterance. Both of these meanings are, in Husserl's terminology, ideal, and neither is dependent on the intuitive presence of the circumstances of the utterance. The plausibility of Derrida's "deconstruction" is a function of the neglected details of Husserl's own text.

These are only some of the distortions I found to be at work in *Speech and Phenomena*. None of them have been pointed out by the philosophers who have lavished such praise on the book. And the book has had an enormous impact in some circles. Writing from the point of view of literary criticism, Frank Lentricchia writes that "sometime in the early 1970s we awoke from the dogmatic slumber of our phenomenological sleep to find that a new presence had taken absolute hold over our avant-garde critical imagination: Jacques Derrida". (Lentricchia, *After the New Criticism*, p. 159) The reference to "phenomenological slumber" makes it clear that *Speech and Phenomena* played a crucial role in this awakening. But one has to wonder if anyone read the book carefully, going back to the Husserlian texts that are so lavishly, if selectively, quoted in the book.

Saussure

Like his work on Husserl, Derrida's reading of Saussure has been widely praised as being, for example, "brilliant and scrupulous" (Jonathan Culler) and "incisive" (Robert Strozier), though there have been other voices as well, including Strozier himself and John Ellis. However, Derrida's central claim about Saussure, namely that he is the heir to the logocentrism and specifically phonocentrism of the Western tradition, has not, to my knowledge, been challenged. Saussure argues that the proper object of linguistics is the spoken word only, but that the written word "manages to usurp the principal role". (Saussure, *Course in General Linguistics*, p. 45/25) Saussure's language here is very hard. He speaks of "the tyranny of the written form". "Its influence on the linguistic community may be strong enough to affect and modify the language itself....the written form may give rise to erroneous pronunciations. The phenomenon is strictly pathological" (Saussure, *Course in General Linguistics*, p. 53/31).

Now what is going on here? How is this rabid language to be explained? Derrida argues that the only explanation is that Saussure is a victim of the phonocentric tradition, and is thus committed to a "*natural bond* of the signified (concept or sense) to the phonic signifier" (Derrida, *Of Grammatology*, p. 53/35). In view of this natural bond, the subordination of writing to speech becomes self-evident, and an influence of the written word on the spoken word becomes unnatural, pathological, tyrannical.

Now when Derrida's treatment of Saussure is read carefully, it becomes clear that it is based on a single crucial text. Thus he writes,

> 'The natural bond', Saussure says, 'the only true bond, the bond of sound'. This natural bond of the signified (concept or sense) to the phonic signifier would condition the *natural relationship* subordinating writing (visible image) to speech. (Derrida, *Of Grammatology*, p. 53/35, quoting Saussure, *Course in General Linguistics*, p. 46/25).

The passage from Saussure reads:

> But how is the prestige of writing to be explained? First, the graphic image of words strikes us as being something permanent and stable, better suited than sound to constitute the unity of language through time. Although that bond is superficial and creates a purely artificial unity: it is much easier to grasp than the natural bond, the only true one, that of sound. (Saussure, *Course in General Linguistics*, p. 46/24)

Thus, the topic under discussion is "the unity of language throughout time." What does this have to do with a "natural bond of the signified (concept or sense) to the phonic signifier"? Saussure has been discussing primarily the relationship between phonetic writing and *pronunciation*, and what is at issue is how changes in pronunciation are to be explained. Saussure's thesis is that there are laws governing the evolution of pronunciation. If these laws are to be discovered, the linguist must direct attention precisely to this field of the spoken word, refusing to be distracted by other—from *this* point of view "external"—influences. Thus, the "natural bond" does not concern the relation between signifier and signified, sound and meaning, but rather a natural bond between sound and sound as pronunciation evolves over time.

Indeed, it should have been obvious that Derrida's reading is at variance with Saussure's text, since Saussure explicitly questions the claim that "the function of language, as it manifests itself when we speak, is entirely natural". (Saussure, *Course in General Linguistics*, p. 25/10) But Derrida's interpretation has not only not been challenged on this point, it seems to have become so canonical that when Roy Harris, a noted Saussure expert, prepared a new, and generally highly superior, translation of the *Course in General Linguistics*, he translated what should read "the natural bond, the only true one, that of sound [*le lien naturel, le seul veritable, celui du son*]" as "the natural and only authentic connexion, which links word and sound" (Saussure, *Course in General Linguistics*, p. 46/26, Harris translation), thus reading a misinterpretation back into the text under the guise of translating it. I cannot demonstrate that it was Derrida's misreading of Saussure that lead to this translation, but there has to be some reason why a translator whose competence cannot be questioned adds two words to a text.

Aristotle and the Now

As my last text, I would like to turn to the essay entitled "*Ousia* and *Gramme*: Note on a Note from *Being and Time*", originally published in *Margins of Philosophy* in 1972. This essay is a "reading" of a footnote in Heidegger's *Being and Time* discussing Aristotle's and Hegel's treatments of time. It has played a fairly important role in discussions of Derrida, and has been taken seriously and praised (by Bernet, Rapaport, Wood, Chantner, Harvey, among others).

In *Being and Time*, Heidegger distinguishes the "vulgar" and traditional understanding of time—which determines time as a series of nows, and beings as having their being "within time"—from the primordial time of the authentic temporality of *Dasein*. His charge is that the metaphysical tradition, in interpreting Being in terms of presence, overlooks primordial time.

In "*Ousia* and *Gramme*" Derrida develops a complex strategy. On the one hand, he offers deconstructive readings of the treatments of time in Aristotle and Hegel, with the aim of showing that precisely as they commit themselves to the primacy of the present, moments in their texts simultaneously undermine this very commitment.

> What Aristotle has set down, then, is both traditional metaphysical security, and, in its inaugural ambiguity, the critique of this security…Aristotle furnishes the premises of a thought of time no longer dominated simply by the present… (Derrida, *Margins of Philosophy*, p. 49).

But, Derrida argues, Heidegger overlooks these moments, which when recognized make "anything like an originary [or primordial] temporality impossible". (Derrida, *Margins of Philosophy*, pp. 45-46) Thus, Derrida can claim to have taken an important step in his two-pronged radicalization of Heidegger. On the one hand Derrida accuses Heidegger's destruction of the history of ontology of being naive, since it fails to see that precisely in the tradition's commitment to presence there is contained a moment of critique of this commitment. On the other hand, Derrida accuses Heidegger of the naive assumption that his thought can move beyond metaphysics while remaining the thought of Being. The demonstration that there can be no primordial temporality undercuts this assumption.

Derrida begins with a basic assumption which he shares with Heidegger. Both begin with the claim that "Aristotle sees the essence of time in the *nun* [the now]" (Heidegger, *Being and Time*, p. 432; cf. Derrida, *Margins of Philosophy*, p. 39). And both of them base this claim on Chapter 10 of Book IV of Aristotle's *Physics*, where Aristotle gives "the common arguments [*dis ton exoterikon logon*]" concerning time.

In *Being and Time* Heidegger does not offer an extended interpretation of Aristotle. However, the year after the publication of *Being and Time* he returned to Aristotle, this time in giving an extended interpretation of Aristotle's treatment of time, and it is clear that it is this interpretation which underlies the brief comments in *Being and Time*. It should be noted that when *"Ousia and Gramme"* was written in the early 1970s, the lectures entitled *Basic Problems of Phenomenology* had not yet been published, so Derrida was necessarily unfamiliar with them. While it is fair to use the lectures to flesh out the reading of Aristotle in *Being and Time*, care must be taken that Derrida not be held responsible for reading a text unavailable to him.

Heidegger begins by noting that the first chapter of Book IV offers a provisional discussion of the problems concerning time, doing so with reference to "previous attempts at a solution". (Heidegger, *Basic Problems of Phenomenology*, p. 233) Following Aristotle's custom, the approach is historical and aporetic. The first of these arguments runs:

> That time is either altogether nonexistent, or that it exists but hardly or obscurely, might be suspected from the following: One part of it has come to be but no longer exists; the other part will be but does not yet exist; and it is of these two parts that infinite time, or any time one might take, is composed. But it is thought that what is composed of nonbeings cannot participate in substance [*ousia*]. (Aristotle, *Physics*, 217b34-218a3)

Heidegger's summary of this argument is: "Past and future, by their very concepts, are exactly non-existent; at bottom it is only the present, the now, that *is*", (Heidegger, *Basic Problems of Phenomenology*, p. 233) which can be taken as an at least partial explication of the thesis stated in the footnote in *Being and*

Time. It should be noted that Aristotle himself does not explicitly draw this conclusion.

Derrida begins his discussion of Aristotle's Chapter 10 by connecting Heidegger's notion of a vulgar or ordinary concept of time with Aristotle's *exoterikon logon*, a more than problematic move:

> First let us reestablish contact. The contact of the concept of *vulgarity* or ordinariness in the expression the 'ordinary concept of time' with the stated point of departure of the Aristotelian interpretation. Precisely with the point of its *exotericness.* (Derrida, *Margins of Philosophy*, p. 39)

To suggest a direct connection between Heidegger's claims about the ordinary or vulgar concept of time, that of intra-temporality [*Innerzeitigkeit*] with Aristotle's *exoterikon logon* is at least a bit surprising. There is a clear tradition of how Aristotle is to be understood at this point. Thomas Aquinas, for example, writes,

> For as with the foregoing, likewise, with time, it is first necessary to proceed by proposing extraneous arguments, that is, sophistical arguments, or arguments given by others, as to whether time exists or not, and if it exists, what its nature is. (Thomas Aquinas, *Commentary on Aristotle's Physics*, 251)

Heidegger's reading of the passage in the *Grundprobleme* clearly stands in this tradition. In suggesting a "contact" between Heidegger's vulgar concept of time and Aristotle's *exoterikon logon*, Derrida is, among other things, rejecting this tradition, though no reasons for this are given.

Derrida then reads the Aristotelian exoteric as moving between two "hypotheses". According to the first hypothesis, which is stated in the passage from the Physics quoted above, the now is an "elementary part" of time (Derrida, *Margins of Philosophy*, p. 40). "The manner in which the first question is formulated indeed shows that the Being of time has been anticipated on the basis of the now, and of the now as part". (Derrida, *Margins of Philosophy*, p. 47)

According to Derrida's reading, the first hypothesis is followed immediately by a second hypothesis, which puts the first in question. He writes of "...the moment when Aristotle seems to overturn the first hypothesis and to contend instead that the now is not a part, or that time is not composed of nows (*to de nun ou meros...ho de khronos ou dokei sungkeisthai ek ton nun*—218ª)" (Derrida, *Margins of Philosophy*, p. 47). The Greek text Derrida quotes is in the passage which immediately follows the "first hypothesis": "And as for the now, it is no part of time;...but it is thought that time is not composed of nows". (218ª7-8) The passage between these two sentences gives the reason for the claim: "...for a part measures the whole, and the whole must be composed of the parts...".

Now the question that has to be raised is why Derrida treats these passages as presenting two hypotheses, the second at least "seeming" to "overturn" the first. I want to suggest that this is not a marginal issue in the deconstructive argument of "*Ousia* and *Gramme*," but is rather the turning point of the entire essay. On the one hand Derrida claims, explicitly agreeing with Heidegger, that Aristotle (at least in the first hypothesis), "giv[es] in to the obvious, that time is, that time has as its essence, the *nun* [now]". (Derrida, *Margins of Philosophy*, p. 39). On the other hand, according to Derrida, Heidegger misses the "second hypothesis", and Derrida clearly thinks that this is of crucial importance.

> Our question, then, is the following: in overturning the [first] hypothesis, in demonstrating that the now is not a part of time, does Aristotle extract the problematic of time from the 'spatial' concepts of part and whole, from the predetermination of the *nun* as *meros* [part] or even as *stigme* [point]?" (Derrida, *Margins of Philosophy*, pp. 46-47).

The conclusion Derrida arrives at in confronting the first hypothesis with the second as its overturning (and the story is of course much more complex than I can suggest here), is that "What Aristotle has set down, then is both traditional metaphysical security, and, in its inaugural ambiguity, the critique of this security". (Derrida, *Margins of Philosophy*, p. 49) The result is that Aristotle's text both institutes the metaphysical interpretation of time and subverts this interpretation:

> Although understood on the basis of Being as presence in act, movement and time are neither (present) beings nor (absent) nonbeings. The categories of desire or movement as such, and the category of time as such, therefore are already or yet again *submitted* and *subtracted* in Aristotle's text, belonging as much to the de-limitation of metaphysics as the thought of the present, as to the simple overturning of metaphysics. (Derrida, *Margins of Philosophy*, p. 62)

The metaphysical account of time deconstructs itself. It is not "destroyed" or "de-structured" (to use the Heideggerian term) from without, from the point of view of an original temporality, but from within, and can thus more properly be said to *deconstruct* itself. Here the manner in which Derridean deconstruction departs from Heideggerian destruction is presented with exemplary clarity.

At this point Derrida's text circles back on itself, picking up a seed carefully planted earlier in the text. It was noted above that Derrida begins his discussion of Chapter 10 of Aristotle's *Physics* by establishing a "contact" between Heidegger's "ordinary concept of time" and the Aristotelian exoteric. Now, having argued that the Aristotelian exoteric both establishes and undermines the metaphysical security of the centrality of the now, Derrida feels that he can suggest "that perhaps there is no 'vulgar concept of time'" (Derrida, *Margins of Philosophy*, p. 63), since the establishment of the now as the essence of time, which is to constitute the vulgar concept of time, subverts itself. A corollary would be that there cannot be an original time either.

> Therefore we can only conclude that the entire system of metaphysical concepts, throughout its history, develops the so-called 'vulgarity' of the concept of time (which Heidegger, doubtless, would not contest), but also that an *other* concept of time cannot be opposed to it, since time in general belongs to metaphysical conceptuality. (Derrida, *Margins of Philosophy*, p. 63)

At this point we can return to the question of the legitimacy of Derrida's reading of Aristotle. The entire passage in question, encompassing both the first and second "hypotheses" (as well as the introductory sentences opening the discussion of time), reads as follows:

> Next to what has been said comes the discussion of time. Concerning time, we would do well, by using the common arguments [*exoterikon logon*], to go over the difficulties (a) as to whether it is a being or a nonbeing and (b) as to what its nature is.
> That time is either altogether nonexistent, or that it exists but hardly or obscurely, might be suspected from the following: One part of it has come to be but no longer exists; the other part will be but does not yet exist; and it is of these two parts that infinite time, or any time one might take, is composed. But it is thought that what is composed of nonbeings cannot participate in substance [*ousia*].
> In addition, if any thing with parts is to exist, then, when it exists, all or some of its parts must exist. But, although time is divisible, some parts of it have been and the others will be, and no part of it exists. And as for a now, it is no part of time; for a part measures the whole, and the whole must be composed of the parts, but it is thought that time is not composed of nows. (Aristotle, *Physics*, 217b29-218a8)

Now it only takes a little reflection to see that we do not have two opposing arguments or hypotheses here, the second attempting to "overturn" the first. Indeed, the claim that is made explicit in the second argument, namely that the now "is no part of time," is already implicit in the first, which asserts that time is composed of *two parts*, namely the past and the future. This is simply inconsistent with Derrida's claim that in the "first hypothesis" the now is a part of time, and this is the claim that Derrida takes to be the crucial part of the first hypothesis. A study of Book IV of the *Physics* shows that Aristotle never considers the now to be a part of time, and when he compares the now to a point, he explicitly notes that points are not parts of a line (220a18-20). Derrida's entire approach to Aristotle, based as it is on the supposition of the two opposing "hypotheses", is imposed on the Aristotelian text.

Hegel and Intratemporality

I would like to make one last observation in concluding this brief look at *"Ousia and Gramme"*. In his discussion of Hegel's account of temporal categories in his *Philosophy of Nature*, an account Heidegger calls a "paraphrase" of Aristotle (Heidegger, *Being and Time*, p. 432), Derrida quotes Hegel's statement that "…it is not *in* time (*in der Zeit*) that everything comes to be and passes away, rather time itself is the *becoming*, this coming-to-be and passing away". (Hegel, *Philosophy of Nature*, §258Z, p. 35) Derrida then comments, "Hegel takes multiple precautions of this type. By opposing them to all the metaphorical formulations that state the 'fall' into time (which, moreover, are not to be denied all dignity), one could exhibit an entire Hegelian critique of intratemporality (*Innerzeitigkeit*)". (Derrida, *Margins of Philosophy*, p. 45) This claim is aimed directly at Heidegger's discussion of Hegel in *Being and Time*, where Heidegger claims that Hegel's treatment of time follows the vulgar concept of time, which is precisely the conception of time as intratemporality.

Now if Derrida's claim can be upheld, it is indeed a devastating criticism of Heidegger. It would be the correlate concerning Hegel of Derrida's "two hypotheses" interpretation of Aristotle. However, I think that there is reason to question it. In the *Zusatz* to section 258, Hegel writes, "Time is not, as it were, a receptacle in which everything is placed as in a flowing stream…" (Hegel, *Philosophy of Nature*, §258Z, p. 35). This makes it clear that what Hegel is rejecting is Newton's absolute time, which for Heidegger would be one way of understanding intratemporality, but only one. At the very least, Derrida would owe his reader some reason to think that a critique of Newtonian absolute time amounts to a critique of what Heidegger called the vulgar concept of time. It could also be shown that Hegel is not criticizing a position that could plausibly be attributed to Aristotle. This would require a look at Aristotle's discussion of what it means "to be in time" (*Physics*, 221ª1-221ᵇ3; cf. Heidegger's interpretation in *Basic Problems of Phenomenology*, 251-252.)

CONCLUSION

What conclusions can we draw from these readings of Derrida's texts? Well, I have not shown, nor have I tried to show—either here or in *Strategies of Deconstruction*—that deconstruction is either wrong, wrongheaded, or worthless. What I have shown, if my arguments are successful, is that a few deconstructionist texts—though very central and influential ones—fail to live up to their own standards of rigor. I would hope that this makes it clear that there is a pressing need for serious, close readings of other Derridean texts. They may fare better. We will have to see.

What is clear, however, is that the reception of Derrida's works for more than two decades has rarely lived up to the standards Derrida himself established for his own work. Derrida's work on Husserl, Saussure, Aristotle, and Hegel—that is, precisely that work I have been discussing—has been widely praised for being careful, rigorous, professional, etc., but it is increasingly clear that at least these texts have not been read carefully by those who have praised them, where care involves going back to the texts Derrida is "deconstructing"— or which are supposed to be deconstructing themselves—and giving them a serious, independent reading. There is no doubt that the discussion of Derrida's work has been poisoned by unfounded charges raised by people who have not seriously read his work, and Derrida himself has justifiably protested against this demonization. But there is equally no doubt that public discourse is poisoned by the repeated and habitual praise of texts when that praise is not based on serious reading. This contributes to misology: the scorn of reason and rigor...and reading. And it does so even when the people involved are themselves committed, as indeed Derrida himself insists that he is, to the life of reason.

J. Claude Evans

Department of Philosophy
Washington University
One Brookings Drive
Campus Box 1073
St. Louis, MO 63130.

REFERENCES

Aristotle, *Physics*, in *Aristotle: Selected Works*, tr. Hippocrates G. Apostle, Grinnell, Iowa: Peripatetic Press 1982. I have changed Apostle's translation of '*nun*' from 'moment' to 'now' in order to bring it in line with Derrida's text. None of the claims I am making depends on questions concerning translation.

Gustav Bergmann, "The Ontology of Edmund Husserl", in Bergmann, *Logic and Reality*, Madison: University of Wisconsin Press 1964, pp. 193-224.

Jonathan Culler, *On Deconstruction*, Ithaca: Cornell University Press 1982.

Jacques Derrida, *La voix et le phenomene*, Paris: Les Editions de Minuit 1967. English translation by David Allison: *Speech and Phenomena*, Bloomington: Indiana University Press 1973.

Jacques Derrida, *Of Grammatology*, tr. Gayatri Chakravorty Spivak, Baltimore: Johns Hopkins University Press 1976.

——, *"Ousia* and *Gramme*: Note on a Note to *Being and Time"*, in Derrida, *Margins of Philosophy*, tr. Alan Bass, Chicago: University of Chicago Press 1982.

——,. "Letter to a Japanese Friend", tr. David Wood and Andrew Benjamin, in David Wood and Robert Bensaconi (eds.), *Derrida and Difference*, Evanston: Northwestern University Press.

John Ellis, *Against Deconstruction*, Princeton: Princeton University Press 1989.

J. Claude Evans, "Deconstructing the Declaration", *Man and World* 23 (1990), 175–189.

——, *Strategies of Deconstruction.*, Minneapolis: University of Minnesota Press 1992.

G.W.F. Hegel, *Philosophy of Nature*, tr. A.V. Miller, Oxford: Clarendon Press 1970.

Martin Heidegger, *Sein und Zeit,* Max Niemeyer: Tübingen 1972, English translation by John Macquarrie and Edward Robinson, *Being and Time*, New York: Harper and Row 1962.

——, *Die Grundprobleme der Phänomenologie*, Frankfurt: Vittorio Klosterman. English translation by Albert Hofstadter, *Basic Problems of Phenomenology*, Bloomington: Indiana University Press 1982.

Edmund Husserl, *Logische Untersuchungen*, Tübingen: Max Niemeyer Verlag, 1901. English translation by J.N. Findlay, *Logical Investigations*, London: Routledge and Kegan Paul, 1970.

Edmund Husserl, *Formale und Transzendentale Logik*, ed. Paul Janssen, The Hague: Martinus Nijhoff 1974. English translation by Dorian Cairns, *Formal and Transcendental Logic*, The Hague: Martinus Nijhoff 1969.

Carl Knüfer, *Grundzüge der Geschichte des Begriffs 'Vorstellung' von Wolff bis Kant*, Hildesheim: Georg Olms 1975.

Frank Lentricchia, *After the New Criticism*, Chicago: University of Chicago Press 1980.

Andrew Parker, " 'Taking Sides' (On History: Derrida Re-Marx)", *Diacritics* 11 (1981), 57-73.

Richard Rorty, "Is Derrida a Transcendental Philosopher?", *Yale Journal of Criticism* 2 (1989), 207-271.

Ferdinand de Saussure, *Cours de la linguistique generale*, ed. Charles Bally and Albert Sechehaye, Paris: Payot, 1955. English translations by Wade Baskin, *Course in General Linguistics*, New York: McGraw-Hill 1966, and by Roy Harris, *Course in General Linguistics*, La Salle, Illinois: Open Court 1983. Unless otherwise noted, quotes are taken from the Baskin translation.

Robert M. Strozier, *Saussure, Derrida, and the Metaphysics of Subjectivity*, Berlin: Mouton de Gruyter 1988.

Thomas Aquinas, *Commentary on Aristotle's Physics*, tr. R.J. Blackwell, R.J. Smith, W.E. Thirlkel, New Haven: Yale University Press 1963.

HEIDEGGER'S "QUESTION OF BEING": A CRITICAL INTERPRETATION

Whenever we reflect on the relation between "European Philosophy and the American Academy", we find ourselves backstage contending with Martin Heidegger.[1] This happens because Heidegger so decisively influenced the manner and matter of modern continental philosophy, particularly post-war French and German thought.

But discussing Heidegger is difficult. The very "question of being" that he wanted to raise is hard to grasp, because, as he repeatedly stressed, "being" is as yet not understood. Thus it is that we live in "oblivion of being".[2]

My argument in this paper is that Heidegger's question of being appears to defy interpretation mainly because it is not one single question. Borrowing an expression from musical theory, I hold that at least five leitmotivs are interwoven in the question of being. Much of what Heidegger says will sound obscure as long as the question is considered in the light of one such leading motive only. We have to put the leading motives together in order to grasp the full significance of Heidegger's texts, because in this respect, his works are like Wagnerian overtures. The reader may be captivated by their spell without being able to recognize the interplay of leitmotivs—that is, without fully understanding what Heidegger wants to say. I shall thus call the view of the question of being to be defended in what follows the Wagnerian interpretation.

In Section 1, five leitmotivs are listed and elucidated. Next, their interplay is sketched (Section 2). Because there is no compelling reason why they should be rolled into one, I shall evaluate Heidegger's question of being by evaluating the leading motives separately (Section 3). Finally, in (Section 4), I shall discuss some philosophical stratagems based on two leitmotivs which prevail in the later Heidegger, leaving it to the reader to reflect upon the ways in which philosophers influenced by Heidegger, such as Jacques Derrida, use similar stratagems.

I. ANALYSIS

In the order in which they appear in *Being and Time* and in Heidegger's later works, the five leitmotivs of the question of being are the following:

A. *The meta-Aristotelian theme.*

According to Aristotle's *Metaphysics*, 'being' is said in many ways (*pollachôs*), and always in relation to one thing or nature (*pros hen*).[3] As a consequence,

Aristotle's question of being has two opposite poles, a pole of differentiation and a pole of unification. The pole of differentiation (*pollachôs*) motivates the programme of developing the different ways in which 'being' is used. It embraces the system of categories, the notion of truth, the distinction between actual and potential being, and that between matter and form. Unification (*pros hen*), on the other hand, consists in showing how the different ways of using 'to be' are interrelated, and how they depend on one fundamental sense of 'being'. According to Aristotle, this fundamental sense is that of being as a substance, and, in the final analysis, being as the deity.[4]

I call Heidegger's question of being meta-Aristotelian because Heidegger is more radical than Aristotle regarding both differentiation and unity.[5] As far as differentiation is concerned, he holds that Aristotle tried to understand the many different types of being on the model of one type only, which Heidegger names a "present thing" (*das Vorhandene*). This is what Heidegger calls Aristotle's "ontology of presence" (*Ontologie der Vorhandenheit*), which he articulated in his system of categories, and in which 'being' is construed as "constant presence". According to Heidegger, it is impossible to understand in terms of the ontology of presence our own being, or the way tools exist, for example. This is why we have to "destroy" or deconstruct the ontology of presence and elaborate a proper system of " existential categories" for human existence (i.e. a system of what Heidegger calls existentials). The published part of *Being and Time* is mainly devoted to this task.[6]

As far as the pole of unification is concerned, Heidegger holds that the most fundamental sense of 'being', to which all the other senses are related, cannot be being-as-a-substance or being-as-deity.[7] According to Heidegger, one should acknowledge a radical difference between the totality of beings (*Seiendes*) on the one hand, to which substances and gods belong, and being itself, being in the sense of the verb 'to be' (*das Sein*) on the other hand. I shall indicate this second sense by an upper-case initial: 'Being'. Heidegger calls the difference between beings and Being the "ontological difference".[8] He holds that Aristotle, and with him the entire metaphysical tradition of the West, has thought about the totality of beings only, so that Being has been "forgotten". This is the famous oblivion of Being (*Seinsvergessenheit*). Heidegger's question of being in the sense of the pole of unification is concerned with Being, not with beings.

B.   *The phenomenological theme.*

In *Being and Time*, Heidegger seems to equate Being with the manner of being (*Seinsweise*) of types of beings. This is why Being is called a phenomenon, although not a phenomenon in the "vulgar sense".[9] Because we usually concentrate on beings and their properties, the manner of being of these beings is concealed. We rarely reflect, for instance, on the difference between our own manner of being, which Heidegger calls existence, and the manner of being of inanimate things. This explains the predominance of the ontology of presence, which seeks to understand human existence on the model of things (e.g., the Cartesian *res cogitans* and *res extensa*).[10] It is the aim of phenomenological ontology to elucidate the ontological status of types of being by analyzing their manner of being. Because there "are" many manners of being, the phenomenological leitmotiv seems to have dissolved the unity of Being. Unity is restored, however, via themes C, D, and E below, albeit in different ways.

C. *The transcendental theme.*

According to Kant and Husserl, the sciences are "founded in" synthetic *a priori* ontologies, and these ontologies are founded in turn in a science of the transcendental subject. In §§3–4 of *Being and Time*, Heidegger endorses this tripartite structure of knowledge.[11] He argues that the phenomenological ontology of our existence or *Dasein* is *fundamental* ontology. This implies that it is impossible to understand ontologically non-human types of being except by interpreting them in the light of the ontology of *Dasein*. The world, for example, is primarily a meaningful structure that is revealed or opened up in human moods (*Stimmungen*) and understanding (*Verstehen*). It is the world of daily life, the world in which we must live our lives, in which we use tools, attend conferences, etc. The scientific understanding of the world as a multiplicity of in themselves meaningless events is a secondary and impoverished kind of understanding which, according to Heidegger, is derived from our primary understanding, and which is, therefore, *also secondary in the ontological sense.*[12]

D. *The neo-Hegelian theme.*

Hegel says in the preface to his *Philosophy of Right* that philosophy should express the essence of its epoch in thought.[13] Notably in the works after *Being and Time*, Heidegger assumes in a Hegelian vein that each epoch has a fundamental structure (*Grundstellung*),[14] which manifests itself in *all* aspects of that epoch.[15] The sequence of these structures is "real history". Traditional metaphysics would have been an articulation of such fundamental structures, in which the whole of being is conceived of in a certain way,[16] even though metaphysics did not dwell upon the sense of Being which is fundamental to each epoch and which constitutes its unity.[17] This is why the metaphysical tradition excludes an "experience of the truth of Being" and has been oblivious of Being.[18] Heidegger's post-metaphysical "thinking" aims at grasping the fundamental structure of the present epoch in such a way that we may question it and become free for a new experience of Being.[19] Thinking in this sense would be more fundamental than the investigation of our culture by history, economics, or the social sciences, so that it would not depend on these disciplines.[20]

E. *The post-monotheist theme.*

Between Hegel and Heidegger stands Nietzsche, who became the greatest challenge for Heidegger's thought. Whereas Hegel's history of Being is progressive and culminates in a unification of our soul with the Absolute, Heidegger's history of Being is one of decline or fall (*Verfall, Verfallen*), in which Being becomes ever more concealed.[21] Heidegger endorses the Nietzschean dictum that God is dead. That is, that the idea of a transcendent realm has lost its force, which is why the world now manifests itself merely as a meaningless field for technical domination, exploitation, and consumption by man's will to power (*das Wesen der Technik*).[22] Nonetheless Heidegger does not resign himself to this situation. I suggest that just as Luther blamed the influence of Greek philosophy on Christian theology for the crisis of faith in his time,[23] so Heidegger thought that the eclipse of Being ("nihilism") was due to the Greek ontology of presence, from which the fundamental structure of our epoch is derived.[24] Because, in the ontology of presence, Being is represented as an eternal and immutable substance (God), the sudden and unexpected coming (*Ankunft, Ereignis*) or advent of Being in our life is precluded. Therefore, in order to prepare for such an advent, we have to "destroy" or deconstruct the tradition of metaphysics, which conceals Being. But of course we cannot force Being to come,[25] and in fact Being has concealed or withdrawn *itself* in the history of metaphysics (the *Deus absconditus* theme).[26] Therefore, we have to ask for Being (to ask the question of Being) with resignation (*Gelassenheit*),[27] in order to *prepare* for a future advent of Being (the John the Baptist theme),[28] in which Being will manifest itself to us (the theme of grace).[29] It belongs to the logic of the post-monotheist leading motive that Heidegger on the one hand dismisses all assimilations of his question of Being to traditional (onto)theology, which is held responsible for our abandonment by Being,[30] whereas on the other hand there is a strong structural and terminological similarity between his discourse on Being and the very theology he rejects. By substituting 'God' for 'Being' in Heidegger's later texts, one quite often obtains traditional statements of monotheist theology.

II. SYNTHESIS

How are these five leitmotivs connected together in *the* question of being? Heidegger introduces the question (A) in *Being and Time* as what do we mean by the *word* 'being'.[31] But then he immediately drops the quotation marks and asserts that we have to ask the question about the sense of being (*die Frage nach dem Sinn von Sein*). And indeed, in *Being and Time* Heidegger asks both for the sense of 'being' and for the sense of being.[32]

This apparent ambiguity in the question of being may be understood against the background of Husserl's *Logical Investigations*.[33] According to Husserl, all meaningful expressions have both meaning and referent. Husserl assumes that in order to elucidate an expression's meaning, acquaintance with its referent(s) is crucial. Because he applies this view to logical constants such as 'to be', we have to look for the ("categorial") *phenomenon* of Being if we want to clarify the sense of the verb 'to be'.[34] That is, a search for the meaning of 'being' has to be a quest for Being. This Husserlian assumption links the meta-Aristotelian theme (A) to the phenomenological theme (B): to elucidate the sense(s) of 'being', Heidegger has to analyze a phenomenon: the Being of beings (*Seinsweisen*).[35]

In sections 2 and 4 of *Being and Time*, Heidegger argues that there is a primacy of one particular being in the developing question of Being: the being that we humans are, because we already have an understanding of (')Being(').[36] This links the phenomenological theme (B) to the transcendental theme (C). Interpreting our existence ontologically, Heidegger discovers that the ontological sense (*Sinn*) of our existence resides in what he calls concern (*Sorge*), and that the sense of, or the condition of the inner possibility of, concern is authentic time, that is, time as it unfolds itself in our authentic being-to-death. Time in this sense, then, is the sense of our being-there (*Dasein*). This notion of time is very different from and allegedly more fundamental than our usual concept of time as a measurable quantity.

Because in *Being and Time* Heidegger holds that the ontology of Dasein is fundamental or transcendental, the sense of Being revealed by this ontology should point to the fundamental sense of Being tout court, from which the other senses are somehow derived. This is why the original scheme of the book contained a turn or reversal (Kehre), which is announced in section 83: after having interpreted the sense of Being from the point of view of our human understanding of Being (*Seinsverständnis*), Heidegger planned to interpret Dasein and all the other modes of being from the point of view of the temporality of Being itself. This notion of a turn is crucial for understanding Heidegger's development, and, indeed, for understanding how themes A, B, and C are linked to themes D and E. However, the notion of a turn in Heidegger is a complex one, and perhaps the turn as planned in *Being and Time* was never realized.[37]

In the first place, there is a turn after *Being and Time* from the transcendental theme (C) to the neo-Hegelian theme (D), a turn which may be compared with Hegel's reaction to Kant. According to *Being and Time*, the fundamental ontology of *Dasein* articulates the essence of human existence, which underlies all ontic or factual manifestations of human life.[38] This implies that the ontology of *Being and Time* claims to be universally valid for all times and cultures. However, the "historicity" of human existence belongs to the essence of *Dasein*, and the ontological concepts Heidegger uses in *Being and Time* are rooted in the Christian and philosophical tradition of the West. Should one not conclude that a universally valid analysis of human existence is impossible, because human existence is entirely determined by the historically variable fundamental structures of the relevant epoch, a conclusion that turns one from C to D? If so, then it comes as no surprise that French structuralists such as Michel Foucault were so deeply influenced by the later Heidegger.

Heidegger seems to construe the turn from C to D in yet another way. The fundamental ontology of *Dasein* (C) is impossible unless we are able to deconstruct our inherited common sense or self-understanding derived from the ontology of presence, because the ontology of presence conceals the real nature of human existence by conceptualizing it on the model of a present thing. In the later writings, however, Heidegger seems to claim that the fundamental structure of our epoch has become such that it is now impossible to break through the ontology of presence. We are dominated by a way of understanding the world and ourselves which Heidegger calls "the reign of technology" (*das Wesen der Technik*).[39] As a consequence, we understand everything in the world as a matter for calculation and exploitation, so that the way to authentic Being is barred.

On this point, theme D is connected with E, the post-monotheist leitmotiv. According to Heidegger, the technical and scientific understanding of the world, which is due to the reign of technology, and which dominates our era, is the climax of the oblivion of Being. However, he holds out the hope that by meditating on this climax, we may prepare for a new advent (*Ankunft*) of Being. This is the aim of Heidegger's later "thinking" or "questioning".[40] The post-monotheist theme (E) is also connected with (C) via yet another kind of "turn". At this point, comparing Heidegger with Pascal is instructive. In the *Pensées*, which were meant to be an *apologia* for Christianity, Pascal first showed, by an analysis of human existence, that man is miserable and incomprehensible to himself. Crucial to Pascal's analysis is his notion of diversion (*divertissement*), because he tried to convince us that *everything* we do is diversion except meditation on our mortality, which will make us miserable. He then argued that Christianity offers the consolation and understanding we need, provided that it is liberated from its contamination by Greek ontology. Similarly, Heidegger's analysis of human existence in *Being and Time* purports to show that we are "inauthentic" unless we consciously confront our death. The time-structure of such a confrontation is called *Augenblick* (instant, moment), and some commentators suppose that Heidegger modeled this notion on the Christian idea of *kairos* (the supreme moment of the advent of God).[41] If so, the interpretation of human existence in *Being and Time* may be seen as a preparation for a "turn": by showing the finiteness of human existence, Heidegger would incite us to a resolute openness (*Entschlossenheit*) for Being in the post-monotheist sense. Because we cannot force Being to come, what we experience in resolute openness for Being is *Angst* and nothingness.[42] Having realized this first turn, we will hope for a second one: that Being will turn itself to us again. And indeed Heidegger says that the turn (*Kehre*) should be seen as a turn *of Being itself*.[43] This interpretation of the Heideggerian turn by analogy with Pascal's *apologia* for Christianity has the advantage that it accounts for the unity of Heidegger's *Denkweg*, a unity on which Heidegger often insisted.[44]

What the example of Heidegger's notion of a turn shows is the amazing polyvalence of his key expressions,[45] a polyvalence which corroborates our Wagnerian interpretation of the question of being. It is responsible for the characteristic combination of darkness and richness in Heidegger's texts.[46] In particular, the polyvalence of key expressions enables Heidegger to make smooth transiations between the different leitmotivs of the question of being, and indeed to conceal to the reader that there is a plurality of such leitmotifs. Polyvalence makes interpretation difficult especially when the various meanings of a key expression are incompatible. And in fact they often are. If, for instance, one takes Being phenomenologically (theme B) as the Being (*Seinsweise*) of types of beings, 'oblivion of Being' means that we usually do not *notice* different manners of Being. We can cancel this oblivion of Being by doing phenomenological ontology. But if Being is taken post-monotheistically (E), oblivion of Being is a "fate" Being itself bestows on us, and which Being alone can undo.[47] Whereas Being in the second sense is radically transcendent to the totality of beings, Being in the first sense may be elucidated by investigating beings.[48]

III. CRITICISMS

There is no compelling reason to interweave the five leitmotivs into the symphony of the question of being. The post-monotheist attempt to rescue the essence of religion in an age of atheism and technology can do without neo-Hegelian structuralism; a phenomenological analysis of the Being of beings is not necessarily tied up with transcendentalism; and in fact none of the five leitmotivs requires any of the other four. Because they are often even in conflict, as I showed at the end of section II, we may just as well evaluate each of the themes separately.

A.   No one will object to the pole of differentiation in the *meta-Aristotelian theme*. Logicians teach us that 'to be' as a logical expression is used in at least three senses, identity, predication, and existence. Moreover, there are many non-logical uses of 'to be', 'to exist', and 'being', for instance when we speak of 'human existence', or use 'Being' as a post-monotheist substitute for 'God'. As far as the pole of unity is concerned, however, I suggest that we should have strong reservations concerning Heidegger's question of being. To begin with, it is a mistake to think that 'to be' in the logical sense is used as a referring expression. Moreover, the logical uses of 'to be' are not internally related to the non-logical uses. In particular, it is erroneous to think that a notion of time is essential to the logical uses, and that this notion of time is derived either from the ontology of presence or from human "understanding of Being".[49] Consequently, an ontology of human existence or a post-monotheist discourse on Being will throw no light upon our ordinary logical uses of 'to be' and 'to exist', so that the unity of the meta-Aristotelian question of being is an illusion.[50]

B.   On the other hand, the importance of Heidegger's *phenomenology of human existence* cannot be overestimated. Heidegger convincingly showed in *Being and Time* that we tend to misinterpret the ontological "sense" of our existence under the influence of metaphysical and scientific conceptions. The rich and detailed ontology of *Dasein* is a remedy against superficial reductionisms and eliminative materialisms which abound in the modern philosophical tradition. It seems impossible, at least in the light of our present scientific knowledge, either to *reduce* our existence and the world as meaningful phenomena to "meaningless" material systems, or to *eliminate* the ordinary "meaningfulness" of our world and human life in favour of a purely scientific world-view.[51]

C.   However, it does not follow from the phenomenology of *Dasein* that human existence is ontologically more fundamental than nature as science understands it. This anti-naturalist thesis is as essential to Heidegger's transcendental theme, as to the neo-Hegelian and the post-monotheist leitmotivs. I think that we should reject Heidegger's anti-naturalism, whether it is motivated by the transcendental, the neo-Hegelian, or the post-monotheist theme. We also should dismiss Heidegger's dogma that science is based on *a priori* ontologies, on a "scheme" (*Entwurf*) which cannot be empirically justified, or on a particular neo-Hegelian fundamental structure, a dogma which is instrumental in Heidegger's argument for the non-binding nature of scientific knowledge.[52] In short, we should try to reconcile naturalism to anti-reductionism concerning human life.[53]

D. It cannot be denied that technology more and more dominates our culture and it is certain that, in conjunction with overpopulation, technology tends to destroy the ecosystem of the Earth. But this does not entail that we should accept Heidegger's neo-Hegelian thesis of the *reign* of technology (*das Wesen der Technik*). According to this thesis, the domination of technology is due to the dominance of a specific fundamental structure which would manifest itself in all aspects of our epoch, and which makes us consider everything in the world merely as a matter for calculation, exploitation, and consumption. According to Heidegger, this structure itself can be explained by studying the "logic" of Western metaphysics,[54] and can be known or experienced in specific "moods" (*Grundstimmungen*), such as boredom.[55] This experiential knowledge of the reigning fundamental structure would be independent of, and indeed *a priori* in relation to, empirical investigation of modern culture by the social sciences, for instance.

I suggest that we reject this neo-Hegelian theme for at least three reasons. First, Heidegger's thesis that the fundamental structure of the "reign of technology" governs *all* manifestations of our epoch lands him in a dilemma. If we take in their usual sense terms like 'technology', 'exploitation', 'consumption', 'calculation', and the other terms used by Heidegger to characterize the way beings manifest themselves in the era of technology, then it is empirically false that in our epoch we always regard everything as a matter for exploitation, consumption, etc.[56] Or, Heidegger stretches the meaning of these terms indefinitely, until their extension embraces everything. But if he does this, then the terms will lose their significance. In short, like all universal theses of this kind, Heidegger's thesis of the essence of technology is either false or meaningless.[57]

This semantic objection is related to a second, moral, objection. Heidegger's neo-Hegelian theme may be called "totalitarian" in that Heidegger pretends to know in advance what the manifestations of his fellow human beings mean ultimately: they all express the reign of technology. For instance, in "The Question of Technology" Heidegger claims that the tourist who enjoys the landscape of the Rhine, or the forester who loves the woods as his ancestors did, are entirely dominated by the tourist or timber industry "whether they know it or not".[58] This totalitarian feature of the neo-Hegelian motive is most irritating, because it means that Heideggerians will never take at face value what their critical interlocutors are saying, and will never pay proper respect to the declared intentions of others. For a Heideggerian, a champion of human rights will be just another marginal manifestation of the all-embracing technological will to power.[59]

Finally, there is a crucial epistemological objection to the neo-Hegelian theme. If one pretends that one may somehow experience the fundamental structure of our epoch by means of privileged moods (*Grundstimmungen*), inde-

pendently of empirical research, one will uncritically trust one's own preconceptions and hypostatize them into privileged objective insights. This explains
the extraordinary self-confidence with which Heidegger professed his reactionary stance on technology and his anti-democratic stance in politics.[60] But of
course there "are" no unified fundamental structures to be "experienced" in fundamental moods. Modern culture is complex and pluralistic, and only those
longing for a simplistic world-view will be attracted by the idea of neo-Hegelian fundamental structures, whether Marxist, Foucauldian, or Heideggerian. A
philosophical critique of modern culture is perhaps more urgent than ever, but it
should be developed in interaction with the empirical sciences.

E.   Heidegger's later writings will appeal in particular to those who have for-
sworn traditional Christianity but somehow preserved a religious attitude.[61] If
specific moods (*Stimmungen*) are fundamental epistemic sources, as Heidegger
suggests, the post-monotheist theme may be indisputable. If, on the other hand,
rational argument should prevail in philosophy,[62] the post-monotheist leading
motive must be rejected for many reasons. Let me state two of them.

In the first place, there is a semantic objection. Talking about Gods in poly-
theistic religions may be or have been empirically meaningful, although scientific advance has shown in many cases that what was said, for instance that
Apollo causes the plague, is false. However, the competition between religions
led to the invention of ever more powerful Gods. In the end it gave rise to the
idea of an infinitely powerful God who would tolerate no other Gods, that is, it
led to monotheism. Because the monotheist God is infinite, he is wholly transcendent, and our language ceases to be applicable to him. God becomes the
Deus absconditus. One may try to say something meaningful about the infinite
God by analogy, but if he is really infinite, analogies with finite beings will
break down. Monotheist theology, therefore, is infected by (empirical) mean-
inglessness. Heidegger's post-monotheist Being is even more transcendent than
the monotheist God, because Heidegger says that Being transcends the sphere
of beings as a whole. Being is *das transcendens schlechthin*.[63] Moreover,
'Being' should be understood in the verbal sense; it does not refer to an entity or
to an agent. If this is so, how can Heidegger say that we have to let Being
address us again,[64] that Being *is waiting* until we humans will deem it worthy
of our attention,[65] that Being *conceals itself*,[66] etc.? These predicates can be
meaningfully applied to (finite) agents only. We must conclude that Heidegger's post-monotheist discourse on Being can have no meaning.[67]

Secondly, the post-monotheist discourse on Being confronts Heidegger
with a dilemma, a dilemma which infects all absolute and non-empirical epistemic claims. Let me call it the *sectarians'* dilemma, the one that arises as soon
as one's own absolute epistemic claim is contradicted by another equally abso-

lute epistemic claim. For instance, one religiously inspired politician pretends that God prohibits abortion in all cases, and another retorts that God sometimes allows abortion. In such a situation, either we have to admit that both absolute claims are equally valid, which means that they are both invalid and useless because they destroy each other, or we may pretend that one of them (usually the claim one shares) is somehow more valid than the other. But this second option is dogmatic, and it cannot be justified by argument. Heidegger chose the second option.[68] This explains why he could never say that his former convictions had been mistaken and why he had to account for changes in his philosophy by postulating changes in Being itself. For the possibility of a mistake by the private person Martin Heidegger would invalidate his absolutist epistemology, according to which Heidegger's discourse of Being somehow expresses the voice of Being itself. The sectarian's dilemma also explains why Heidegger refused to discuss his political past in public, although there may be other explanations for this fact also. Heidegger's absolutist epistemology, according to which he had privileged access to the reigning fundamental structure and to Being itself, is inseparable from his anti-democratic and authoritarian attitude. A commitment to rational argument in philosophy and to democracy in politics is incompatible with the essence of Heidegger's later thought.

IV. STRATAGEMS

Even if we reject the leitmotivs in Heidegger's question of being, with the exception of the pole of differentiation in the meta-Aristotelian theme (A), and the phenomenological theme (B), as I suggest we should, we may still be mesmerized by the extraordinary expressiveness and rhetorical power of his works. The spell will be broken only by an explicit analysis of Heidegger's rhetorical stratagems, which are rooted mainly in the neo-Hegelian and the post-monotheist theme. At least seven characteristic stratagems may be distinguished.

1. *The Stratagem of the Fall.*

Heidegger often suggests, as indeed the neo-Hegelian theme and post-monotheist oblivion of Being imply, that modern man is somehow fated to "err" (*Irren*), because everything he says or does is governed by the fundamental structure of the reign of technology.[69] Of course this is not a sound argument. Its premiss is either false or meaningless, as I argued above. But it is a powerful rhetorical device, since it will be used to transform each and every critical observation into a confirmation of Heidegger's views, by unmasking or deconstructing it as a typical expression of "the reign of technology", "information", "logocentrism", or whatever other all-embracing depreciation one prefers. Logically speaking, the stratagem of the Fall is an instance of the informal fallacy called "poisoning the well".

2.   *The Stratagem of the Radical Alternative.*

If everything we think and do is contaminated by the Fall, redemption must consist in an alternative which is *radically* different from anything we are able to conceive of. The conjunction of stratagems (1) and (2) puts the Heideggerian in a comfortable, because unassailable, "position": he may condemn all other philosophical movements and conceptions in the name of an alternative which is ineffable because it is *radical*. But then, because an ineffable alternative cannot be criticized, he is able to criticize while being himself immune against criticism.

In Continental universities, undergraduates are greatly charmed by this powerful non-position, until they discover that it is obtained at the price of emptiness. As there are no compelling *reasons* to be convinced by stratagems (1) and (2), one is tempted to give a psychological explanation for their astonishing rhetorical success. Clearly, the unassailable "position" obtained by these stratagems will appeal to weak or immature personalities, who are longing to feel both superior to others and safe against criticism. If conditions are favourable, teachers craving for power may use Heidegger's writings to reinforce their irrational authority over students and to form a Heideggerian sect.

The stratagem of the radical alternative is particularly pernicious in relation to the problem of technology. It is vital for mankind to develop new types of technology which are ecologically stable, so that in, say, fifty years time mankind will have found a sustainable mode of life which offers a reasonable level of prosperity. Heideggerians will tend to condemn and depreciate all attempts to find such solutions to the problem of technology for being not sufficiently radical and for remaining within the "reign of technology". I would say, therefore, that Heideggerian thought may corrupt juvenile minds in our universities, because it tends to divert their intellectual energy from constructive approaches to urgent problems mankind has to solve.

3.   *The Stratagem of Indifferentiating Abstraction.*[70]

We have seen how Heidegger tries to characterize the fundamental structure of our epoch by stretching indefinitely the extension of nouns such as 'technology', 'information' and 'exploitation'. These nouns thereby become so abstract that they lose their meaning, though Heidegger simultaneously suggests that they keep the senses they usually have. I call this kind of abstraction "indifferentiating", because Heidegger also suggests that the fundamental structure is the only thing that counts, so that all differences *within* the framework of the alleged fundamental structure of the present epoch become a matter of indifference. Accordingly, Heidegger did not acknowledge any interesting difference between, for instance, Stalin's totalitarian regime and Roosevelt's democratic America.[71] In other words, the neo-Hegelian theme implies a repulsive degree of moral indifference or unconcern.

4. *Strategies of Immunization.*

Apart from the conjunction of stratagems (1) and (2), Heidegger uses two other stratagems in order to immunize his thought against criticism. One is the claim *that criticism is due to misunderstanding.* Of course this may be true in many cases, but it cannot be always true unless Heidegger were infallible. Heidegger repeatedly said that the question of being is not (yet) understood. One thing he might mean is that modern man is not attempting to hear the voice of Being, because man is preoccupied with the world of beings and technology. Or perhaps Heidegger meant that Being itself does not yet respond to our questioning and that it withdraws itself from us. But surely both of these claims presuppose that Heidegger's question of being has the post-monotheist meaning I attributed to it. If one says that this interpretation is based on a misunderstanding, one must offer another interpretation of the many passages which so strongly suggest it. Secondly, Heidegger often poured explicit calumny upon the very ideas of criticism and discussion.[72] Both stratagems, the notion that criticism is a symptom of misunderstanding and the straightforward calumnies against discussion and criticism are inherent in the (post)monotheist tradition. For if God or Being is infallible, criticism of his Word is sinful and must be due to incomprehension.

5. *Stratagem of the Obedient Ear.*

Heidegger's post-monotheist thinking would be inspired by the voice of Being. This is why Heidegger as a private person is not responsible for his thought, and why Heideggerians usually eschew discussion. Changes in Heidegger's philosophy are said to be due to changes in Being itself. They should not be explained by saying that Heidegger changed his mind for such and such reasons. According to Heidegger, this irresponsibility is the highest form of responsibility, because it is supposed to be a responsiveness to Being. Kant and Sartre would reply that such a radical heteronomy is a form of self-deception. For each ear is responsible at least for its choice of what or whom to obey.

6. *Stratagem of the Forest Trails (Holzwege).*[73]

A post-monotheist thinker should always deny that his thought is post-monotheist, for otherwise he will be classified as belonging to the very tradition he wants to overcome, the tradition of monotheism. This is why the post-monotheist thinker has to fight a spiritual guerilla war against the intellectual establishment, and can never reveal where he really stands. He should on the one hand use forms and locutions of the monotheist tradition, but on the other hand disguise them beyond recognition. Instead of 'religion', he should say *'Bezug'*; instead of 'revelation' he should say *'Lichtung'* or *'Eröffnung'*; instead of 'Fall' he uses *'Verfallen'* or *'Irre'*; instead of 'advent' *'Ankunft'*, *'Angang'*, or *'Ereignis'*; instead of 'conversion' he says *'Wende'*, *'Wandlung'*,[74] or *'Wandel'*; and at best he uses all these expressions in a polyvalent way, so that in some contexts they do not have their post-monotheist significance. These contexts may then be used to "refute" the post-monotheist interpretation.[75]

7. Stratagem of the Elect.

Where we are all caught up in the fundamental structure of technology, so that our thinking is wholly perverted, Heidegger seems to have gained access to the impenetrable Place from where he is able to experience the Truth of Being, a Truth which remains concealed from ordinary mortals.[76] If so, why should we not blindly believe him, after all?

Herman Philipse

Leiden University,
Postbus 9515,
NL-2300 RA Leiden,
Netherlands

NOTES

1.   I am grateful to Joop Doorman (Delft Technical University), to Han Adriaanse, Arent Baron van Haersolte, Don Kwast and James McAllister (Leiden University), and to Barry Smith (Buffalo) and Eloise Segal (New York), for comments on an earlier draft. For references, see the list at the end of the paper.
2.   E.g. Heidegger, *Was ist Metaphysik?*, pp. 18-19; Neske, Kettering (eds.), *Antwort*, pp. 23-24; Heidegger, *Einführung in die Metaphysik*, p. 30.
3.   Aristotle, *Metaphysics* VI.2, 1026$^{a\text{-}b}$, and IV.1, 1003^a, respectively.
4.   This is why traditional metaphysics may be called onto-theology. Cf. Heidegger, "Die onto-theologische Verfassung der Metaphysik", in Heidegger, *Identität und Differenz*, pp. 56-57 and 66-69.
5.   At the end of *Sein und Zeit*, §1.1, Heidegger reproaches Hegel for having neglected the Aristotelian problem of the unity of being in relation to the plurality of cat-

egories. I am suggesting that Heidegger wanted to solve this Aristotelian problem in a radically new way.

6. There is some analogy between Heidegger's radicalization of the pole of differentiation, coupled to the destruction of the ontology of presence, and the later Wittgenstein's analysis of a multiplicity of language-games, coupled to a critique of the "Augustinian picture of language". See my "Heidegger's Question of Being and the 'Augustinian Picture' of Language".

7. Heidegger frequently identifies the question of being with the pole of unification, that is, with the question regarding the "guiding fundamental meaning" of 'to be'. See Heidegger, "Mein Weg in die Phänomenologie", in Heidegger, *Zur Sache des Denkens*, p. 81; Heidegger, *Sein und Zeit*, p. 17; Heidegger, Letter to Richardson, p. xi.

8. See, for example, Heidegger, "Vom Wesen des Grundes", in Heidegger, *Wegmarken*, pp. 21, 30.

9. Heidegger, *Sein und Zeit* §7. Cf. "'Seinssinn", for instance in *Phänomenologische Interpretation/Einführung*, pp. 58-61.

10. Because we are usually preoccupied with (things in) the world, it is "natural" that we try to understand ourselves by analogy with such things (animals, machines, computers). In *Sein und Zeit*, Heidegger calls this tendency *Verfallen* (the term 'Verfallen' echoes the Christian doctrine that being preoccupied with the world is the human predicament since the Fall: see my leitmotiv E, and also Heidegger, "Vom Wesen des Grundes", in Heidegger, *Wegmarken*, p. 40). Heidegger would hold that modern cognitive science is dominated in its entirety by the ontology of presence, and that it therefore fundamentally misunderstands human existence. His critique of the Aristotelian and Cartesian tradition applies *mutatis mutandis* to much contemporary philosophical psychology.

11. Cf. Heidegger, "Vom Wesen des Grundes", in Heidegger, *Wegmarken*, pp. 29–30.

12. Heidegger objects to the modern epistemological tradition that it is implicitly based on this secondary ontology, which dominated Western philosophy since the scientific revolution. He therefore claims that his question of being is more fundamental than epistemology, which had been considered as "first philosophy" at the end of the nineteenth century.

13. Hegel, *Philosophie des Rechts*, pp. xxi–xxii: "so ist auch die Philosophie, *ihre Zeit in Gedanken erfasst*".

14. See, for example, Heidegger, *Die Frage nach dem Ding*, pp. 33, 52, and passim; Heidegger, "Die Zeit des Weltbildes", in Heidegger, *Holzwege*, p. 96.

15. See, for example, Heidegger, "Die Zeit des Weltbildes", in Heidegger, *Holzwege*, p. 69: "Dieser Grund durchherrscht alle Erscheinungen, die das Zeitalter auszeichnen", and p. 101: "kann sich nichts entziehen". Cf. "Wozu Dichter?", in Heidegger, *Holzwege*, p. 272; Heidegger, "Die Frage nach der Technik", in Heidegger, *Vortraege und Aufsaetze*, pp. 19–21, 31 ("Wo dieses herrscht, vertreibt es jede andere Möglichkeit der Entbergung"), and *passim* in the later works. This is why the neo-Hegelian theme also brings about a unity in the plurality of "manners of being".

16. See, for example, Heidegger, *Die Frage nach dem Ding*, pp. 38, 50, 74ff.; Heid-

egger, "Die Zeit des Weltbildes", in Heidegger, *Holzwege*, p. 69.

17. Taking the traditional periodization of Western history as unproblematic, Heidegger says that 'Being' in Ancient Greece was understood as *alêtheia* and *physis*, in the Roman era as being the product of an operation, in Medieval times as being created, and in the modern epoch as being represented by a subject. What all these senses of Being have in common is the ontology of presence. Because the Greek ontological model was in fact derived from artefacts (a substance is a form impressed on matter), the era of technology, in which everything is regarded as a matter for exploitation, calculation, and consumption, is only the logical outcome of the history of Western metaphysics. The era of technology is the "reign" of the "end" of metaphysics, the final consummation of the metaphysical tradition. See Heidegger, "Überwindung der Metaphysik" in Heidegger, *Vortraege und Aufsaetze*, and *passim* in the later works.

18. See, for example, Heidegger, "Nietzsche's Wort 'Gott ist tot'", in Heidegger, *Holzwege*, pp. 195–196, 243; Heidegger, "Überwindung der Metaphysik", in Heidegger, *Vortraege und Aufsaetze*, p. 67, and passim in the later works.

19. Heidegger, *Die Frage nach dem Ding*, pp. 8, 30–34, 37–38, 73–74. This is "geschichtliches Fragen", which prepares a decision (*Entscheidung*). Cf. Heidegger, *Einführung in die Metaphysik*, pp. 33–39, 153.

20. See Heidegger "Wer ist Nietzsches Zarathustra?", in Heidegger, *Vortraege und Aufsaetze*, p. 115:

> Wir Heutigen sind durch die eigentümliche Vorherrschaft der neuzeitlichen Wissenschaften in den seltsamen Irrtum verstrickt, der meint, das Wissen lasse sich aus der Wissenschaft gewinnen und das Denken unterstehe der Gerichtsbarkeit der Wissenschaft. Aber das Einzige, was jeweils ein Denker zu sagen vermag, lässt sich logisch oder empirisch weder beweisen noch widerlegen.

21. See Heidegger, "Das Ende der Philosophie und die Aufgabe des Denkens", in Heidegger, *Zur Sache des Denkens*, p. 66; the seminar on "Zeit und Sein", in *Zur Sache des Denkens*, p. 56; *Einführung in de Metaphysik*, pp. 11, 28–29. Heidegger, *Beiträge zur Philosophie*, contains particularly clear expressions of the post-monotheist theme.

22. Heidegger, "Nietzsches Wort 'Got ist tot'", in Heidegger, *Holzwege*, pp. 193–247; "Überwindung der Metaphysik", in *Vortraege und Aufsaetze*, pp. 67–95; "Wer ist Nietzsches Zarathustra?", in *Vortraege und Aufsaetze*, pp. 97–122; "Die Frage nach der Technik", in *Vortraege und Aufsatze*, pp. 9–66; and *Nietszche*. Heidegger took the idea that the "reign of technology" is connected to the metaphysics of the Will to Power from Ernst Jünger's *Der Arbeiter*. Cf. Heidegger, "Zur Seinsfrage", in *Wegmarken*, pp. 217–219. Whereas Jünger seemed to applaud the reign of the Will to Power, Heidegger saw it as the climax of the Fall, and tried to overcome it by preparing for a new advent of Being.

23. Heidegger refers to Luther on crucial points, e.g. *Sein und Zeit* p. 10. In *Was ist Metaphysik*, p. 20, he refers to St. Paul's statement that God turned the wisdom of the world (i.e. Greek philosophy) into folly.

24. In "Brief über den 'Humanismus'", Heidegger calls the Nietzschean conception of God as the highest value, and thinking in terms of values in general, "die grösste Blasphemie, die sich dem Sein gegenüber denken lässt" (Heidegger, *Wegmarken*, pp. 179–180). In *Identität und Differenz*, pp. 70-71, Heidegger opposes the traditional con-

ception of God as *causa sui* to the "Göttlicher Gott".

25. See Heidegger, "Brief über den 'Humanismus'", *Wegmarken*, pp. 145, 154; *Was ist Metaphysik?*, pp. 49-50: "Das Opfer ist der Abschied vom Seienden auf dem Gang zur Wahrung der Gunst des Seins. Das Opfer kann durch das Werken und Leisten im Seienden zwar vorbereitet und bedient, aber durch solches nie erfüllt werden...", and *passim* in the later works.

26. See Neske, Kettering (eds.) *Antwort*, pp. 23-24; Heidegger, "Nietzsches Wort 'Gott ist tot'", in Heidegger, *Holzwege*, p. 244; Heidegger, "Wozu Dichter?", in Heidegger, *Holzwege*, p. 251, 254; Heidegger, "Was heisst Denken?", in Heidegger, *Vortraege und Aufsaetze*, p. 133; Heidegger, "Zeit und Sein", in Heidegger, *Zur Sache des Denkens*, pp. 9, 31–32, 44; and *passim* in the later works. This is why Heidegger's Überwindung (overcoming) of metaphysics becomes a Verwindung (coping with, as one has to cope with the loss of one's father) of the oblivion of Being in metaphysics. Cf. Heidegger, "Zur Seinsfrage", *Wegmarken*, p. 243–244.

27. See Heidegger, *Einführung in die Metaphysik*, p. 157: "Fragen können heisst: warten können, sogar ein Leben lang"; "Wissenschaft und Besinnung", in *Vortraege und Aufsaetze*, p. 64: "Besinnung ist Gelassenheit zum Fragwürdigen". Elsewhere Heidegger defines "Gelassenheit" as an attitude to the technical world in which we simultaneously accept and refuse technical artefacts, so that we will remain receptive to the hidden meaning of things ("Offenheit für das Geheimnis"): Heidegger, *Gelassenheit*, pp. 23–24.

28. See Neske, Kettering (eds.), *Antwort*, p. 28; Heidegger, "Die Zeit des Weltbildes", *Holzwege*, pp. 103–104; "Nietzsches Wort 'Gott ist tot'", in *Holzwege*, pp. 194–195; "Wissenschaft und Besinnung", in *Vortraege und Aufsaetze*, p. 66; "Brief über den 'Humanismus'", in *Wegmarken*, p. 160; "Das Ende der Philosophie", in *Zur Sache des Denkens*, pp. 66–67; Seminar on "Zeit und Sein", in *Zur Sache des Denkens*, p. 38; "Vom Wesen der Wahrheit", in *Wegmarken*, p. 97; *Beitraege zur Philosophie*, p. 421.

29. Heidegger, "Brief über den 'Humanismus'", *Wegmarken*, p. 145, 155, 165–167 ("Schickung des Seins selbst"); *Was ist Metaphysik?*, p. 49. ("Gunst des Seins")

30. Heidegger, *Identität und Differenz*, p. 51: "Wer die Theologie aus gewachsener Herkunft erfahren hat, zieht es heute vor, im Bereich des Denkens von Gott zu schweigen."

31. Heidegger, *Sein und Zeit*, p. 1. This text, which opens with a quotation from Plato's *Sophistes*, bears no title and does not occur in the table of contents.

32. This of course makes the word 'sense' (Sinn) ambiguous. It may refer to the meaning(s) of the expression 'to be', or to the ontological status of beings (Husserl used 'Sinn' in this sense in his *Ideas* I), or to transcendental structures, implicitly grasped in the *Seinsverständnis* of Dasein. Heidegger defines 'Sinn' in this latter sense as "das Woraufhin des primären Entwurfs des *Verstehens von Sein*". (Heidegger, *Sein und Zeit*, pp. 151–161, 323–325) The third meaning of 'Sinn' is the transcendentalized version of the second, which belongs to the phenomenological theme. In "Brief über den 'Humanismus'", Heidegger uses the word 'Sinn' in yet another, post-monotheist, sense, as an equivalent for 'truth of Being' (Heidegger, *Wegmarken*, pp. 168, 172; *Was ist Metaphysik?*, p. 18).

33. Heidegger says in "Mein Weg in die Phänomenologie" that he was greatly influenced by Husserl's *Logical Investigations* in developing the question of being. See especially Heidegger, *Zur Sache des Denkens*, p. 86, and also Heidegger's seminar at Zähringen, *Vier Seminare*, p. 116:

> Um die Frage nach dem Sinn von Sein überhaupt entfalten zu können, musste das Sein *gegeben* sein, um bei ihm seinen Sinn zu erfragen. Husserl's Leistung bestand in eben dieser Vergegenwärtigung des Seins, das in der Kategorie phänomenal anwesend ist. Durch diese Leistung, fährt Heidegger fort, hatte ich endlich einen Boden: 'Sein' ist kein blosser Begriff, ist keine reine Abstraktion, die sich auf dem Weg der Ableitung ergeben hat.

See also Heidegger, *Prolegomena zur Geschichte des Zeitbegriffs*, p. 93, and *Zur Sache des Denkens*, p. 47.

34. I have argued for this Husserlian connection in detail in my "Heidegger's Question of Being".

35. Husserl sharply distinguishes the logical uses of 'to be' or 'being', such as identity, existence, and predication, from non-logical uses, such as in 'what is the sense of being?' (meaning 'what is the sense of life?'). In Heidegger's thought, this fundamental distinction is often blurred. For instance, Heidegger assumes that logic is somehow connected to a specific "material" ontology, so that it should be disregarded by those who want to deconstruct this ontology. In developing the question of Being in *Sein und Zeit*, Heidegger sometimes suggests that the question of being is concerned with logical uses of 'to be', and at other times he suggests that it is concerned with the "sense" of specific manners of being, which, from a logical point of view, belong to "matter" and not to logical form. Because Heidegger does not clearly maintain Husserl's distinction between "sensual matter" and "categorial form" (Husserl, Sixth *Logical Investigation*, §§59–62), or between material and formal categories (Husserl, *Ideas* I, §13), the question of being seems in Heidegger's work to be concerned with both. See Section IIIA below, and my "Heidegger's Question of Being", §V. Although Heidegger distinguishes in §7 of *Sein und Zeit* between phenomena in the "vulgar" sense and the phenomenological phenomenon of being, it is not clear at all that the latter is purely "categorial" in Husserl's sense. Husserl would regard the fundamental ontology of Dasein in *Sein und Zeit* as a material ontology that is confined to one specific region.

36. This is the argument of *Sein und Zeit* §2, which is inconclusive, as Heidegger himself observes (*Sein und Zeit* §2, p. 8). But the argument of §4, in which Heidegger infers the *ontological* primacy of *Dasein* from the *ontic* fact that there would be no sciences and ontologies without *Dasein*, is equally invalid. The primacy of *Dasein* for the development of the question of Being can best be understood from the post-monotheist perspective. See the comparison with Pascal below.

37. See Grondin, *Le tournant dans la pensée de Martin Heidegger* for a scrupulous analysis. I should add that in fact there are two different "transcendental themes" in SZ. In a *Kantian* sense of 'transcendental', Heidegger's analysis of *Dasein* is a transcendental philosophy, because he assumes that all ontologies are rooted in the ontology of *Dasein* (*Sein und Zeit*, §4). In §3 of *Sein und Seit*, however, Heidegger's argument is transcendental in a pre-Kantian and even scholastic sense: he argues that we should elucidate the meaning of 'to be' in order to develop (by means of a "not deductively constructive genealogy") the various modes of being ("Weisen von Sein"). Being is the

transcendens schlechthin, as he says on p. 38. The turn planned in *Sein und Zeit* relates the first to the second transcendental theme.

38. *Sein und Zeit*, pp. 17 ("wesenhafte Strukturen...die in jeder Seinsart des faktischen Daseins sich als seinsbestimmende durchhalten"), p. 52 ("echte Wesenserkenntnis"), pp. 199-200, and p. 231 ("Wesen des Daseins"). Like Husserl's fundamental ontology, Heidegger's analysis of *Dasein* claims to exhibit timeless fundamental structures, even though time and historicity themselves are such structures.

39. The phrase 'Das Wesen der Technik' is difficult to translate. One of the reasons is that the noun 'Wesen' (essence) is used in an active sense, as an infinitive. This is why the French translate it by 'essance' (with an 'a'). Heidegger means by 'das Wesen der Technik' the alleged fact that in our time we are unable to understand or grasp anything whatsoever except as materials for possible exploitation and calculation.

40. See Heidegger, *Einführung in die Metaphysik,* p. 32, where he defines the objective of the question of Being as follows:

> Es gilt, das geschichtliche Dasein des Menschen und d.h. immer zugleich unser eigenstes künftiges, im Ganzen der uns bestimmten Geschichte in die Macht des ursprünglich zu eröffnenden Seins zurückzufügen; all das freilich nur in den Grenzen, innerhalb deren das Vermögen der Philosophie etwas vermag.

41. See Pöggeler, "'Historicity' in Heidegger's Late Work", p. 56; see also Pöggeler, *Der Denkweg Martin Heideggers*, pp. 36–45, 189ff.; Karl Lehman, "Christliche Geschichtserfahrung"; Klaus Held, "Grundbestimmung und Zeitkritik bei Heidegger", pp. 32, 36–37. In *Beiträge*, Heidegger defines 'Augenblick' as "das Erblitzen des Seyns" (§255, p. 409). One should not forget that 'Augenblick' was Luther's translation of *'kairos'*.

42. See Heidegger, *Was ist Metaphysik*. We then experience that man is "hineingehalten in das Nichts" (p. 35), and that we can liberate ourselves from idols only by letting ourselves go into nothingness (p. 42). According to the postscript to *Was ist Metaphysik*, man is called by the voice of Being, and the courage to experience essential *Angst* opens the possibility to experience Being:

> Einzig der Mensch unter allem Seienden erfährt, angerufen von der Stimme des Seins, das Wunder aller Wunder: Dass Seiendes ist. Der also in seinem Wesen in die Wahrheit des Seins Gerufene ist daher stets in einer wesentlichen Weise gestimmt. Der klare Mut zur wesenhaften Angst verbürgt die geheimnisvolle Möglichkeit der Erfahrung des Seins. (pp. 46-47)

43. In his "Brief über den 'Humanismus'", Heidegger interprets *Sein und Zeit* from the point of view of the *Kehre*: *Wegmarken*, pp. 159ff., 180ff. On p. 181 he says that it was the aim of *Sein und Zeit* to develop an adequate conception of *Dasein* in relation to which one might inquire as to what is Dasein's ontological relation to God. Cf. Heidegger, "Vom Wesen des Grundes", *Wegmarken*, p. 55n. For the turn into Being itself, see "Zur Seinsfrage", *Wegmarken*, pp. 234, 239, and the seminar on "Zeit und Sein", *Zur Sache des Denkens*, pp. 56-57 ("Verwandlung des Seins ins Ereignis"). See also *Beiträge zur Philosophie*, especially §255, and the letter to Richardson, p. xix.

44. See the letter to Richardson, pp. xix-xxi; "Brief über den 'Humanismus'" in *Wegmarken,* and *Sein und Zeit,* p. v: "Deren Weg bleibt indessen auch heute noch ein notwendiger, wenn die Frage nach dem Sein unser Dasein bewegen soll. '

45. Heidegger often stresses the "multiplicity" of his thought (See the letter to Richardson, p. xxiii). But this multiplicity should be understood in a strictly post-

monotheist sense: although Being is one and simple, its "behaving" (*Verhalten*) towards us is multiple, so that our attempt to express Being in words requires polysemic language (*ibid.*). As Heidegger calls Being the "Sache des Denkens", this multiple behaving of Being is called the *mehrfältige Sachverhalt* (*ibid.*). ('Sachverhalt' usually means state of affairs. But here it means the *Verhalten* of the *Sache des Denkens.*) Heidegger's notions of multiplicity and polysemy are very different from my *critical* notion of polyvalence.

46. Heidegger says that his texts cannot be translated. And this is true, for in coining his typical polyvalent neologisms, Heidegger is drawing heavily upon the contingent resources of the German language. To take one example, *'Entschlossenheit'* means both openness or opening up and being firmly resolved. Both meanings are essential to Heidegger's post-monotheist concept of *Augenblick* as *kairos*. In a translation, the typical polyvalence of the German text will be lost, or it will be retained at the price of an unacceptable degree of artificiality. This is why Heidegger scholars should be fluent in German, and why I refer to the German texts only.

47. See Heidegger, "Zeit und Sein", in *Zur Sache des Denkens*, pp. 31–32.

48. In a third, neo-Hegelian sense, oblivion of Being means that the sense of 'Being' which unites the fundamental structure of an epoch remains implicit. Heidegger thought that we may experience the sense of Being in our times in specific moods, such as boredom. Oblivion of being in this sense can also be cancelled by us. But Heidegger connected the neo-Hegelian theme of the history of Being (*Seinsgeschichte*) to the post-monotheist theme of a *fate* which Being "sends" us, so that his *Seinsgeschichte* is also a *Seinsgeschick*. The word-play with 'Geschichte' (history, and *also* happening) and 'Geschick' (fate *and* something sent to us) is untranslatable.

49. Heidegger rejects the formal-logical tradition because he assumes that the uses of 'is' in logic are connected to the Aristotelian ontology of presence. See Heidegger, "Zeit und Sein", in *Zur Sache des Denkens*, p. 19; *Einführung in die Metaphysik*, p. 19; *Was ist Metaphysik?*, pp. 27–28, 36–37, 47ff.

50. See my "Heidegger's Question of Being" for detailed argument.

51. For a critique of Paul Churchland's eliminative materialism, see my "Absolute Network Theory".

52. This dogma is similar to constructivism, neo-Kantianism, or "internal realism" in contemporary Anglo-Saxon philosophy and sociology of science.

53. There are several ways of doing this. See for instance Fodor, "Special Sciences".

54. See Heidegger, "Brief über den 'Humanismus'", *Wegmarken*, p. 171: "Als eine Gestalt der Wahrheit gründet die Technik in der Geschichte der Metaphysik." If, however, the neo-Hegelian *Seinsgeschichte* is also a post-monotheist *Seinsgeschick*, its "logic" will be inscrutable, because it is the logic of a *Deus Absconditus*. Cf. "Zeit und Sein", in *Zur Sache des Denkens*, pp. 6 and 56; *Beiträge zur Philosophie*, p. 11.

55. The German 'Stimmung' is related to 'Stimme' (voice) and 'abstimmen' (tuning in to, attuning). This connection is lost in the English 'mood'. Whereas according to *Sein und Zeit*, "Stimmung" is a primordial disclosure of the world in *Dasein*, "Stimmung" becomes *both* our being tuned in to the voice of post-monotheist Being *and* our experience of neo-Hegelian fundamental structures in the later writings. See for the post-monotheist sense of 'Stimmung' e.g. the postscript to *Was ist Metaphysik?* (1943),

pp. 45–47.

56. See "Die Frage nach der Technik", *Vortraege und Aufsaetze*, p. 31, where Heidegger says of the reign of technology (das *Wesen der Technik*): "Wo dieses herrscht, vertreibt es jede andere Möglichkeit der Entbergung." This is patently false, although it may require a specific form of vigilance in order to protect other ways of "revealing" beings. Although I reject Heidegger's neo-Hegelian theme, I suppose that his works may be fruitful if taken as an exhortation to such a form of vigilance.

57. Compare Nietzsche's thesis that everything is will to power, or Marx's thesis that everything human is an expression of class interests. In fact, Heidegger's neo-Hegelian stance may be seen as an alternative to that of Marx, which in the thirties was regarded as a great danger to German culture. There is much more of a discussion with Marxism in the later Heidegger than the surface of Heidegger's texts reveal. In 1932, for instance, Heidegger stressed the need to "transcend Marxism" (*Vom Wesen der Wahrheit*, p. 325).

58. Heidegger, "Die Frage der Technik", *Vortraege und Aufsaetze*, pp. 19ff.

59. Totalitarianism in this sense is what Heidegger has in common with, in Paul Ricoeur's phrase, the "three masters of suspicion": Marx, Nietzsche, and Freud. It is impossible to discuss with orthodox totalitarians, because their assumption of unconscious all-embracing fundamental structures (of our society, our age, or within our personalities) is immune to empirical falsification and because it implies that the real significance of what we say and do is globally (and not only locally) different from what we think it is.

60. Heidegger shared Nietzsche's contempt for democracy. He thought that democracy would "lead to a loss of human greatness". In his first lectures on Nietzsche (1937), Heidegger wrote that democracy would become "the historical death" of Europe (*Nietzsche: Der Wille zur Macht als Kunst*, p. 193).

61. Cf. Löwith, *Heidegger*, p. 233:
> Was aber allem von Heidegger je Gesagten hintergründig zugrunde liegt und viele aufhorchen und hinhorchen lässt, ist ein Ungesagtes: das religiöse Motiv, das sich zwar vom christlichen Glauben abgelöst hat, aber gerade in seiner dogmatisch ungebundenen Unbestimmtheit um so mehr diejenigen anspricht, die nicht mehr gläubige Christen sind, aber doch religiös sein möchten.

62. According to many commentators, it is one of Heidegger's great "discoveries", in *Sein und Zeit*, that the theoretical attitude is not fundamental, and that the world is revealed to us primarily in moods and pre-theoretical understanding (see *Sein und Zeit* on *Befindlichkeit* and *Verstehen*). Now this discovery is a valid one if one merely claims that *de facto* the theoretical attitude is based on and has developed from something more "primordial". But Heidegger also seems to think that his discovery limits the *validity* of theoretical scientific claims, and that knowledge by means of "moods" is not only *de facto* more fundamental, but also *de iure* prior to and independent from discursive thought and scientific knowledge. However, this does not follow at all. The question whether one should acknowledge moods or rather rational argument as the final arbiter of one's philosophical convictions is a matter of decision, and the option one chooses has great moral and epistemic implications.

63. Heidegger, *Sein und Zeit*, p. 38.

64. Heidegger, "Brief über den 'Humanismus'", *Wegmarken*, pp. 150, 155.

65. Heidegger, "Brief über den 'Humanismus'", *Wegmarken*, p. 154.

66. E.g. Heidegger, "Zur Seinsfrage", *Wegmarken*, pp. 235, 243; *Zur Sache des Denkens*, p. 56; "Was heisst Denken?", *Vortraege und Aufsaetze*, pp. 126, 128; "Nietzsches Wort 'Got ist tot'", *Holzwege*, p. 244; "Zur Seinsfrage", *Wegmarken*, p. 235.

67. Heidegger would reply: "the worse for our language", which allegedly is corrupted by the ontology of presence anyhow. See *Zur Sache des Denkens*, pp. 25, 27, 54. But what I am arguing is that there can be *no* language in which we might meaningfully celebrate Being, whereas Heidegger suggests that there can be such a language. See especially *Unterwegs zur Sprache* and "Brief über den 'Humanismus'" in *Wegmarken*. According to the letter to Richardson, p. xxiii, a "saying" which responds to Being does not require a new language, but only a changed relationship to the essence of the existing language ("ein gewandeltes Verhältnis zum Wesen der alten [Sprache]").

68. Although he very much stresses the "questioning" and non-propositional nature of his thinking, one cannot interpret Heidegger as making no "cognitive" claims at all. The same is true of traditional theology.

69. According to Heidegger, *Zur Sache des Denkens*, p. 54, all our language is "metaphysical". Cf. *Einführung in die Metaphysik*, p. 19.

70. The neologism in the section title is inspired by Jürgen Habermas's coinage of "nivellierende Abstraktion".

71. Heidegger, *Einführung in die Metaphysik*, p. 28: "Russland und Amerika sind beide, metaphysisch gesehen, dasselbe." Cf. pp. 34-35.

72. See, for instance, Heidegger, "Wer ist Nietzsches Zarathustra?", *Vortraege und Aufsaetze*, p. 117: "Die Geschäftigkeit des Widerlegenwollens gelangt aber nie auf den Weg eines Denkers. Sie gehört in jene Kleingeisterei, deren Auslassungen die Öffentlichkeit zu ihrer Unterhaltung bedarf." Cf. Heidegger, "Brief über den 'Humanismus'", *Wegmarken*, p. 167: "Alles Widerlegen im Felde des wesentlichen Denkens ist töricht."

73. *Holzwege* are trails in the forest used by lumbermen or animals, trails which often do not lead anywhere. This is why the German 'Holzweg' also means *wrong track*. Heidegger used the word in order to describe the difficult "ways" of his thought and, perhaps, to suggest that a thinker should be at home in the labyrinth of thought as foresters and lumbermen are at home in the labyrinth of forest trails: *Holzwege*, p. 3. I am using the expression ironically, to designate the fact that the post-monotheist strategy must be hidden (it must use forest trails) in order to be successful.

74. In German, 'Wandlung' also refers to the moment of transsubstantiation in the Catholic Mass, provoked by the words of the consecration. Heidegger uses 'Wandlung' both in a neo-Hegelian and in a post-monotheist sense.

75. Heidegger himself draws an analogy with negative theology: *Zur Sache des Denkens*, p. 51.

76. It is common in philosophical theology and moral theory to claim that one possesses a special extra-perceptual organ which enables one to grasp and verify Higher Truths, which remain concealed from ordinary mortals. Heidegger seems to claim such an organ for himself and his followers:

> Wer für das Erblicken des Gebens einer solchen Gabe an den Menschen, für das Schicken eines so Geschickten keinen Sinn hat, wird die Rede vom Seinsgeschick nie verstehen, so

wenig wie der von Natur Blinde je erfahren kann, was Licht und Farbe sind". (Letter to Richardson, p. xxiii)

Of course, the analogy with (color-)blindness does not hold. For in the case of (color-) blindness we have been able to discover the physical causes for this deviation from normal perceptual abilities. There are, I suppose, no similar bodily causes for "religious blindness" or for blindness for Being. The stratagem of the *special organ for higher truths* (or of a privileged relation to a higher reality) is inherent in many religious traditions. One finds it in Plato and Luther. Husserl's doctrine of a special phenomenological "intuition" may have been another source of inspiration for Heidegger in this respect.

REFERENCES

Jerry Fodor, "Special Sciences, or The Disunity of Science as a Working Hypothesis", *Synthese* 28 (1974), 77-115.

Jean Grondin, *Le tournant dans la pensée de Martin Heidegger*, Paris: PUF 1987.

G.W.F. Hegel, *Grundlinien der Philosophie des Rechts*, Berlin: Nicolaischen Buchhandlung 1821.

Martin Heidegger, *Beiträge zur Philosophie (Vom Ereignis)*, in M. Heidegger, *Gesamtausgabe* 65, Frankfurt: Klostermann 1989.

——, *Einführung in die Metaphysik*, Tübingen: Niemeyer 1966.

——, *Die Frage nach dem Ding*, Tübingen: Niemeyer 1975.

——, *Gelassenheit*, Pfullingen: Neske 1992.

——, *Holzwege*, Frankfurt: Klostermann 1963.

——, *Identität und Differenz*, Pfullingen: Neske 1957.

——, Letter to Richardson, in W.J. Richardson, *Through Phenomenology to Thought*, The Hague: Nijhoff 1963.

——, *Nietzsche*, Pfullingen: Neske 1961.

——, *Nietzsche: Der Wille zur Macht als Kunst*, in Heidegger, *Gesamtausgabe* 43, Frankfurt: Klostermann 1985.

——, *Phänomenologische Interpretationen zu Aristoteles* and *Einführung in die phänomenologische Forschung*, in M. Heidegger, *Gesamtausgabe* 61, Frankfurt: Klostermann 1985.

——, *Prolegomena zur Geschichte des Zeitbegriffs*, in M. Heidegger, *Gesamtausgabe* 20, Frankfurt: Klostermann 1988.

——, *Zur Sache des Denkens*, Tübingen: Niemeyer 1969.

——, *Sein und Zeit*, Tübingen: Niemeyer 1967.

——, *Unterwegs zur Sprache*, Pfullingen: Neske 1971.

——, *Vier Seminare*, Frankfurt: Klostermann 1977.

——, *Vortraege und Aufsaetze*, Pfullingen: Neske 1985.

——, *Was ist Metaphysik?*, Frankfurt: Klostermann 1969.

——, *Wegmarken*, Frankfurt: Klostermann 1967.

——, *Vom Wesen der Wahrheit*, in Heidegger, *Gesamtausgabe* 34, Frankfurt: Klostermann 1988.

Klaus Held, "Grundbestimmung und Zeitkritik bei Heidegger", in Papenfuss and Pöggeler, *Zur philosophischen Aktualität Heideggers* I.

Ernst Jünger, *Der Arbeiter*, Hamburg: Hanseatischer Verlags-Anstalt, 1932.

Karl Lehman, "Christliche Geschichtserfahrung und ontologische Frage beim jungen Heidegger", in Pöggeler (ed.), *Heidegger. Perspektiven zur Deutung seines Werkes*.

Karl Löwith, *Heidegger—Denker in dürftiger Zeit*, in Löwith, *Sämtliche Schriften* VIII, Stuttgart: Metzler 1984.

Günther Neske, Emil Kettering (eds.), *Antwort: Martin Heidegger im Gespräch*, Pfullingen: Neske 1988.

Herman Philipse, "The Absolute Network Theory of Language and Traditional Epistemology: On the Philosophical Foundations of Paul Churchland's Scientific Realism", *Inquiry* 33 (1990), 127-178.

——, "Heidegger's Question of Being and the 'Augustinian Picture' of Language", *Philosophy and Phenomenological Research* 52 (1992), 251-287.

D. Papenfuss, O. Pöggeler, *Zur philosophischen Aktualität Heideggers*, Frankfurt: Klostermann 1991.

Otto Pöggeler, "'Historicity' in Heidegger's Late Work", *The Southwestern Journal of Philosophy* IV (1973).

——, *Der Denkweg Martin Heideggers*, Pfullingen: Neske, 1963.ff.

Otto Pöggeler (ed.), *Heidegger: Perspektiven zur Deutung seines Werkes*, Königstein: Athenäum 1984.

IN DEFENSE OF THE FRENCH

La vraie éloquence se moque de l'éloquence, la vraie
morale se moque de la morale; c'est à dire que la
morale du jugement se moque de la morale de
l'esprit—qui est sans regles.
Car le jugement est celui à qui appartient le sentiment,
comme les sciences appartiennent à l'esprit.
Se moquer de la philosophie, c'est vraiment philosopher.

Pascal

Rousseau, Voltaire, and the "philosophes"

French philosophy has always been different from its Anglo-American counterpart. Montaigne, to begin with, is notoriously difficult to classify, whether as a
writer or a philosopher; and his successors compound the difficulty, for they
multiply the possible categories. Descartes, noteworthy in the history of science
for first getting the principle of inertia right, made significant contributions to
mathematics, and also set the stage for three centuries of Western philosophy.
Pascal, too, contributed to both mathematics and philosophy; but in his case we
must take account of his contributions to literature and to religion as well. The
English scene at the same time was very different. Bacon, perhaps, poses some
of the problems that Montaigne does, but the others mostly fall neatly into categories. Newton, who certainly made contributions to mathematics and physics
at least equal to those of Descartes, wrote little that is considered by philosophers and nothing that belongs to the history of English literature. Hobbes and
Locke, whose metaphysical, moral, and political works are still read with profit,
made no noteworthy contributions to mathematics or physics.

In the brilliant subsequent generation, that of Hume and Rousseau which
dominated the thought of the 18th century, the contrast is different but not less
striking. Hume and Rousseau were both generalists, neither made contributions
to science or mathematics, both were critics of the intellectuals around them,
and both eminently readable and prolific writers; but their styles were vastly
different. Hume (1711-1776) wrote histories, treatises, dialogues, and essays,
each in its appropriate form, except that the dialogues read more like essays
than Plato's dialogues do. Although witty, he was earnest and paid close attention to facts. Rousseau (1712-1778) was above all imaginative. His historical
speculations are generally based on romantic fantasy rather than fact, and he put
forward his ideas about education in works of fiction that can be read for plea-

sure without bothering to assess the intended moral. Rousseau is as difficult to classify as Pascal or Descartes.

We do read Rousseau in philosophy courses as well as in literature courses and consider him, most of the time, a philosopher as well as a writer. Other shining figures of the French 18th century do not fare as well. The greatest of them, and the hardest to classify, was Voltaire (1694-1778). The concept 'philosopher' applies to him only in the broadest sense. Yet he constantly commented on life around him by reference to broad and plausibly universal principles, and was counted by those who knew him to be a lover of wisdom as well as a wit and a lover of life. His style was not that of philosophy; certainly not of Anglo-American philosophy. He wrote poems, plays, letters commenting on life and customs, stories, and historical works—and his best known work of philosophical criticism, *Candide*, a merciless attack on the theodicy of Leibniz, takes the form of a fictional *reductio ad absurdum* rather than proper argument.

Was Voltaire really a philosopher? He certainly shared with philosophers an intense interest in ideas. Although this interest never led him to attempt to construct anything like a philosophical system, there was a coherence, a consistency, an astuteness, and a political bite to the way he dealt with ideas. His attack on Leibniz is an attack on the use of religion to entice people to accept injustice and poverty as necessary. It goes together with his *Lettres anglaises* as part of his attempt to reduce the power of the clergy, and to promote secularism, decentralism, democracy, and individualism. Since he lived much of his life in the long reign of Louis XV, his philosophical writings put him in constant, or recurrent, jeopardy. He spent some time in Potsdam at the court of Frederick the Great, who was more open to new ideas, and lived for many years just outside Geneva, where there was great political liberty (though less social liberty); but he remained French and returned to France for the last two decades of his life. In France, however, he lived in Ferney, close enough to the Swiss border to be out of the country in a few minutes if he heard that the king was especially angry with one of his sallies. Perhaps one should just say that he was a writer; but the French, generally contemptuous of our complaint that his treatment of Leibniz was outrageously unfair, also tend to think of him as a philosopher, and that seems nearly as appropriate as in the case of Rousseau.

Rousseau and Voltaire were only two of the galaxy of intellectual stars of 18th century France. Both are more often known as writers than as philosophers, and are assigned regularly and without embarrassment in courses on French literature as well as in courses in the history of ideas. Many of the others are labeled "philosophes", with what has always impressed me as a sort of sneering deference to the different conception of philosophy in France. Diderot (1713-1784), D'Alembert (1717-1783), Holbach (1723-1789), Turgot (1727-1781), Helvétius (1715-1771), and Condillac (1715-1780) all worked on the encyclopedia that Diderot organized and edited, as did Rousseau and Voltaire, and even Condorcet (1743-1794), though he was a generation younger. All these men combined interest in general philosophical questions with interest in learning as a whole, in education, and in politics. The materialism of Holbach and the hedonism of Helvétius were particularly subversive of the Christian ideology of the French monarchy, and Voltaire was able to win favor with the king by publishing a criticism of the atheistic materialism of Holbach's *Système de la Nature*.

What stands out in this brief mention of these intellectual luminaries is that the great French thinkers and writers of the 18th century were interested in the shape of learning, of human life, of culture, and of society, as well as in the problems of philosophy in the narrower sense. We can also say, though this survey has been too brief to demonstrate it, that their interest in the larger picture led them to be less concerned with the smaller details, and in particular with the exact meaning of statements and the precision and justice of judgments and of arguments.

Much of what was true of 18th century French intellectuals has carried over into the 20th century, though the importation and transformation of German existentialism (beginning especially in the 40's) gives it a vastly different style and tone in Lyotard and Derrida than in Duhem and Poincaré. This partially accounts not only for the style that we find difficult being familiar and unproblematical in France but also for the striking difference between the Anglo-American and French traditions today. Three factors seem likely to have influenced the creation and maintenance of this difference, though I am unsure just how.[1] One is that France has produced relatively more contributions to mathematics than Britain and America, and relatively fewer contributions to experimental science. Another is that in the period during which America experienced a continuity ruffled only by a war of independence and a civil war and Britain an evolving constitutional monarchy, France has undergone at least nine constitutional changes: two monarchies, two empires, and five republics. The third is the differential importations from Germany in the past half century, especially that Hegel, Nietzsche, and Heidegger have been hugely influential on Merleau-Ponty, Sartre, and Derrida, while Kant and Frege have been the dominant German influence in Britain and America.

Sartre

Jean-Paul Sartre is, like Rousseau, a writer and a philosopher. Like all the great figures of the French Enlightenment, he was interested in the shape of culture, thought, politics, and life. He was above all a moralist, and his frequent political forays were generally apocalyptic in tone, designed to damn expediency, com-

promise, bias, and oppression, rather than (as in the case of Turgot) to foster
more efficient and effective government. He is best known as an existentialist.
Existentialism is basically a metaphysical doctrine, but in Sartre's hands it
became more a tool for moral commentary.

The central doctrine of Sartre's existentialism is that humans are always
and ineluctably free, and therefore always responsible; and from this central
doctrine it follows that any idea or thought that attempts to reduce or escape
from this responsibility is "bad faith". There are two ways in which these leading ideas make for a sharp rejection of mainstream moral philosophy. One is
that Sartre regards any rule or principle a person cites as a reason for acting as
an attempt to escape responsibility for the action, and hence as bad faith. If, for
example, a person were to say, "I cannot tell a lie", thereby citing a familiar
moral principle, the person would be claiming to have really had no choice in
the matter—a denial of freedom. Since moral principles quite generally characterize a certain action or seemingly possible action as either necessary or impossible, this type of consideration constitutes a decisive and abrupt rejection of
moral principles, and of all moral philosophy devoted to seeking or justifying
moral principles.

The other sharp divergence from common morality and much moral philosophy is found in Sartre's absolutism. He allows no excuses, since an excuse is
always, by its very nature, an attempt to evade responsibility for one's actions.
Excuses, like principles, are instances of bad faith. This has always appealed to
me as an appalling point of view. Austin argued against it, without mentioning
Sartre, in his essay, "A Plea for Excuses", and also in other works in which he
carefully distinguishes different kinds of excuses from one another. Austin's
arguments are sound considerations against any sort of moralistic absolutism,
not just against Sartre's; and since Austin does not mention Sartre, it remains
uncertain whether or not he took Sartre's point of view on this matter to be a
philosophical view. The alternative is that it is some sort of religious view—
atheistic, to be sure, but religious nonetheless. Since either referring to principles or offering excuses is an instance of bad faith, we are all of us involved in
bad faith all the time. Sartre considers bad faith an inescapable part of the
human condition. "Abandon hope, all ye who enter here!" I cannot help thinking of this as an atheistic equivalent of the Christian doctrine of original sin,
with all hope of salvation withdrawn. This is not a religion I would choose to
join.

So the leading idea of Sartre's moral existentialism, considered in general
terms as a universal claim, is either straightforwardly false, for reasons Austin
has spelled out in detail, or else announces a new religion which there is no reason (of course not!) to accept.

I am sure that the above remarks, however true, do not do justice to Sartre. He was a writer as well as a philosopher. Perhaps we should say that he was a writer first and foremost. One of the most famous passages in *Being and Nothingness* is his description of the waiter, whose behavior as a waiter is determined by his role rather than by himself; that is, rather than by his desires, aims, ambitions, and independent initiatives. In this passage, as in many others, Sartre provides great insight into the anguishes of human existence, and therefore makes a significant contribution to moral psychology. What he contributes, however, is not laws or principles, not anything universal and perhaps not anything universalizable; it is the insight provided by apt stories, and details that are telling because of the way they fit into the stories. I have myself found some of Sartre's plays to be more useful as a basis for presenting and discussing his existentialist outlook than his rather ponderous philosophical prose. That is perhaps a matter of taste, but I think it may also have something to do with differences between French and Anglo-American philosophy.

In *No Exit* Garcin says near the end of the play, "Hell is other people!" It is perhaps the most famous line Sartre ever wrote, and many take it as a key to his existentialism. I agree that it is a brilliant line, and that if one understands it right one will have progressed a good way toward understanding Sartre's philosophy. But I think most people misunderstand it by assuming it to be the straightforward expression of one of Sartre's own beliefs. "Nur im Fluss des Lebens haben die Worte ihre Bedeutung", says Wittgenstein (*Last Writings* §913); and even though the action of *No Exit* takes place after death rather than "in the stream of life", the words spoken by Garcin have their meaning only in the context of the action of the play. To make use of the context we must consider two questions. One is whether there is some character in the play that has the best claim to being considered Sartre's alter ego. The other is what Garcin's motives, aims, and frustrations were at that point in the play.

Garcin is the only male character in the play, and this fact may be taken by some to indicate that he really speaks for Sartre. Such a reading of the play would lead one naturally to accept the famous line spoken by Garcin as an expression of Sartre's existentialist philosophy. I cannot accept this view. For one thing, Garcin is throughout the play engaging in behavior that Sartre disapproves of: he offers excuses for his actions and he seeks "justification" or endorsement through the opinions—almost blessings—of Estelle and Inez. Whatever doubts Sartre may have had about his own life, it seems highly unlikely that he considered himself so egregiously lacking in existentialist integrity as he portrays Garcin. Another consideration is that Inez often says things that seem highly congenial with existentialism. When Garcin seeks her approval for his excuses and rationalizations, she brushes him aside by insisting, rather eloquently, that at death a line is drawn and the sums are totaled up: nothing else makes any difference, and nothing they say to one another now can alter the final balance. Another time she represents herself as a mirror in which he can see *himself* reflected. Though it was not always easy for him, I have no doubt that this is the relation in which Sartre saw himself toward conventional society. Perhaps he would at times have liked to condemn, but he knew he lacked that status of a priest or a preacher, and that the best he could do would be to reflect back to others what they were, what their actions were, so that they could see themselves better. Like Inez, he failed in this attempt because the pride and conceit of the viewers made them deny what they saw in the "mirror", or cast doubt on its reflective capacities.

Perhaps this makes the play too autobiographical. It may be that none of the characters really represents the author. But if any one of them does, I am convinced that Inez rather than Garcin has the greatest claim to being considered Sartre's alter ego in this play.

Garcin utters the famous line after he has again failed to get Inez to endorse his rationalizations, that is, to give him moral praise for his dubious, apparently cowardly, self-serving actions, which he is trying to paint as courageous. So he is frustrated, and the words are an expression of his frustrations. In that context they can only be seen as another expression of bad faith—of attempting to shift the responsibility for his guilt to Inez instead of accepting it himself. Understood in this way I find this line both brilliant and brilliantly funny. It is funny because there is nothing more absurd than still worrying about consequences and reputation after one is dead, after the line has been drawn and the balance added up. It is brilliant for two reasons. First, because of the dramatic force with which it portrays the existentialist idea that the great weakness of humans is their seeking to verify rationalizations rather than accept responsibility. Second, because it so effectively exploits the powerful ambiguity of our relations with *others*, who, like Inez, are both our tormentors and our potential saviors.

I find this play particularly useful for introducing students to existentialist moral ideas—better, for example than *Existentialism is a Humanism*. I also sometimes make use of the wonderfully sensitive study of paternalism in *Altona*. In these plays one does not, of course, find either explicit arguments or carefully defined problems. As my exegesis above makes clear, it is often difficult—as it is also with Plato, Kierkegaard, Derrida, and Wittgenstein—to know whether or not to take the words as Sartre speaking *propria persona*, which is a problematical ambiguity. There is therefore much that is vital to philosophy that is left out. But there is also much that is left out of more rational and logical approaches to philosophy. Sartre's stories and plays may or may not constitute philosophy, but they contribute usefully to a philosophical overview, not because they are entertaining but because they focus thoughtfully and intensely on essential features of human life.

Foucault

In the spring of 1983 I attended what proved to be Foucault's final lectures at the Collège de France prior to his unfortunate death in 1984. Still unpublished, they were devoted to *parrhesia*, the virtue, as Foucault explained it, of speaking the truth forcefully and forthrightly when one's life is in danger; more specifically speaking the truth to one who has power over one's own life. Speaking truth to power, it might be conveniently called for short. Foucault described it as the founding virtue of Athenian democracy, though whether he ultimately believed in it, and what relation it might have to problems of democracy today, are more difficult to say.

The first four weeks of the course of lectures were devoted to an extraordinary exegesis of the *Ion* of Euripides, which Foucault characterized as a play devoted to proclaiming *parrhesia* as the founding virtue of Athenian democracy. This is a bold interpretation, of which there is no hint in the 1958 Chicago edition of *The Complete Greek Tragedies*, so I will reconstruct the main themes as best as I can recall them.

Ion was abandoned at birth by his mother, Creusa, in the very cave where she had conceived him when raped by Apollo. Apollo sent Hermes to take the baby to his temple in Delphi, where he was raised by the priestess. Creusa meanwhile had married Xuthus, an Aeolian (i.e. a foreigner) who had helped Athens in battle, but the couple remained childless. When they went to Delphi to ask Apollo for children, the god gave Ion to Xuthus, but the basket and swaddling clothes preserved by the priestess revealed to Creusa that she was Ion's real mother. At this point, however, Creusa was threatened with death by Ion, and she could come forward and speak the truth only by exposing herself to death. This she did, and her family's native Athenian line was thus preserved as the ruling line in Athens.

Creusa is in many ways the central figure of this drama, and the chorus consists of her servants. She is the only surviving daughter—the only surviving child—of Erechtheus, an Athenian king who (or whose ancestor Erichthonius) reputedly sprang up from the earth. The family origins are important for the reading Foucault gives to the play. Most Greek heroes were children of the gods, and for a line of government to originate from the earth rather than from the heavens signifies something new and different. Euripides was, of course, no atheist, so Apollo and Athene have the roles in preserving the line. But it is not their line originally, and the gods (especially Apollo) are convicted of behaving badly—so badly that Apollo is ashamed to appear at his own temple at the end of the play. It is therefore the new line springing from the earth that provides the roots for democracy, the new form of government.

Although it was the male line of Erechtheus that sprang from the earth, it is his daughter rather than a son who continues and preserves the line. Euripides presents this as a succession of power by justice, for the leading experience of her life was being raped by a powerful god, and she laments:

Unhappy women! Where shall we appeal
For justice when the injustice of power
Is our destruction? (*Ion* 11. 252-254)

And it is Creusa, not any of the men, who decisively confronts life-threatening power with the truth.

No brief summary can do justice to the rich exegesis presented by Foucault. Each of the lectures was inspiring in the clarity of its organization, in its familiarity with sources and with symbols, and in its elaboration of a certain almost ideal relationship between personal virtue and political democracy. At the end of the four weeks I was impressed and inspired.

At the end of the full course of lectures I was less impressed and much less inspired. While not ever directly challenging the lessons learned from Euripides, Foucault went on to discuss Plato's attempt to inspire sound government, as recounted in the 7th Letter. What is principally at issue are his relations with Dion and Dionysius II of Syracuse. Plato made two trips to Syracuse at the behest of Dion, in 367 and again (with some personal danger) in 361–360 BC, but he declined further involvement when Dion seized power in 357. Foucault's comments gave Plato full credit not only for concerning himself with the relation of philosophy to politics but also for personal involvement when Dion first invited him to Syracuse. His main thrust, however, was that Plato's 7th Letter contains a carefully crafted principle that limits the applications of *parrhesia*, roughly, that a philosopher should not waste words speaking truth to someone determined not to listen—as seemed the case in 360 with Dionysius II and in 357 with Dion.

As a matter of intellectual history, as well as a preliminary for philosophical consideration of the relation between personal virtue and democracy—perhaps to follow a study of Sartre's cynical lesson in *Dirty Hands*—the combination of the lectures on Plato with the lectures on Euripides was brilliantly stimulating. Foucault enlarged the scope of the question not only historically but also intimately and personally, by bringing the conflicting principles so vividly to life. The philosophical issue, however, was left unexamined. My recollection is that Foucault did not even comment on the tension between *Ion* and the 7th Letter. Perhaps he saw—but he never explained how—the two principles as complementary features of a comprehensive political or philosophical perspective. Certainly he never, through the course of the lectures, addressed the philosophical issue of the tension between the principles to which he had given such lively articulation.

Is such work philosophy? In the Anglo-American tradition we must count it a philosophy *manqué* at best. Our tradition seems to require that moral and political philosophy articulate principles and precepts—especially precepts—and it is just at this point that Foucault falters. Our tradition also places high value on logic, and hence on the consistency of one's perspective or overview, and the problem of consistency is one that Foucault conspicuously leaves aside. Yet Foucault held what is arguably the most prestigious chair in philosophy in France, and gave the lectures on *parrhesia* as professor of philosophy at the Collège de France. A conflict of traditions? No doubt. But it is a clash of traditions that challenges our conception of what philosophy is.

Foucault's manner of presenting intellectual issues conforms with his published work. He enlarges our vision without making either logical consequences or moral precepts more precise. The picture that he enlarges is therefore not likely to be any clearer, if we were already familiar with its narrower ordinary features. This kind of work leaves some important work still to be done; but it nonetheless contributes something important. If our aim, along with Wittgenstein, is *Übersichtlichkeit*, Foucault's work can easily be seen as providing it. We certainly are not likely to gain perspective or command a clear view of our lives and our world if we take into account only those details that are already clear or already within our daily ken.

Serres

Michel Serres is a philosopher in the French tradition. His first work was a two-volume study of Leibniz, full of good insights and arguments in the regular philosophical manner. More recently he has written nothing more of the kind, has attacked Anglo-American philosophy for its scanty vision, and been elected to the French Academy. Nonetheless there are aspects of Leibniz that have stayed with him: the insatiable encyclopedic curiosity, the search for an inclusive overview, and a special interest in problems of communication (in all the senses of that word). He was a colleague of mine at SUNY/Buffalo for a few years. I got to know him enough to report on his lectures and testify to his philosophical competence. I want to do that before turning to examine his recent discussion of the tasks of philosophy.

The lectures I attended became a part of his recent book, *The Five Senses* (*Les cinq sens*). One of which I retain a particularly vivid memory had to do with the sense of hearing and our need for silence. It was entitled "Guérison à Epidaure", that is, "Healing at Epidavros". Epidavros, which contains the finest ancient theater remaining in Greece, was the city of Asclepius, god of medicine and the healing arts, and it is, within a certain classical tradition, the natural place to go for a healing. Serres began by describing his flight to Epidavros. Approaching the city, the theater appeared like a gigantic ear facing out to the sea, perhaps to hear the sounds of the sea, or of the gods, or of strangers who might approach from the sea. Upon landing he betook himself to the theater to examine this great ear more closely. Instead of capturing sounds, it captured silence, isolating the visitor from the harsh sounds of the city. He walked down to the stage, the center of the amphitheater, and the silence seemed there to be most profound. In the midst of it he sensed the gods approaching, and began to feel that the healing would indeed take place. At this moment he heard faint sounds, which grew into distant whispering and then into human speech. A group of tourists was coming through the tunnel to view the ancient monument. Their words became distinct, and he withdrew from the stage to allow them space, noticing as he did that the gods had also withdrawn.

For, Serres concluded, the gods come to us only in silence.

Serres delivered this lecture with a passion that no report can convey. He never clarified why he needed healing, from what ailment, nor did he elaborate on how, from his 20th century perspective, he intended or understood these references to gods that are no longer part of our culture or daily lives. So the style was through and through evocative rather than analytic, for reasons Serres has explained in a more recent interview to which I refer below. The question is whether and how, from the perspective of Anglo-American philosophy, we can understand and make use of such a lecture.

Let us note first that the lecture was concerned with hearing. The image chosen for the amphitheater at Epidavros was an ear, and the larger context was a discussion of our five senses. So our question reduces to the narrower and more manageable question, how can this lecture be used to increase our understanding of hearing?

We should note second that no general moral or universal conclusions are drawn by Serres. His effort is not put into defining a question, nor into elaborating a doctrine, but into describing an incident. We do not know whether the incident actually occurred, nor just what the nature of these healing gods might be; but that does not matter. The incident is described vividly, and was no doubt chosen with care. It is certainly not the sort of incident most of us would think of if we were asked to tell a story about the importance of hearing to humans. In that respect his story reminds us of a richer range of uses of hearing than might have occurred to us, so enlarges our perspective. There is no reason to think that he had Wittgenstein in mind, but his method could in this reading be thought of as an implementation of Wittgenstein's insistence on the need for intermediate cases, and for a broad range of cases.

One of the ideas suggested by the story is that our ears are for hearing silences as well as sounds. Another is that we need to dwell long on the silences we hear, in order to overcome the effects of clamor and noise on our well-being. Speaking of silence in an interview, Serres says "that in our world it no longer exists. It no longer exists because in the open spaces of the country or the sea, where silence once reigned, motors and the media have filled it with noise. We have to fight against the power of noise, which is immense and frightening".[2] Perhaps there are other thoughts conveyed in the story. The two ideas mentioned are ones we often forget, and that the doctors who examine our ears seldom take into account. They, therefore, enlarge our ordinary horizon about hearing and its relation to our well-being. That seems sufficient reason for philosophers concerned with the senses to take seriously what Serres has to say, even when he tells half fantastic tales that have no explicit moral.

Serres was in Buffalo for only a few weeks at the beginning of each semester. One year I asked him early in September if he would give a lecture to the Department of Philosophy on Leibniz. He said he could do that, he knew what sort of style was needed to lecture to the Department of Philosophy; but it would take a good deal of preparation. We therefore set a date in February. It was again an astonishing performance, but in an entirely different way. The expository style he adopted that day, in English, was entirely different from the passionate manner in which he lectured in French to his literary audiences. He had a clear outline, he proceeded with definitions and explanations, and all in all gave a very fine expository lecture, leaving nothing to be imagined by the listener or called up by evocative images. On the other hand, this lecture had in common with the others a superb sense of timing, and excellent judgment about the choice of topics and about where and when to shift focus so as to bring out the main points. One of my colleagues said afterwards that he had learned more in those two hours than in a whole course on Leibniz in graduate school.

It has been said of some contemporary French philosophers that they are incompetent in philosophy or in logic. Whether that is true or not in other cases, it cannot be said of Serres. That his work pays little attention to the linguistic or the logical, and that he does not consider philosophical theories, is due neither to ignorance nor incompetence but to a conscious decision. He gave the reasons for the style of his work in the interview cited above. French philosophy, he said, "has always had an encyclopedic scope. The real French tradition...which I hope myself to carry on, is that of Descartes, Auguste Comte, Diderot, and of Bergson himself, for whom philosophy must have an encyclopedic base. That is, the philosopher must be a person who knows mathematics, physics, chemistry, biology, and so on, just as in the approach of Auguste Comte." But he adds that this complete picture with its encyclopedic details "must be forgotten before philosophy is undertaken."[3] Serres not only recognizes the existence of this tradition, but he accepts it and treats it as a reason for not being like us: "I think this is an old French tradition, and...I try to work according to this tradition. I have written on mathematics, physics, biology, and the humanities."[4] He goes on to add, "I can't imagine philosophy as a discipline. I think of philosophy as a sum",[5] and adds that he no longer considers himself a specialist on Leibniz (which requires discipline) now that he is a philosopher in the French tradition.

The conception of philosophy expressed in these remarks is not immune from controversy in France. Although he has been elected to the Academie Française, he, like Derrida, lacks a chair of philosophy in Paris, his post being that of professor of history at the Sorbonne. He nonetheless has a clearly articulated conception of philosophy, which he does not limit to the French tradition. He holds that "the foundation of philosophy is encyclopedic and its goal is synthesis",[6] explaining that this implies a rejection of the analytic, since "the goal of philosophy should be to create a synthesis, whereas analysis goes off into detail".[7] There is, however, an aspect of the ordinary language philosophy of Wittgenstein, Ryle, and Malcolm that he finds congenial: "As I get older I am more and more attracted by ordinary language, a philosophy that does not need terms other than those drawn from everyday language to express itself."[8] So the synthesis based on encyclopedic knowledge, which certainly requires the mastery of several disciplines and very specialized terminology, is then to be expressed in everyday language.

Serres is, however, not above inventing terminology when the need, or opportunity, arises. A bit of specialized terminology that Serres introduces, in his wonderful contribution to environmental philosophy, *Le contrat naturel*, is the distinction between "subjective violence" and "objective violence". He calls all the violence humans do to each other "subjective", on the grounds that they know that it is violence they are doing. It is subjective because it counts as violence in the human consciousness. He calls "objective", on the other hand, violence which humans do to the world around them without ever taking account of the fact that it is violence. It includes all the damage humans do to the earth when we believe that we are just being productive and efficient—or just living in a normal and ordinary way. There was attention called to this "objective violence" (though not in those terms) by *Consumer Reports* in its environmental quiz last fall. The question was which of the following actions would contribute most to lessening the burden on the environment: recycling newspaper, avoiding plastic products, using passive solar heating, or not having another child. The correct answer, lessening the burden far more than any of the others, is not having another child. Hardly anyone thinks of having a child as a burden to the environment. It is not in our consciousness that having children might be a violence to the earth. That is just the point Serres wants to make.

The kind of overview Serres seeks has a good deal in common with what Wittgenstein seeks. There is of course considerable difference in method and in starting place; but each seeks to gain a clear overview of the whole human scene, each thinks it utterly necessary to notice differences and to consider a wide range of phenomena, and each thinks jargon mostly injurious to philosophy though not always to be avoided. The account Serres gives of the French tradition to which he adheres gives a cogency to his stance, something that is lacking in Sartre (because of the shrillness and implausibility of some of his main themes) and Foucault (because of his indifference to the issues). No one brought up in the Anglo-American analytic tradition will find the style of Serres familiar or easy. But his work does constitute a fine example of what is worthwhile in the unfamiliar philosophic tradition of the French.

Weil

Simone Weil belongs to the French tradition. Like that of Montaigne and Serres, her work is intensely personal, almost embarrassingly so for an Anglo-American philosopher accustomed to divorcing arguments and ideas from personal commitments and attitudes. Like Foucault she dips back into Greek literature and at times identifies herself more with Greek than with contemporary culture, her essay *"The Iliad*, Poem of Force" being one of the memorable essays of the century and a stirring pacifist document. What she synthesizes includes a deep admiration for the Greeks, a native Jewishness, a profound identification with Christian Catholicism, Marxism, experience as a factory worker as well as a teacher, and a patriotism that led to her early death. In her work the particular is always intermingled with the universal, the scholarly with the practical, the religious with the secular, and the personal with the social.

Weil is particularly challenging about the relation of religion to philosophy, a matter that Peter Winch examines in his admirable study of Weil, *The Just Balance.* Weil's book *The Need for Roots: Prelude to a Declaration of Duties Toward Mankind* (*L'enracinement*) was done as a study of the principles that ought to guide the reconstitution of French society following World War II, but the astonishing historical and philosophical scope of her thought—the encyclopedic dimension, as Serres might put it—makes it applicable quite generally. In it she articulates a neglected bit of philosophy of mind, the needs of the soul, drawing heavily on her own complex roots in Jewish, Christian, and Greek culture. She then formulates social policies that take into account these personal needs as well as the needs of society and government. The work defies categorization: it is a deeply religious work that nonetheless addresses secular problems in secular terms, it is a social philosophy that sees social reality as involving individual psychology, and a philosophy of mind that sees healthy individual psychology as dependent on rightly ordered society.

None of Weil's work is easy, especially if one is trying to decide into which course of our academic curriculum it fits. It is, however, eminently accessible, at least for any reader willing and able to adjust to her special uses of common words and to accept the reality and vitality of the spiritual dimension of humanity, which she presupposes throughout her work. She lacks the faults of the others: the dated partisan commitments of Sartre, the avoidance of clarity and commitment of Derrida, the blind eye to philosophical issues of Foucault, and the occasionally untranslatable literary flourishes of Serres. More than any of the others, Weil is a representative of the French tradition who deserves to be more fully incorporated into ours; to that end Winch's book is much to be welcomed.

Conclusion

In concluding I want to reflect on the achievement of Monet in painting. I never tire of looking at works by Monet, particularly the later works. What impresses me about them is partly their realism, their faithfulness to the natural forms of rivers, ponds, trees, hills, buildings, and water lilies. Monet has the capacity to convey just what the scene was. Sometimes, of course, I only surmise this, since I was never there; but sometimes a comparison can be made. Photographs of the recently reconstructed gardens of Monet's home at Giverny, for example, show some of the scenes that Monet painted over and over. Viewing both, it becomes apparent how wonderfully exact the paintings are.

The other thing that impresses me about Monet's paintings is the distinctive way in which this exactness of representation is conveyed. Its medium is pictorial rather than verbal, but it is pictorial in a way that is not photographic. Photographs have a kind of digital exactness, which now lets them be transmitted by electronic means.[9] From the point of view of the viewer, the key thing about photography is that one can get a magnifying glass and examine the details. The closer one can examine the details, the higher the resolution, we say. Satellite photography is now capable of such high resolution that one can identify a vehicle in a photograph taken from a thousand miles up. The photographs I have seen of Monet's garden do not have such a high resolution, but one can still examine details with a magnifying glass. Monet's paintings, by contrast, have hardly any resolution at all. To see them, and especially to see the exactness of the details in them, one must stand at a considerable distance, often twenty or thirty feet. When one approaches the paintings, the details vanish. That is to say, the details of what is represented in the painting vanish, although the details of the brush strokes and the points of color remain. It astonishes me—and astonishes me over and over again when I look at these paintings—

that there can be a form of representational exactness so lacking in resolution, so utterly different from photographic exactness.

One could characterize photographic exactness as having mereological transitivity: If a picture is an exact representation of X, and if Y is a part or detail of X, then the picture is also an exact representation of Y. Because of this principle of mereological transitivity, photographs are analytic in a particular way. One can, up to a limit that varies with the degree of resolution of the film and the print, break a photograph into elements, and conceive it (as is done in electronic transmission) as composed of its elements.

What of Monet's exactness? One might say that it is a sort of holistic rather than analytic exactness. That strikes me as true but misleading. The main reason it is misleading is that the paintings are, of course, composed of elements, namely the brush strokes, or the elements of color applied to the canvas by the brush strokes. This was a point Monet stressed in letters and interviews. He insisted that there was an exactness of representation in his paintings, and that it consisted in placing on the canvas the exact colors that were there in the scene. I am inclined to credit this account, and therefore to characterize Monet's exactness as being analytical as well as holistic, and as being the result of elements that are exactly chosen and exactly arranged. But this sort of analytic exactness differs from photographic exactness in that it is not subject to the principle of mereological transitivity.

I continue to regard photography as providing the paradigm for representational exactness, and I believe that representational exactness is one virtue of painting and of photography, though far from the only one and not necessarily the most important one. For reasons given above I do not believe that the representational exactness found in Monet's paintings can be reduced to photographic exactness nor satisfactorily explained in terms of it. Monet, it seems to me, must be credited with making an astonishing and unexpected contribution to our understanding of representational exactness—even if we do not yet understand exactly the nature of the elements with which he worked.

Let us suppose that photographic exactness corresponds to logical and analytic precision in meaning. It is easy to imagine that an association of photographers, dominated perhaps by geographers who rely on satellite photography, might protest vehemently against the idea presented above that Monet's paintings present any kind of exactness at all. They might even organize a protest against an honorary degree for Monet, on the ground that his alternative claim to exactness had the foreseeable, and no doubt intended, consequence of undermining the logic and rationality of every distinction between what is vague and what is exact. The grounds for a reply by Monet and his followers, bound to be full of complexities and uncertainties, would not be likely to persuade the protesters. In addition to the considerations I have sketched above, further claims, equally problematic, could no doubt be added. One is that the protesters confuse a sound paradigm for exactness with the only possible one. Another is that their highly successful photographic tradition has understandably led them to resist any change having to do with our ideas about the nature of representation or exactitude. But they could come back with the reply that Monet and his ilk are after all called *impressionists*, as such often being contrasted with representational artists, and that the supposed new sort of exactitude lacks the sort of replicable technique that would allow it to become the basis for a practice or tradition.

I do not know how this controversy would play out, nor how it should. It has a partial analogue in the insistence on exact definitions, by Kant, Frege, C. I. Lewis, and others, and Wittgenstein's well known rejection of the requirement in the *Philosophical Investigations*. Wittgenstein insists that the revision need not compromise logic or inference, but he has been ignored or rejected by many Anglo-American philosophers who continue to require exact definitions, to give priority to formal logic and formal inference, and to defend the hegemony of epistemology in philosophy. I have chosen Monet as a person who has as much authority with respect to seeing and representing scenes as Wittgenstein has with respect to matters of speaking and meaning. But authority is not enough. One can hardly expect one to have more success than the other in overcoming adherents of traditional conceptions of exactness and of proper standards within their disciplines.

Monet is also French to the core. His landscapes differ as radically from Constable's as Sartre's views on excuses differ from Austin's. I greatly admire Constable and found Austin to be among the most impressive intellects and the most rewarding teachers I have known. But I refuse to be bound by a false logic of admiration, or an either/or version of philosophic commitment, that would infer from my admiration of Constable or Austin that I must abhor or reject Monet and Sartre.

In the end a defense of French philosophy must focus on two strengths of the tradition I have sketched. One is the search for synthesis on an encyclopedic base, such as we find in Montaigne, Descartes, Diderot, Comte, Bergson, Poincaré, Serres, and Weil. Such a search may—at its peril, to be sure—overlook or even scorn details. But it is a search that has also been undertaken by those who have honored details and have been guided by them in their search, such as Aristotle, Kant, Austin, and Wittgenstein—and, indeed, some of the French philosophers just named. The other attractive dimension in the French tradition is the striving for a style that will attract rather than repel a very wide range of intelligent readers. *Candide* is a splendid example of this aspect of French philosophy, as are the *Meditations* of Descartes, all the works of Rousseau, the plays and novels of Sartre, the recent work of Serres, and much of Weil. The most recent example is Michel Tournier's *Vendredi*, a retelling of the Robinson Crusoe story by a writer *agregé en philosophie*, published in paperback with an afterword by one of the most prominent professors of philosophy in France (Gilles Deleuze), and regularly assigned to high school students throughout the country. These works are contributions to literature as well as philosophy, a combination rarely achieved in Anglo-American philosophy, although the works of William James and Bertrand Russell (who won the Nobel Prize for Literature) are prominent exceptions, and more recently we have the two British biographies of Wittgenstein and the novels of Robert Pirsig.[10]

There is a method and rationale in the Anglo-American rejection of these characteristics of the French tradition, and *vice versa*. Each method has its dangers, each its advantages. The French tradition appeals to me as one we should try to become more familiar with, partly because its modern members as well as its great figures can enrich our own search, and partly because emulating its literacy and its social relevance can strengthen the role of philosophy in American life.

Newton Garver

State University of New York
Buffalo, NY

NOTES

1.   There is useful discussion of these and other factors by Tony Judt in his recent book, *Past Imperfect*. See also John Wightman's review of that book in *The New York Review of Books*, February 11, 1993. For a brief account of the subsequent years (1953-1987), see Pavel, "The Present Debate".

2.   Mortley (ed.), *French Philosophers in Conversation*, p. 56.

3.   This complex attitude is reminiscent of a famous remark by Simone de Beauvoir, "In order to understand anything, you must understand everything; but in order to say anything, you must leave out a great deal."

4.   Mortley (ed.), p. 48.

5.   Mortley (ed.), p. 49.

6.   Mortley (ed.), p. 59.

7.   Mortley (ed.), p. 58.

8.   Mortley (ed.), p. 59. Serres could perhaps agree with Malcolm's famous slogan, "Ordinary language is correct language."

9.   Monet's paintings can, of course, be photographed, and these photographs can be electronically transmitted with astonishing faithfulness. In this case, however, the faithfulness of the representation is to the details of Monet's painting itself rather than to

the details of what is represented in the painting.

10. Pirsig's two novels, *Zen and the Art of Motorcycle Maintenance* and *Lila*, have both been bestsellers, and the former made the rounds among university students when it came out in paperback, though rarely as a text. Pirsig's theme is, roughly, the relevance of Aristotle to ordinary lives, and it is conceivable that he could play a role in America similar to that of Tournier in France. Three differences remain, however, striking reminders of the cultural chasm I have been describing: whereas Tournier has the most prestigious philosophy degree in France, Pirsig has a degree in English from the University of Montana; although some philosophers have written about Pirsig, no edition of either novel has ever included an essay by one; and Pirsig circulates subversively among students rather than as an assigned text.

I have not mentioned Iris Murdoch, a philosopher who writes novels, because her novels do not work philosophical problems and themes into their fictional development in the way that the works of Tournier and Pirsig do.

REFERENCES

J.L. Austin, *Philosophical Papers*, ed. J. O. Urmson and G. J. Warnock, Oxford: Clarendon Press 1961.

Euripides, *Ion*, tr. Ronald Frederick Willetts, in *The Complete Greek Tragedies*, Chicago: University of Chicago Press, 1958.

Tony Judt, *Past Imperfect: French Intellectuals, 1944-1956*, Berkeley: University of California Press 1992.

Raoul Mortley, *French Philosophers in Conversation*, New York: Routledge, 1991.

Thomas G. Pavel, "The Present Debate: News from France", *Diacritics* (1989), 17-32.

Blaise Pascal, *Pensées*, Paris: Garnier Frères 1964. The motto is quoted from page 75.

Robert M. Pirsig, *Lila: an inquiry into morals*, New York: Bantam Books 1991.

——, *Zen and the Art of Motorcycle Maintenance: An Inquiry Into Values*, New York: Morrow 1974.

Michel Serres, *Le contrat naturel*, Paris: François Bourin 1990.

——, *Les cinq sens*, Paris: B. Grasset 1985.

Michel Tournier, *Vendredi, ou les limbes du Pacifique*, Paris: Gallimard 1972.

Simone Weil, *The Need for Roots: Prelude to a Declaration of Duties Toward Mankind*, tr. Arthur Wills, with a preface by T. S. Eliot. New York: Harper and Row 1971.

——, *The Simone Weil Reader*, ed. George A. Panichas. New York: David McKay, 1977. Contains the Elisabeth Chase Geissbuhler translation of "*The Iliad*, Poem of Force".

Peter Winch, *The Just Balance*, Cambridge: Cambridge University Press 1989.

Ludwig Wittgenstein, *Last Writings on the Philosophy of Psychology* I, ed. G. H. von Wright and Heikki Nyman, tr. C. G. Luckhardt and Maximilian A. E. Aue, Oxford: Blackwell 1982.

Part Two

THE APOCALYPTIC TONE IN PHILOSOPHY:
KIERKEGAARD, DERRIDA AND THE RHETORIC OF
TRANSCENDENCE

'Apocalypse': etymologically a shedding of veils, a revelation of truths hitherto concealed, a coming-to-light of some sacred or secret wisdom vouchsafed only to the elect few. This is the realm of hermeneutics, rather than philosophy, to the extent that philosophy has mostly been thought of—at least since Socrates—as a process of reasoned and disciplined enquiry aimed toward establishing valid propositions in the sphere of enlightened understanding. And indeed the philosophers have not taken kindly to the 'apocalyptic tone', regarding it as a renegade or upstart discourse, a mode of address that ignores all the protocols, all the criteria and validity-conditions that properly determine what shall count as a competent (good-faith) contribution to debate. These characters offend against reason and justice alike by claiming a privileged access to truth that renders them exempt from any such requirements. Moreover, their language is so cryptic and obscure—so akin to the rapturous afflatus of the poets, prophets and other soothsaying adepts—that it brooks no correction from the critical tribunal of plain-prose reason. They can wax eloquent on any topic you care to name without the least show of supporting argument or proof that they know what they are talking about. Worse than that, they affect an arrogant belief that they, and they alone, have attained true wisdom through this power of mystical-intuitive insight that rejects any challenge on grounds of mere logic, consistency, or evidential warrant.[1]

In short, the apocalyptic tone is nothing more than a species of rhetorical imposture, a strategy for evading peer-group review among those—the genuine philosophers—who submit their judgment to the *sensus communis* of informed participant exchange. So little do its zealots care for such debate that they positively glory in the gulf of mutual incomprehension—the lack of any shared grounds for discussion—between their own rhapsodic-inspirational style and the kinds of philosophizing mostly carried on in the academies, the journals, or other such reputable quarters. Quite simply, they think themselves above such commonplace or workaday standards of assessment, presuming as they do—on no better authority than sheer intuitive self-evidence—that what is true or right is what is revealed to them through possession of the requisite hermeneutic skills.[2] Hence the long series of philosophical put-downs, from Plato's dialogues—where Socrates is shown running expert dialectical rings around the poets, rhetoricians, sophists and other such false claimants to truth—to the latest bout of hostilities between thinkers in the Anglo-American, "analytic" camp and those, like Derrida, who are taken to embody the worst excesses of that whole misbegotten "continental" tradition of thought. The idioms may have changed, and the lines of demarcation been drawn rather differently from time to time. Nevertheless the charge-sheet remains much the same if one compares (say) Plato's case against the poets—and more crucially, those who mix the genres of poetry and philosophy—with the typical response of analytic philosophers when invited to air their views on the topic. Here again it is primarily a question of style, of the choice as these latter see it between, on the one hand, a language that respects the philosophical requirements of clarity, precision, and the good-faith will to communicate, and on the other a language (Derrida's) that exploits the maximum possible degree of obscurity, bafflement, and high-toned "literary" pretension. By the same token such pseudo-philosophy is held to constitute a standing affront to all those regulative notions (of truth, method, conceptual adequacy, argumentative rigour, etc.) which define the very nature of the philosophic enterprise, and in the absence of which—so it is urged—any jumped-up charlatan can always lay claim to the truth as revealed to his or her powers of unaided intuitive vision.

Hence the frequent tonings of moral outrage—the talk of corrupting influence, of "nihilism", irrationalism, decadence and so forth—which reached a climax in the recent campaign to prevent Derrida from receiving an honorary doctorate at Cambridge.[3] One may suspect that such opinions very often went along with a determined refusal to read Derrida's work, since to do so would clearly place these parties at risk of succumbing to that virulent contagion. But despite its more absurd aspects this episode provides a useful index of the defences that philosophy still seeks to muster against any intrusion of the "apocalyptic tone" as perceived—with whatever degree of distorting prejudice—by those within the current professional fold. What makes the case still more interesting is the fact that Derrida has always maintained a highly complex, ambivalent yet critical relation to that "tone" in its various modalities, sometimes through a kind of multi-layered intertextual dialogism such that his opponents might almost be forgiven for lumping him together with the latterday zealots and mystagogues.[4] But these opponents are demonstrably wide of the mark when they fail to observe how Derrida is *citing* certain instances of apocalyptic discourse, and how they thus come to figure, in the analytic idiom, as "mentions" rather than "uses" of the tone or style in question. That is to say, we shall get Derrida wrong if we think to read his arguments straight off from the page without first asking such elementary questions—"elementary" at least for literary critics—as, What is the function of this utterance in context? What determines where the relevant context begins or ends? Who is speaking here and to what (overt or implied) purpose? How are we to take the various signs of non-coincidence between manifest meaning and meaning as construed with ironic reference to those same texts that Derrida is citing or mentioning? For we shall otherwise end up in the unfortunate position of those novel-readers who naively assume that any statement not attributed to some (named or identified) fictive character must therefore reflect the author's own views on this or that topic of thematic concern.

Of course this may be taken as yet further evidence—if any were needed—that Derrida's work scarcely merits serious (philosophical) attention. For it can always be assigned to that hybrid genre of so-called "literary theory" which treats philosophy, in Richard Rorty's phrase, as just another optional "kind of writing" on a level with poetry, fiction, *Kulturgeschichte* or what have you, and which is therefore best left to those tender-minded (or muddle-headed) types who nowadays congregate in departments of Comparative Literature.[5] But whatever its justice as applied to some of Derrida's less philosophically informed disciples, this view is quite inadequate in his own case. For nobody has gone further toward thinking through the relationship that exists between philosophy, literature, and the "apocalyptic tone". And he has done so *not*–as neopragmatists like Rorty would approvingly claim, along with detractors like Jürgen Habermas—in a spirit of post-philosophical scepticism that sets out simply to demolish or collapse such generic boundary-markers.[6] On the contrary: the questions that Derrida raises with regard to the "apocalyptic tone" are questions that have haunted the discourse of philosophy from Plato to Kant, Husserl, J. L. Austin, and even (or especially) those who would nowadays exclude it *de iure* from the forum of "serious" intellectual debate. What is distinctive about Derrida's work—and what has often provoked such fierce antagonism—is the way that he both enacts (or mimics) that tone through all manner of "literary" allusions, citations, parodic references, etc., and at the same time subjects it to a deconstructive reading of the utmost philosophical acuity. In Austin's terms his writing is both *performative* and *constative*: a putting-into-play of various speech-act modalities (among them the discourse of revealed or apocalyptic truth) while maintaining a certain critical reserve, a capacity to stand back and remark their more wayward, extravagant or questionable forms.

It is this calculated mixing of genres—this extreme virtuosity of style allied to a constant reflexive critique of its own performative implications—which Derrida's opponents have mostly written off as so much "literary" verbiage. Small wonder that his texts have caused great offense to exponents of a would-be systematic speech-act theory—notably John Searle—who, unlike Derrida (and indeed unlike Austin), wish to draw a firm disciplinary line between performatives and constatives, standard and non-standard ("deviant") cases, "felicitous" and "infelicitous" modes of utterance, "ordinary language" as properly deployed in the conduct of our everyday lives and those other speech-act genres—literature among them but also, more vexingly, the discourse of "ordinary language" philosophy—that cite such examples in a different (artificial or deviant) context of usage, and which thus tend always to suspend or problematize the usual speech-act conventions.[7] For it was Austin—not Derrida—who first remarked on this tendency of performatives to "play Old Harry" with received philosophical ideas, among them (to begin with) the truth/falsehood distinction and then, as he followed out the logic of his own argument, the very possibility of assigning any firm categorical status to constative and performative modes. This is why the best, most intelligent and responsive readings of Austin are those that decline to take refuge in the comforts of system and theory, and which follow his example by remaining alert to the various anomalies, deviant cases, communicative "misfires", etc., that can always arise to complicate the project of speech-act philosophy. For as Derrida insists—again *contra* Searle—it is only by taking account of such "marginal" instances that theory is able to define the requirements of normal (felicitous or good-faith) performative utterance. Which is also to say that one will never come up with an exhaustive set of criteria—or necessary and sufficient conditions—whereby to establish what should rightfully count as a genuine, authentic example of the kind.

Hence the oscillation, in Austin's text, between sincerity-conditions, based on the idea that speakers should genuinely mean what they say, and contextual criteria which make it a matter of uttering the appropriate form of words in the right situation, with adequate authority, institutional warrant or whatever. In each case there will always be instances that give room for doubt, that are simply undecidable by any such appeal to intentions or validating context. And this applies above all to that most problematical genre of discourse which Derrida—taking his cue, as it happens, from a little-known polemic by Kant—refers to as the "apocalyptic tone".[8] For it is here that philosophy (and speech-act theory in particular) comes up against the greatest imaginable challenge to its powers of conceptual grasp. After all, what use is the appeal to sincerity-conditions—to good-faith utterance or speaker's intent—in the case of a discourse that acknowledges no such criteria, whose truth is a matter of inward revelation (whether vouchsafed directly through divine grace or through the inspired reading of scripture), and which therefore renders such questions wholly redundant? What room is there for talk of utterer's meaning, speech-act implicature, commitment to honour one's word, etc., if the apocalyptic tone is *by very definition* such as to suspend all notions of assignable origin, all attempts to construe it in subjective, intentionalist, or humanly accountable terms? And again: what is to count as a relevant context where the speech-act in question (or the genre of discourse) is one that would claim to transcend all the limiting conditions of historical place and time?

Not that Derrida wishes us to take such claims on faith, or to be understood himself as practising a form of divinatory textual hermeneutics. Nor should he be taken as suggesting—with regard to Austin—that issues of context or speaker's intent are utterly beside the point, since language is always and everywhere subject to this kind of radical undecidability. On the contrary: he knows that in most situations, and for most practical purposes, we do get along quite reliably on the basis of imputing good-faith intentions (or reckoning with their possible absence), and also by taking due stock of the relevant contextual factors. For otherwise we could never make a start in understanding even the simplest of verbal communications, let alone those immensely complex forms of utterance that constitute the domain of philosophical argument. So his opponents are wrong—Searle and Habermas among them—when they think to catch Derrida out by invoking the standard *tu quoque* argument deployed against sceptics down through the ages, that is to say, by pointing out that he requires his own work to be read with a decent regard for context, generic constraints, authorial intentions etc., while (supposedly) allowing himself all manner of hermeneutic licence with the works of others. What they ignore is Derrida's reiterated point: that the claim to respect those imperative values can become a pretext for simply reproducing the established interpretive tradition, and thus remaining blind to any discrepant or anomalous details in the text that would threaten to disrupt that prevailing consensus view. For it is precisely in the "margins of philosophy"—in those aspects which are deemed marginal on the standard (doxastic) account—that an alert reading may hope to gain access to philosophy's "unthought axiomatics", its hitherto occulted systems of value and priority.[9] Such is at any rate Derrida's contention, a case borne out (as I have argued at length elsewhere) by readings that exhibit the highest qualities of philosophical rigour, acuity, and insight.[10]

It is important to be clear about this since the critics have gained some polemical mileage from the idea of deconstruction as a species of all-out (and hence self-refuting) scepticism. One could assemble quite a dossier of statements—beginning with some well-known passages from *Of Grammatology*—where Derrida very firmly rejects any idea that deconstruction can somehow dispense with the standards of interpretive validity, of right reading, of consistency, logic, or truth.[11] Nor can these be written off as mere pious declarations patently at odds with Derrida's actual practice. For what typifies his writing at best—as in the books and essays on Plato, Rousseau, Kant, Husserl, Austin and others—is a scrupulous attentiveness to the letter of the text, combined with an a keenness of analytic insight that are seldom matched in the commentary of mainstream exegetes.[12] That his arguments so often run counter to the received wisdom—raising questions that understandably provoke strong resistance among those wedded to the orthodox view—is scarcely good reason for reject-

ing them out of hand. And this applies even (or especially) to those instances
where the question has to do with such deep-grained philosophical assumptions
as the priority of literal over metaphoric meaning, the principle of sufficient reason, the existence of determinate felicity-conditions for the various classes of
speech-act, or again—subsuming all of these—the privilege traditionally
accorded to logic and grammar (as opposed to "mere" rhetoric) in the analysis
of language under its truth-functional aspect. In each case Derrida arrives at his
heterodox (and often counter-intuitive) conclusions through a process of metic-
ulous textual close-reading allied to a detailed working-through of the rhetorical
and the logico-grammatical complexities involved. Such is his procedure—to
cite just a few examples—when analysing the relation between concept and
metaphor in his essay "White Mythology", when examining Husserl's phenomenological distinction between "expressive" and "indicative" signs, or when
expounding the strange (but none the less rigorously demonstrable) "logic of
supplementarity" that inhabits Rousseau's various writings on language, culture, civil institutions, and the genealogy of morals.[13] Commentators may well
balk at Derrida's findings, especially when these are taken out of context or
cited—as too often happens—in reductively encapsulated statements of the kind
"there is nothing outside the text", "all concepts are metaphors", "all interpretation is misinterpretation" etc. But such readings find no warrant in Derrida's
work, least of all in those texts (like the essay on Austin or his second-round
response to John Searle) where the argument turns explicitly on questions of
context and authorial intent. For it is here, more than anywhere, that Derrida is
at pains to dissociate deconstruction from any version of the free-for-all
hermeneutic creed—promoted by some of his literary-critical admirers—which
would cheerfully bid farewell to such irksome constraints upon the infinitized
"freeplay" of textual meaning.

II

So much by way of cautionary preamble, lest it be thought that Derrida exploits
the "apocalyptic tone" as yet another ruse (along with *differance*, "dissemination", intertextuality and the like) for deflecting attention from his own failure
to offer cogent or adequate philosophical arguments. What it does serve to
emphasize—perhaps more pointedly than any of those other terms—is the problem that philosophy has always encountered with speech-acts, discursive genres
or modes of utterance that cannot be assigned with confidence to any one (e. g.
constative or performative) category. Hence Plato's chief objection to the poets,
sophists and other purveyors of a false (unphilosophical) wisdom. All very well
had these characters preserved a due modesty with regard to their own inferior

role, their task of providing occasional solace or instruction in the arts of public speaking. But this was not at all the limit of their ambition. Rather, they imposed upon ignorant or credulous minds by mixing up various sorts of true-seeming statements—moral *sententiae* and so forth—with a hopeless farrago of myth, metaphor, personification and suchlike deceptive tropes. So the wise (philosophically instructed) lawmaker had no choice but to counsel their speedy banishment from the well-ordered republic, albeit with token expressions of regret. And he was also obliged—as part of this same exercise in intellectual hygiene—to set about purging philosophy of those residual poetic elements that compromised its own dedication to the interests of virtue, justice, and truth. Of course the issue was by no means closed, as witness the long succession of brooding commentaries—most recently by Iris Murdoch—that have sought to re-adjudicate this "ancient quarrel" between poetry and philosophy.[14]

Among them must be counted Derrida's remarkable essay "Plato's Pharmacy", his deconstructive reading of the *Phaedrus* as a dialogue which implicitly pursues that quarrel through all manner of oblique, allegorical, and self-reflexive strategy.[15] For the essay is concerned not only with speech *versus* writing as a problematic *topos* in the legacy of Platonist thought. It also has to do with that whole complex of associated themes—origins, presence, truth, *mimesis*, the paternal *logos* of authorized knowledge as against its upstart progeny, rhetoric and metaphor—which together provide an interpretive matrix for what has seemed to many commentators a somewhat unconvincing or loosely-constructed piece of argument. In particular, it casts fresh light on that troublesome episode in the *Phaedrus* where Plato resorts to an Egyptian myth about the origins of writing, despite his own strictures on mythic explanation as a pre-philosophical (and hence highly suspect) form of pseudo-knowledge. What Derrida is thus able to show is firstly the structural complicity that exists between these various opposed pairs of terms (speech/writing, *logos*/*doxa*, concept/metaphor, reason/rhetoric, philosophy/myth etc.), and secondly the way that those same oppositions are destabilized—rendered strictly undecidable—by Plato's recruitment of myth, metaphor and other such "literary" devices as a necessary adjunct to his own philosophical argument. The ambivalence of the key-term *pharmakon* (writing as both poison and cure) is just one among the numerous textual signs that Plato is here drawn into issues of language, knowledge and representation that in some way exceed his conceptual resources for determining the philosophic outcome in advance. Which is also to say—as many readers have felt—that the stylistic qualities of Plato's writing (his images, metaphors, flights of allegorical invention) are such as to qualify his overt allegiance to Socrates' teaching, and to place him in the poets' party despite his doctrinal unwillingness to acknowledge the fact.

I would not of course claim that this summary does justice—or anything like it—to the extraordinary subtlety, the intricate detail and the sheer analytical intelligence brought to bear in Derrida's reading of Plato. But there are several points that may usefully be stressed by way of leading us back to the "apocalyptic tone" and its significance for Derrida's work. One is its kinship with those "literary" elements—myth, rhetoric, metaphor etc.—which likewise involve an appeal beyond the Socratic tribunal of reason and truth as established through a process of disciplined dialectical thought. Another is the way that this "ancient quarrel" has been played out repeatedly down through the history of western philosophical debate, from Kant's polemic against the mystagogues, the hierophants and adepts of revealed religious truth, to those current denunciations of Derrida's work—by Habermas, Searle and Iris Murdoch among others—which take him to task for adopting an irrationalist stance (a contemporary update of the "apocalyptic tone") quite beyond the pale of civilized, truth-seeking discourse.[16] And lastly, there is the notion of his having "deconstructed" the distinction between philosophy and literature, thus exposing philosophy (as Plato feared) to all the alien intrusions of a mystical afflatus—an "inner voice" of revealed, self-authenticating truth—that would block any appeal to the *sensus communis* of enlightened inter-subjective debate. On this account the tonings of apocalypse that occasionally surface in Derrida's work—no matter how ironically qualified or hedged about with intertextual allusions—must be seen as gestures intended to promote a species of hermeneutic mystery-mongering or a wholesale irrationalist creed.

Hence Habermas's oft-repeated charge against Derrida, that his philosophy regresses to a phase in the pre-Kantian history of thought when religion, so far from being properly confined within the "limits of reason alone", was permitted to encroach upon domains of thought where it had no right to obtrude. "If this suspicion is not utterly false", Habermas writes, "Derrida returns to the historical locale where mysticism once turned into enlightenment".[17] And he does so in order to revoke the philosophical discourse of modernity, to undermine the truth-claims of enlightenment critique, and to level those various genre-distinctions—as between epistemology, ethics, and aesthetics, or thought in its problem-solving, moral-evaluative, and poetic or "world-disclosive" aspects—which have served at least since Kant as a regulative framework for the conduct of genuine, responsible enquiry. What this amounts to is the grave accusation: that Derrida has promoted *just one* of those aspects—the "world-disclosive"—to a point where it effectively dissolves all the others into so many forms of metaphoric or poetico-rhetorical discourse, devoid of any normative or critical force. Thus the rhetorical element occurs *in its pure form* only in the self-referentiality of the poetic expression, that is, in the language of fiction specialized for world-disclosure. Even the normal language of everyday life is ineradicably rhetorical; but within the matrix of different linguistic functions, the rhetorical elements recede here. The same holds true of the specialized languages of science and technology, law and morality, economics, political science, etc. They, too, live off the illuminating power of metaphorical tropes, but the rhetorical elements, which are by no mean expunged, are tamed, as it were, and enlisted for special purposes of problem-solving.[18]

What Derrida simply ignores, on Habermas's account, is this process of increasing specialization within and between discourses, this attainment of a differential "public sphere" wherein the various languages can expect to be assessed each according to its own evaluative criteria, its appropriate validity-conditions, or distinctive orders of truth-claim. So far from respecting such differences, Derrida "holistically levels these complicated relationships in order to equate philosophy with literature and criticism". From which it follows, yet more damagingly, that "[h]e fails to recognize the special status that both philosophy and literary criticism, each in its own way, assume as mediators between expert cultures and the everyday world".[19]

In Habermas's view it is here—through their various "mediating" roles— that such relatively specialized discourses can feed back into the currency of ordinary language with the effect of enhancing its capacity for informed, responsible, or discriminating judgment. But in so doing they must also retain some degree of autonomy, some critical distance that sets them apart from both expert cultures (science, law, political theory etc.) and the language of the everyday world. And this is where Derrida goes so disastrously wrong, according to Habermas.

Because [he] over-generalizes this one linguistic function—namely, the poetic—he can no longer see the complex relationship of the ordinary practice of normal speech to the two extraordinary spheres, differentiated, as it were, in opposite directions. The polar tension between world-disclosure and problem-solving is held together within the functional matrix of ordinary language; but art and literature on the one side, and science, morality, and law on the other, are specialized for experiences and nodes of knowledge that can be shaped and worked out within the compass of one linguistic function and one dimension of validity at a time.[20]

I have perhaps said enough already to indicate why this is a false (or at any rate very partial and misleading) account of Derrida's work. It ignores—among other things—his continued engagement with the legacy of Kantian-enlightenment thought; his insistence (*contra* postmodern "textualists" like Rorty) that deconstruction can never justifiably dispense with the values of truth, right reading, and interpretive fidelity; and above all the precise analytical grasp that

Derrida brings to his writings on metaphor, on the rhetorical, performative aspects of philosophic discourse, and on the "ancient quarrel"—resumed with such partisan vigour by Habermas—between philosophy and literature. In short, there is good reason for Derrida's sharp-toned rejoinder to Habermas, Searle and others who would accuse him of muddying philosophical distinctions, or of failing to respect those elementary protocols which they (his opponents) are curiously apt to abandon when confronted with Derrida's texts.[21]

But my concern here is not so much to vindicate Derrida's case as to ask just what it is about his writing that has engendered this latest resurgence of polemics around deconstruction and its perceived threat to the conduct of serious, civilized philosophical debate. The most obvious starting-point for any such enquiry is Derrida's essay "Of an Apocalyptic Tone Recently Adopted in Philosophy", a text that not only rehearses the issue as raised by philosophers from Plato to Kant, but which also includes some sidelong reflections on this age-old "contest of the faculties" in its present-day guise. However, that essay is such a gift for my purpose that I shall defer the pleasure of expounding it for just a while longer, and preface my discussion with some further remarks about the "literary" reading of philosophic works. For it is this question that most exercises critics like Habermas and Searle, committed as they are to a definite view of the proper relationship between "ordinary" (or "everyday") language on the one hand, and on the other those relatively "specialized" languages—philosophy among them, but also (more problematically) poetry and fiction—whose benefits are available only on condition that they observe the requisite division of discursive domains. With Searle, this requirement takes the form of a speech-act philosophy that aims to define the criteria for felicitous (good-faith) performative utterance, together with a theory of fictive (literary) discourse which specifies the ways in which such language departs from those same real-life standards of veridical utterance.[22] For Habermas—who always has Heidegger in view as the chief modern enemy of enlightenment—it is more a matter of preventing the metaphorical (or "world-disclosive") aspect of poetic language from overreaching its competence to the point of annulling all distinctions between those realms.

Thus in Derrida's work, as Habermas construes it,

> linguistically mediated processes within the world are embedded in a *world-constituting* context that prejudices everything; they are fatalistically delivered up to the unmanageable happening of text-production, overwhelmed by the poetic-creative transformation of a background designated by archi-writing, and condemned to be provincial.[23]

What provokes this charge—as so often in philosophy's troubled dealings with poetry and metaphor—is the idea of a language wholly given over to the "apocalyptic tone" of some inner revelation, some voice of inspired (self-authenticating) utterance that defies all the standards of rational accountability. And it also has to do with those issues that Derrida raises with regard to Austinian speech-act theory. For in the case of such apocalyptic language one can never know for sure who is speaking, in the name of what authority, with what precise intent (or institutional warrant), in fulfillment of what obscure prophecies, or with cryptic allusion to how many source-texts, arcane prefigurings, typological correspondences, and so forth. It is as if—to take up Habermas's argument —philosophy were in danger of being thrown back to a stage of unthinking pre-enlightenment faith when intuition (not reason) was the oracle of truth, and when the mere appeal to scripture (Derrida's *archi-écriture*) sufficed to silence any criticism. Or again, it would risk endorsing that strain of post- or counter-enlightenment thought which abandoned the imperatives of critical reflection and embraced various forms of quasi-transcendental monism, whether grounded (like Fichte's idealist variant) in the solipsistic world-creating subject or else (like Schelling's) in the idea of nature—the "objective" pole of this pseudo-dialectic—as the ultimate horizon of being and truth.

> Unabashedly [Habermas writes], and in the style of *Ursprungsphilosophie*, Derrida falls back on this *Urschrift* which leaves its traces anonymously, without any subject...As Schelling once did in speculating about the timeless temporalizing internesting of the past, present and future ages of the world, so Derrida clings to the dizzying thought of a past that has never been present...He too [like Heidegger] degrades politics and contemporary history to the status of the ontic and the foreground, so as to romp all the more freely...in the sphere of the ontological and of archi-writing.[24]

Such might indeed be the consequence if Derrida were arguing—as he doesn't—that concepts or truth-claims are *nothing but* sublimated metaphors; that philosophy is *purely and simply* a "kind of writing"; and that there is no appeal beyond the rhetorical (or "literary") aspect of philosophic discourse. One could cite any number of passages from his work —especially from "White Mythology"—that go clean against this vulgar-deconstructionist line. It is, to say the least, ironic that Habermas takes no account of them while he criticizes Derrida for supposedly infringing all the maxims and ground-rules of communicative reason or good-faith dialogical exchange.

III

Still one has to ask: can there be any reason in principle—as distinct from reasons of professional self-esteem—for supposing that philosophy need have no truck with such "literary" notions as narrative voice, the unreliable narrator, or

the implied author and his/her counterpart, the implied reader? The example of
Kierkegaard is perhaps most telling in this respect since he adopts a whole
range of oblique narrative strategies —multiple viewpoint, repetition, incongru-
ous perspectives, unstable irony, pseudonymous authorship etc.—in order to
confound any straightforward reading that would pass directly from the "words
on the page" to ascriptions of authorial intent. Of course this is not the whole
story, since Kierkegaard (according to his own retrospective account in *The
Point of View for My Work as an Author*) was from the outset fully in control of
his literary production, deploying such strategies always in the service of a
higher self-justifying cause, that of revealed religious truth.[25] Thus his ultimate
design was to point a way *through and beyond* these stages of aesthetic indeci-
sion—of artfully suspended judgment—to a moment when at last all pretences
would be set aside, when Kierkegaard would speak in *propria persona* (as in
the "edifying" or "upbuilding" discourses), and when the reader would confront
a necessary choice between "authentic" and "inauthentic" modes of existence.

Such is at any rate Kierkegaard's claim, his challenge to the unregenerate
hypocrite lecteur who might well be tempted to value the "aesthetic" productions (especially Volume One of *Either/Or*) above anything belonging to the
ethical stage—like Judge William's virtuous reflections in Volume Two—or
even (worse yet) above the works of redemption authored by Kierkegaard
ipse.[26] At this point art must indeed conceal art, or literature disown—by all the
means at its disposal—whatever might still be construed as in need of "literary"
(narrative or rhetorical) decoding. For eternal salvation, no less, depends upon
the reader's capacity to perceive this qualitative difference of realms, this need
to pass over—by an existential "leap of faith"—from the aesthetic domain of
ambiguity, irony, unreliable narration and so forth, to a hermeneutic quest for
truth as revealed to those with the requisite powers of inward or spiritual understanding. Failing that, his authorship will stand condemned in every aspect of its
intricate development. It will be shown up as a vain and delusive enterprise, not
only at the ultimate (all-justifying) stage of religious conversion, but also as
providing—in the aesthetic or pseudonymous works—such a range of pretexts
for sceptical readers who can then claim Kierkegaard as one of their own, an
ironist and aesthete *malgré lui* whose powers of literary invention got the better
of his merely didactic ("edifying") purpose. And nothing could be worse, from
Kierkegaard's viewpoint, than for his authorship to suffer this perverse misconstrual in matters that bear upon the reader's prospects of attaining salvation
through faith.

This is why he goes to such lengths, in *The Point of View*, to explain what
prompted his various modes of oblique or pseudonymous narration, to justify
those writings with reference to a higher (providential) sense of governing
intent, and to caution any reader drawn to the idea that maybe the *entirety* of

Kierkegaard's authorship can be read as a species of aesthetic (or "literary") production. In his own day this was the approach of those romantic ironists, Friedrich Schlegel among them, who saw no end—and no ethical objection—to the enticing prospect of an infinitized irony that would undermine every last standard of interpretive validity or truth.[27] And the same would apply, give or take a few shifts of rhetorical idiom, to the present-day exponents of deconstruction in its literary or ultra-textualist guise. Such readings are the Devil's work, Kierkegaard implies, since they acknowledge no difference—no absolute requirement to choose—between the aesthetic way of life conjured up so brilliantly in the "Seducer's Diary" of *Either/Or,* Volume One, and the religious vocation that involves a total break with such frivolous "life-styles" or cultivated forms of self-deception. For the stakes in this matter are pitched uncommonly high. On Kierkegaard's account the issue of right reading—or true divination of authorial intent—becomes nothing less than a touchstone of spiritual grace, a means of separating the sheep from the goats among his various (more or less receptive or educable) readers. As with Milton, his writings are intended for that elect group of individuals, fit though few, who will not be seduced by aesthetic blandishments or mere story-telling interest. To put it bluntly, this author will see you damned if you persist in mistaking his purpose, as for instance by reading a work like *Fear and Trembling*—Kierkegaard's sombre meditation on the parable of Abraham and Isaac—as if it were just another piece of fictive experiment, handy material for literary talk about the "implied author", levels of irony or textual *mise-en-abîme*, frame-narratives, the "rhetoric of dubious authority", or suchlike tools of the trade.[28] For to do so is to side with the romantic ironists of his time—and the deconstructive adepts of our own—in treating the most serious choices of existence as if they were fictive episodes contrived to the end of mere aesthetic delectation.

And yet, as Kierkegaard ruefully acknowledges, there is a sense in which his writings are sure to be misread on account of those same duplicitous strategies (or techniques of literary indirection) which should properly lose their seductive appeal once the reader has been brought to this stage of true religious inwardness. Thus: "I held out *Either/Or* to the world in my left hand, and in my right the *Two Edifying Discourses*; but all, or as good as all, grasped with their right hand what I held in my left."[29] In other words, what can prevent the "sophisticated" reader from ignoring Kierkegaard's overt professions of intent, rejecting the idea of a providential "governance" at work throughout the authorship, and choosing to treat the *entirety* of that authorship—first-person "edifying" works included—as so many literary texts that call for expert hermeneutical treatment? This problem has three main aspects, all of them tending to compound the difficulty of taking Kierkegaard at his word, or following him through the "stages of existence" set down for the benefit of his good-faith read-

er in *The Point of View*. To begin with there is the awkward fact—noted by
Adorno, among others—that the first-person discourses are often plain boring,
delivered in a heavily didactic, repetitive and moralizing style which apparently
goes out of its way to repel those readers who have already been seduced by the
artfulness of Kierkegaard's pseudonymous (literary) writings.[30] Second, there is
the problem that attends all uses of irony as a propadeutic technique: namely,
that of knowing for sure when the irony is supposed to have an end and give
way to the voice of authentic, self-authorized, first-person truth. Of course
Kierkegaard was acutely aware of this problem, having devoted much of his
life's work to a sustained engagement with the various practitioners of irony,
from Socrates to Friedrich Schlegel.[31] But this is not to say—as *The Point of
View* would so strenuously seek to convince us—that on an adequate reading
(i.e., one attuned to its deepest governing intent) the authorship provides indu-
bitable warrant for distinguishing these two modes of utterance. Nor does one
have to be a romantic ironist like Schlegel (or a thoroughgoing sceptical
debunker like Stanley Fish) in order to perceive this difficulty with
Kierkegaard's position.[32] For it is here that the third major problem arises: in
the fact that Kierkegaard has himself offered a whole range of highly effective
strategies—ironic, rhetorical, "literary", aesthetic, proto-deconstructive and so
forth—by which to subvert (or to render "undecidable") any such clear-cut distinction. And these are likely to exert all the more appeal when contrasted with
what Adorno describes, not unfairly, as the "loquacious boredom," the "tiresome and unpleasant reading," and the "verbosity of an interminable monologue" that often overtake the *Edifying Discourses*.[33] In which case Kierkegaard
would indeed be at risk not only of failing to separate the sheep from the goats
among his target readership, but also—much worse—of excluding from the fold
a sizable number of likely or potential converts.

The "apocalyptic tone" is never far away when Kierkegaard's critics (and
Kierkegaard himself) seek to clarify this issue of authorial intent in relation to
his literary strategies on the one hand, and his claims of divine or providential
"governance" on the other. After all, what authority can they (or he) possess to
pronounce on the authentic meaning of his work unless guided by some ultimate voice of truth beyond all the obstacles and mazy detours which that work
places in their way? Only at this moment of revealed truth will the literary production cease—along with the pseudonyms, aesthetic devices, narrative alibis,
ironic disclaimers, etc.—and the authorship assume its true vocation as a work
of first-hand spiritual witness. For otherwise there is simply no end to what "literature" can get away with; no end, that is, to the strategies of self-evasion that
readers may practise by taking with their left hands what Kierkegaard offers
with his right. But the question remains: can even the good-faith reader who
seeks to comprehend Kierkegaard's edifying purpose be certain of not falling

prey to the snares of aesthetic illusion or literary semblance? What makes this question so urgent for Kierkegaard is the necessity, as he sees it, that all communication must nowadays adopt such an oblique approach to matters of serious concern, since the "present age" is so far given over to irony, fictive role-playing, and other forms of inauthentic existence. "If the apostle's personal character is one of noble and pure simplicity (which is the condition for being the instrument of the Holy Spirit), that of the reviser is his ambiguous knowledge."[34] And again: "[i]f the apostle is in a unique and good sense entirely in the power of providence, the reviser is in the same power in an ambiguous sense."[35] But the time is not propitious for "apostles," at least, not for those who refuse all commerce with the secular spirit of the age. For only the "reviser"— the adroit exponent of ambiguity, irony and aesthetic indirection—can hope to communicate effectively with readers who share his or her unfortunate plight, that of living in an epoch whose chief characteristic is the excess of self-conscious reflection over authentic commitment.

Hence another crucial tenet of Kierkegaard's thought, most conveniently summarized in a passage from *The Point of View*:

> Teleological suspension in relation to the communication of truth (i.e., to suppress something for the time being that the truth may become truer) is a plain duty to the truth and is comprised in the responsibility a man has before God for the reflection bestowed upon him.[36]

This "suspension" has been in effect—or so we are now given to understand—at every point in the pseudonymous authorship. Its purpose (and sole justification) was Kierkegaard's avowed intent of coaxing the reader onward and up through the various stages of aesthetic, ironic, reflective, and ethical awareness, to that moment of ultimate choice between "religiousness A" and "religiousness B", or the dictates of conventional Christian observance as against the starkly uncompromising faith enjoined by a work like *Fear and Trembling*. For there would then be no need of further prevarication, the reader having at last won through to a state of authentic inwardness and grace whereby to comprehend the edifying works at their true (albeit aesthetically unappealing) worth.

Fear and Trembling is the crucial test-case here, since it deploys every means to interpellate that reader—to set him or her up, so to speak—in a position that allows of no possible escape-route from the choice between those two kinds of religiousness. Thus Kierkegaard subjects the parable of Abraham and Isaac to a series of speculative or experimental readings, all but one of them tending to soften or humanize its ethico-religious implications. Of the various sermons that might be preached on this theme, most would take the decently accommodating line of assuming that God or Abraham (or both) were from the outset looking for some way to save Isaac, some happy issue out of Abraham's hideous predicament. Their aim, in other words, is to commensurate the orders of divine providence and human understanding, or to offer a more "civilized" account of the parable that seeks to bridge the otherwise appalling gulf between God's command to Abraham (that he should sacrifice Isaac) and Abraham's agony of conscience as viewed from the natural standpoint of fatherly love, of familial and ethico-social responsibility, or even of "religiousness A" as a perspective that takes due account of those secular interests. But having entertained a number of such conjectural readings, Kierkegaard—or rather his pseudonym, Johannes de Silentio—rejects them as simply not measuring up to the demands of the biblical narrative. What we should see in them, rather, is a series of instances designed to illustrate (and implicitly discredit) that easygoing form of religious belief that the Sunday-best preachers and their right-thinking audience would substitute for the rigours of authentic Christian faith. It is at this point that "religiousness A" (with its residues of Hegelian *Sittlichkeit* or civic-institutional morality) passes over into the bleak and comfortless terrain of Kierkegaard's "religiousness B."

Thus the only adequate reading of the parable is one that discounts its saving *dénouement*, that rejects any form of sentimentalizing pathos or "human" appeal, and which moreover insists on Abraham's absolute willingness to carry out the sacrifice, along with God's inscrutable purpose in willing that this should be the case. Nor should the reader be tempted to suppose that God, in his divine prescience, must surely have known all along that an alternative object of sacrifice would present itself, and therefore that the test of Abraham's faith would not involve the actual killing of his son. For this is just another strategy of evasion, an interpretive ruse designed to get God off the hook, as it were, from the viewpoint of secular ethics or "religiousness A". There is simply no room, as Kierkegaard reads it, for applying any principle of charity or best-case scenario that would reconcile this parable to our everyday notions of virtue, decency, or civilized conduct. Any reader who seeks to do so—with whatever good motive, humanly considered—is thereby signalling his or her failure to comprehend both the parable itself and Kierkegaard's own strenuous exercise in the hermeneutics of faith.

And yet, as I have remarked, this text cannot be counted among the "edifying" works, at least according to the standard distinction (as laid down in *The Point of View*) between pseudonymous and first-person modes of discourse. Johannes de Silentio is the "knight of faith", a would-be convert at the highest preparatory stage, but one whose approach is philosophical and reflective, rather than grounded in the absolute certitude of revealed religious truth. In the words of one commentator, *Fear and Trembling* is written in the form of an indirect religious communication from the poetic per-spective...[Thus] Johannes confesses from the outset that he cannot understand the faith of Abraham. Compared to the Hegelians who want to go beyond Christian faith, Johannes could only imagine faith...The "knight of faith" is only a hero of imagination unable to empower the leap of faith or to sustain a poised faith that does not vacillate continually between leap and fall. Kierkegaard wants the reader with a religious disposition—one who already knows Bible stories and who wor-ships regularly—to acknowledge that it is one thing to know stories of faith heroes, but it is quite another to experience genuine faith. Faith is the highest passion, but how is such faith attained? For the receptive reader the book might initiate a quest with a seriousness of intent transcending the trivializing effect of those who would "go beyond faith".[37]

This is of course a fideistic commentary that takes Kierkegaard very much at his word concerning the various choices of existence. Thus it proceeds in accordance with his own directives as to how his texts should be read, what pur-poses governed his project from the outset, and where exactly the dividing-line falls between indirect ("aesthetic" or "reflective") productions and works of achieved religious inwardness or faith. By the same token—and likewise at Kierkegaard's behest— it implicitly reproves those non-compliant readers (Hegelians, aesthetes, romantic ironists, speculative thinkers of various persua-sion) who reject his advice and treat the entire authorship as fit material for sub-tilized techniques of interpretive self-evasion. What they ignore is the absolute requirement that one accept his strong providentialist account as offered in *The Point of View*, and that one not take refuge—like present-day sophisticates—in such notions as the "implied author" or "implied reader." For these again pro-vide any number of convenient bolt-holes for the secular exegete keen to avoid facing up to that moment of choice between the aesthetic, the ethical and the religious realms of existence.

And yet, as Kierkegaard is uncomfortably aware, his readers might be thought to have every excuse for missing the point, since the authorship pro-vides so many opportunities for communicative breakdown or cross-purpose understanding. Like some of Jesus' more cryptic parables, it seems wilfully designed to place obstacles in the way of those interpreters—the great majori-ty—who lack the prerequisite spiritual grace to divine its authentic meaning.[38] "To them that have, shall more be given; but from those that have not, shall that little they have be taken away." For it is a feature of apocalyptic writings in whatever (religious or quasi-secularized) mode that their truth is meant only for those few elect readers who are somehow already in possession of that truth as a matter of divinatory skill or hermeneutic foreknowledge. And in Kierkegaard's case this exclusion zone is drawn with uncommon severity and rigour. It applies not only to the unregenerate hedonists who preferred Volume One of *Either/Or* and whose interests were no doubt reflected in the much higher sales of that

volume when printed separately, as well as in the fact that one particular section
—the "Diary of a Seducer"—has on occasion been published as a separate text.
From Kierkegaard's viewpoint there is not much to choose between these seek-
ers after mere erotic titillation and those other, albeit more sophisticated types
who perversely insist on applying the wrong (i.e. aesthetic or literary) criteria
when they interpret his ethico-religious writings. They are all of them display-
ing that same disastrous failure to remark the qualitative shift that occurs—at
least on the fideist account —as Kierkegaard abandons his various techniques of
ironic, indirect or pseudonymous communication and engages his reader at the
level of authentic first-person address. Whatever their motive such readers place
themselves utterly beyond reach of Kierkegaard's redemptive ministry. And
they do so, he speculates, more often through excess of hermeneutic or interpretive subtlety than through sheer obtuseness or failure to grasp the plain sense of
what he is saying.

But there is a further problem here if the reader then asks what *authority*
Kierkegaard can offer for his claim that these texts give access to a truth, an
order of spiritual wisdom beyond any pleasures or stimulus to be had by reading
them as if they belonged to the aesthetic production. For that reader could
adduce several arguments in support of his or her revisionist stance. First (and
most familiar): Kierkegaard's declared intentions are not the last word on this
matter, since the authorship might always turn out to have meanings more
oblique, ambiguous or rewardingly complex than anything that Kierkegaard
overtly or willingly acknowledged. This standpoint is commonplace among literary critics though not so much among philosophers. Second: the very character of Kierkegaard's writings —their degree of rhetorical and narrative complexity—is such as to preclude any confident appeal to his governing purpose as
supposedly manifest in this or that passage of overt authorial comment. From
which it follows (third) that an ethics of reading gets no direct purchase on
Kierkegaard's work, since we may in fact do him an injustice—interpret that
work at less than its full creative or indeed philosophical stretch—if we privilege those passages of first-person statement that would narrow the range of
possibilities elsewhere.

Of course Kierkegaard *ipse* does everything in his power to represent this
as a bad-faith response, a retreat to aesthetic or literary grounds of judgment
which thereby disqualifies the reader from attaining a genuine understanding of
his work. But one could just as well argue that the principle of charity extends
to moral issues also, since Kierkegaard's writings and his troubled life-history
(in particular the break with his fiancée, Regina Olsen) scarcely make an edifying spectacle if one takes him at his word in *The Point of View*. For on this
account Kierkegaard, like Eliot's Tiresias, knew and foresuffered all that would
be subsequently enacted in the course of his dealings with Regina. It requires us

to believe that the whole sad affair—the courtship, the engagement, the self-lac-erating break—was embarked upon from the outset (like Kierkegaard's erotic, pseudonymous, or literary productions) as a kind of controlled experiment with the various possibilities of indirect discourse, an episode whose charms were coterminous with the "aesthetic" stage, and whose upshot marked his point of transition to authentic inwardness and faith. Thus Regina is to be sacrificed, like the Isaac of *Fear and Trembling*, in order that Kierkegaard/Abraham can there-by vindicate his own elect calling and his readiness to endure the utmost degree of moral and social disgrace in pursuit of that high vocation. All in all—and despite his fervent protestations to the contrary—one might feel justified on eth-ical as well as on aesthetic grounds in rejecting Kierkegaard's version of events and treating *The Point of View* as an ingenious piece of narrative fiction or (what amounts to much the same thing) as an *ex post facto* self-justifying account contrived to place a providentialist gloss on his own past actions.

This reading would of course go flat against Kierkegaard's claim to have been guided always—in every last detail of his life and authorship—by that supreme "governance" whose instrument and mouthpiece he aspired to become. But at least it would present him in a morally and humanly preferable light, that is to say, as having suffered these prophetic delusions only after the event, and not as having planned the whole episode with Regina as part of some mon-strously elaborate ruse under the pretext of divine guidance. Moreover, it would answer more fully to our sense that Kierkegaard is often saved from his own worst devices—from arrogance and self-righteous zeal—by precisely those "lit-erary" doubts and scruples that characterize the pseudonymous texts. This applies above all to *Fear and Trembling*, where Johannes de Silentio plays the role of doubting intermediary, and where the sheer inhuman harshness of Kierkegaard's teaching (his interpretation of the Abraham and Isaac narrative) is at least somewhat offset by the presence of one who confesses himself unable to fathom this mystery. With *The Point of View* likewise there is reason to main-tain (on what I have called this ethico-interpretive "principle of charity") that the work is better read with a measure of scepticism—of ironic reserve—as regards its more self-assured intentionalist claims. Only thus can one avoid attributing to Kierkegaard a degree of premeditated cruelty in his relations with Regina which finds a parallel in his willingness to seduce the reader through forms of cunningly contrived aesthetic beguilement which leave him or her per-petually at risk of nothing less than eternal damnation. Much better—one might think—to discount this protestation of divinely authorized purpose, and to regard all his works —the "edifying" discourses included—as subject to a high degree of motivational ambivalence.[39]

At least this approach will have much to recommend it for secular readers who remain unconvinced by his claim to speak as God's proxy, or as the voice of a "governance" whose purpose is at first revealed obscurely, through various devices of aesthetic indirection, and then—at the last—in the authentic accents of divine inspiration or a certain "apocalyptic tone". For it is only by invoking this God-given surety as the last refuge behind aesthetic appearances—as an ultimate source of meaning and truth beyond all the fallible devices of human understanding—that Kierkegaard can justify his having adopted such a range of seductive "literary" stratagems. Once remove that presumptive ground of appeal and the authorship will then be open to assessment in literary-aesthetic and secular-ethical terms. That is to say, we shall value it either for its brilliance of rhetorical and narrative execution, or—on the principle of charity—for the extent to which (borrowing a phrase from William Empson on Milton) Kierkegaard's intensely ambivalent moral feelings can be seen as "crying out" against the demands of his "appalling theology."[40] In fact these approaches—the aesthetic and the ethical—are by no means incompatible, despite his great effort (from the God's-eye perspective of achieved religious inwardness) to hold them apart as qualitatively distinct existential stages on life's way. For a secular criticism is perfectly entitled to reverse Kierkegaard's express order of priorities, to esteem the complications of his pseudonymous authorship, and to count it a positive virtue in narrators like Johannes de Silentio that they maintain such a doubting or ambiguous attitude in the face of those inhuman sacrificial demands that God places upon Abraham and Kierkegaard (not to mention Isaac and Regina). The "apocalyptic tone" would then figure as a species of destructive messianic delusion, albeit to some extent redeemed—in Kierkegaard's case—by the countervailing presence of an "implied author" whose feelings (and whose complex narrative strategies) are engaged to quite contrary effect. What is thereby lost to Kierkegaard in terms of his self-avowed governing purpose is more than made up for—so these critics might claim—by respecting not only the "literary" aspect of his work but also its range of ethical defences against that illusory voice of conscience.

IV

No doubt such a reading can easily lean over into the kind of all-forgiving yet ultimately cynical wisdom summed up in the tag *tout comprendre, c'est tout pardonner*. It can also give rise to that deconstructive variant which Paul de Man exploits to ingenious (if ethically dubious) effect in his rhetorical dismantling of the truth-claims advanced in a text like Rousseau's *Confessions*.[41] For according to de Man it is always the case that such discourse has a "literary" component, a tendency to generate narrative pretexts for the author to mount a self-admiring display of his or her exemplary readiness to confess. It is thus forever "undecidably" suspended between the factual and the fictive, the referential and the rhetorical, or the constative and performative modes of utterance. "There is never enough guilt around for the textual machine to excuse", no end of this desire—on the author's part—to recall (or invent) ever more shameful episodes whereby to exhibit his truth-telling credentials. But as the scandalous revelations pile up so the suspicion inevitably grows—"inevitably" at least on de Man's ultra-sceptical view—that what is offered is not so much a piece of honest self-reckoning as a roundabout means of excusing the utterer through the sheer weight of self-reproach. "The more there is to be exposed, the more there is to be ashamed of; the more resistance to exposure, the more satisfying the scene, and, especially, the more satisfying the revelation, in the later narrative, of the inability to reveal."[42] For one can never be sure of the speech-act genre to which such utterances belong; whether they are an instance of good-faith confession (owning up to some veritable fact of past experience), or whether—as de Man would more often have us believe—they are a fictive contrivance adopted for the sake of absolving the confessor from his present feelings of obscure and unfocused guilt. Thus it is possible "to face up to any experience (to excuse any guilt) because the experience always exists simultaneously as fictional discourse and as empirical event".[43] Moreover, when we read such narratives, "it is never possible to decide which possibility is the right one". In which case there is always the risk that such discourse "will indeed exculpate the confessor, thus making the confession (and the confessional text) redundant as it originates".[44]

In de Man's late (and so far unpublished) essay "The Concept of Irony" there is a curious—not to say outrageous—remark to the effect that the entire modern discipline of *Germanistik* grew out of a refusal to read Friedrich Schlegel's novel *Lucinde*.[45] What de Man has in mind, more generally, is the failure to engage with that vertiginous mixture of eroticism and romantic irony which Schlegel's interpreters had managed to contain by resorting to reductive (i.e. "thematic") modes of analysis, readings which ignored the spiralling complexity—the moments of rhetorical *mise-en-abyme*—engendered by the novel's endlessly shifting and elusive ironic stance. His point was aimed partly against proponents of "stable" irony like Wayne Booth, those who thought to offer a worked-out method, a set of interpretative techniques for reliably detecting the presence of ironic intent and thus convincing readers (themselves included) that they wouldn't be cast in the embarrassing role of victim, fall-guy, or dupe.[46] Such attempts would always fail, so de Man argued, when confronted with the kind of radically unstable irony exemplified not only in Schlegel's fiction but wherever language in its figural ("tropological") aspect threatened to exceed the interpreter's powers of self-assured hermeneutic grasp. But his hyperbolic claim about the avoidance of Schlegel among professional *Germanisten* would apply more justly to the way that Kierkegaard has been conspicuous by his absence in most quarters of present-day philosophico-literary debate. And the reasons, I think, have to do quite as much with the "apocalyptic tone" as with Kierkegaard's own propadeutic uses of irony—of that same seductive and dangerously potent resource—by way of countering adepts like Friedrich Schlegel.

This is not just an issue of two opposed styles (the ironic and apocalyptic) whose antagonism results from the former's appeal to an ethos of secularized sceptical doubt and the latter's to an order of religious or intuitive truth beyond the furthest reach of unaided human intellect. For one thing, the relationship between them is much more complex, making it often very difficult if not impossible to tell (as with Kierkegaard) whether a statement is intended ironically or whether it issues—as we are meant to believe—from some transcendent source of self-authorized meaning and truth. For another, there is a sense in which all understanding of language, philosophical and literary alike, is caught up in this tension between what Derrida calls "hyperbole and finite structure".[47] Booth's idea of "stable irony"—and the problems he encounters in making it stick —can then be understood as a hard-pressed attempt to contain such exorbitant linguistic perspectives (ironic and apocalyptic alike) within a reassuring framework that allows the interpreter to ignore their more wayward or unsettling implications. It is in this sense that, in Derrida's words, "a certain structuralism has always been philosophy's most spontaneous gesture".[48] But at the same time philosophers—like literary theorists—have often been aware of that within language which cannot be brought under adequate concepts or reduced to the order of some abstract explanatory paradigm. This issue has been joined by just about every party to the long-running debate between philosophy and literature down through the history of western thought. Such was Plato's quarrel with the poets, his reproach that they substituted mere inspiration (along with delinquent figures like metaphor and allegory) for the serious business of philosophic argument and truth-seeking enquiry. That Plato himself made liberal use of those figures—not to mention other such "literary" devices as dialogue, mimesis, myth, imagery, personification, etc.—is of course one of the puzzles that have exercised his commentators from Philip Sidney to Iris Murdoch and Derrida. The "ancient quarrel" was resumed by Aristotle, who found more reason to respect poetry for its different kind of truth-telling virtue, but who did so strictly on the terms laid down by his commitment to a methodological ideal of high formalist rigour. Thereafter it was mainly theorists of the sublime—from Longinus to Shelley and their latest postmodern progeny—who contested that approach in a language much given to apocalyptic tonings and gestures.[49]

But the issue, as I say, is one that recurs in a range of philosophical contexts beyond this debate between classicism and romanticism as rival interpretive paradigms. It is often within reach of the larger question: how far is it possible to theorize (or conceptualize) the conditions of possibility for language, given the excess—the creative surplus—of *parole* over *langue*, or of utterer's meaning over that which (in some sense) precedes and enables every act of utterance? Nowadays this question is posed most acutely in the wake of Saussure's influential re-statement of linguistic aims and priorities. But it remains problematic for those (like Chomsky) who reject a good deal of Saussure's theoretical programme, and who would shift the emphasis from *langue* to *parole*, or from language considered in its abstract generality to language as a matter of speakerly "competence", of the way that speakers can generate a huge (potentially infinite) range of well-formed grammatical utterances from a finite stock of "deep" syntactic structures.[50] For this still gives rise to a version of the old freewill/determinism issue, a problem—to put it very crudely —in reconciling Chomsky's account of these ultimately rule-governed (recursive) structures with our intuitive sense of what it actual feels like to talk straight ahead and sort out the grammar as we go along.[51] As with Saussure— who is quite explicit on this point—the antinomies are not so much resolved or transcended as conveniently shelved for the purpose of attaining a clearer, more adequate explanatory grasp. But they are always liable to resurface and generate perplexity at the level of reflective philosophical thought. Under various descriptions—*langue* and *parole*, structure and genesis, system and meaning, "indicative" and "expressive" signs—they constitute the range of binary terms that figure so often as problematic *topoi* in Derrida's early books and essays.[52] Thus the "apocalyptic tone" is just one example—albeit an extreme case—of the tension that exists between "hyperbole and finite structure", or the individual speech-act (idiomatically construed) and those constitutive structures— whether of Saussure's *la langue* or Chomsky's "competence"—that presumably subtend every such utterance.

Of course, it is not a question, for philosophy at least, of simply choosing one or the other perspective. Like Kant's antinomies (or their Derridean equivalent, the aporias discovered in a deconstructive reading) they each follow by the strictest necessity from certain likewise ineliminable presuppositions about the topic in hand. All the same it is difficult not to pose the issue in terms of an either/or choice between alternate possibilities, in consequence of which there have emerged entire schools of philosophico-linguistic thought. That is to say, language can either be conceived (on the structuralist-systemic model) as a closed repertoire of signifying elements, a purely differential economy of sound and sense, or again (following the expressivist or phenomenological path) as a field of open-ended creative possibility where every new utterance somehow transcends those structures of in-place meaning. On the first view it is assumed that any adequate linguistic theory will have to go by way of a structuralist ascesis which, faithful to Saussure, treats language as an object of scientific study and which thus—for this purpose—brackets all questions of speaker's intent, context of utterance, idiomatic variations, linguistic creativity, etc. On the second (adopted sometimes by Husserl but also, more consistently, by Merleau-Ponty) it is only by taking account of those moments of expressive transcendence—the way that meaning surpasses or exceeds all the limits of pre-constituted sense—that philosophy can do justice to language and other forms of human creative potential.[53]

> The relief and design of structures [Derrida writes] appears more clearly when content, which is the living energy of meaning, is neutralized. Somewhat like the architecture of an uninhabited or deserted city, reduced to its skeleton by some catastrophe of nature or art. A city no longer inhabited, not simply left behind, but haunted by meaning and culture.[54]

But we would be wrong, he cautions, to set this up as a straightforward conflict of interpretations between structuralism (or the tyranny of concepts) on the one hand and phenomenology (or the claims of creative transcendence) on the other. For what emerges from Derrida's reading of Saussure and Husserl—taking these as the most "advanced" and "rigorous" proponents of each tradition—is the fact that their projects exist in a relationship of close and reciprocal dependence, each of them deconstructing the other's preconceptions through a process of mutual interrogative exchange.

Thus "[b]y virtue of its innermost intention, and like all questions about language, structuralism escapes the classical history of ideas which already presupposes structuralism's possibility, for the latter naively belongs to the province of language and propounds itself within it".[55] And again: "[i]t is always something like an opening which will frustrate the structuralist project...What I can never understand, in a structure, is that by means of which it is not closed."[56] This impossibility of closure has to do with the expressive surplus in language—the movement beyond all pre-given codes and structures of signification—which involves an appeal to intention or utterer's meaning, and which therefore cannot be interpreted (much less conceptualized) according to the *a priori* dictates of structuralist method. All of which might well appear, on a cursory reading, to place Derrida very firmly in the phenomenological camp. But it is also the case—as argued in his various writings on Husserl—that the project of Transcendental Phenomenology must itself have recourse to certain structuralist (or proto-structuralist) concepts if it is to offer any workable account of how language articulates those meanings in the public sphere of communicative utterance. Husserl may have wished—and explicitly required—that "expressive" signs should take priority over mere "indicative" uses of language, since the former are genuinely meaningful (imbued, so to speak, with the animating spirit of utterer's intent), while the latter belong to a lifeless realm of conventionalized routine signification.[57] However, this distinction proves impossible to maintain, since it is precisely by virtue of its "indicative" aspect—its partaking of a generalized "iterability" or capacity to communicate meaning quite aside from any present intention in the utterer's mind—that language exists as a medium of public (intersubjective) exchange. If expression *always and everywhere* exceeds the limits of structural analysis—and this by an intrinsic necessity of language—still there is no escaping the converse conclusion: that expressive signs can only acquire meaning as elements in a pre-given structural economy of differential terms and relationships.

In short, Husserl "had to navigate between the Scylla and Charybdis of logicizing structuralism and psychologistic geneticism." His project required that he open up "a new direction of philosophical attention", one that might permit the "discovery of a concrete, but nonempirical, intentionality, a 'transcendental experience' which would be 'constitutive', that is, like all intentionality, simultaneously productive and revelatory, active and passive".[58] Which brings us back to the apocalyptic tone and its role as a standing provocation to philosophy. A "provocation", that is, in the twofold sense that it calls forth enquiry into issues of language, meaning, utterer's intention, "expressive" *vis-à-vis*, "indicative" signs, etc, and also that it conjures up deep-laid anxieties concerning philosophy's competence to resolve or adequately address those issues. For the antinomies that characterize language as conceived by Husserl—"simultaneously productive and revelatory, active and passive"—are those that emerge to more disquieting effect when language takes the apocalyptic turn toward a mode of utterance that seemingly defies all the normative constraints upon good-faith rational discourse. Hence (as I have argued) the "ancient quarrel" between philosophy and poetry, one that rumbles on in our current faculty wars and whose echoes are clearly audible when a thinker like Habermas reproaches Derrida for wilfully blurring that genre distinction, or for allowing language in its poetic ("world-disclosive") aspect to override the interests of conceptual clarity and reasoned philosophical debate. What Habermas chiefly objects to— like Plato before him—is the idea of a language "simultaneously productive and revelatory, active and passive", or laying claim to an order of imaginative truth beyond any appeal to utterer's intent or suchlike regulative notions. It is one thing for poets to enjoy a certain privilege in this matter of not knowing precisely what they mean, or not always meaning precisely what they say. But it is quite another—so Habermas maintains—for philosophers (or those who abuse that title) to comport themselves stylistically in a way that insinuates doubts as to just who is speaking and with what argumentative warrant.

This is Derrida's theme in the essay that I mentioned earlier, "Of an Apocalyptic Tone Recently Adopted in Philosophy."[59] The title is taken over in modified form from a little-known pamphlet by Kant, "Von einem neuerdings erhobenen vornehmen Ton in der Philosophie." The word "apocalyptic" might seem a loose—not to say a downright tendentious—rendering of what appears in the latest English translation as a "newly raised superior" tone. But this is one of Derrida's points in the essay: that when Kant attacks the purveyors of apocalypse, the fake illuminati, the mystagogues, adepts and apostles of the inner light, he is also attacking their lordly pretensions and their refusal to abide by the civilized rules of open democratic debate.[60] Thus, they "scoff at work, the concept, schooling: to what is given they believe they have access effortlessly, gracefully, intuitively or through genius, outside of school". (Derrida, *Apocalyptic Tone*, p. 34) It is on these grounds that Habermas criticizes Derrida: for breaking faith with the entire post-Kantian tradition of enlightenment thought—the "philosophical discourse of modernity"—and thereby reverting to what he (Habermas) regards as a species of irrationalist mystery-mongering.[61] It takes no very subtle or sagacious reading to perceive this as the polemical subtext of Derrida's essay, a strategy that would substitute Habermas for Kant, or—not to personalize the issue quite so crudely—which would play off the present-day upholders of enlightenment against the "apocalyptic tone" in its latest modality. Thus everything that Kant has to say about Jacobi and other such perverters of reason and truth is reproduced point for point in the charge-sheet that Habermas draws up by way of countering deconstruction and its supposedly malign influence.[62] That he gets Derrida wrong on just about every issue—relying for the most part on secondary sources or a cursory reading of the texts in question—is a case that I have argued at length elsewhere and which Derrida presents most forcefully in his "Afterword: toward an ethic of discussion".[63] At the moment my concern is not so much with the philosophic rights and wrongs of this quarrel as with Derrida's oblique re-staging of it through the return to Kant and his *Auseinandersetzung* with an earlier phase of counter-enlightenment thought. For in all the vast corpus of Derrida's writings to date there is no other text that engages so revealingly with the "apocalyptic tone" and its unsettling effect on the discourse of self-assured reason and truth.

This is *not* to say—as a simplified reading might have it—that Derrida sides with Jacobi as against Kant, or with those who would appeal to the privilege of genius (of intuitive or revelatory access to truth) as against the merely prosaic virtues of conceptual exegesis and critique. After all, in Derrida's words, paraphrasing Kant:

> [t]he hierarchized opposition of gift to work, of intuition to concept, of genius's mode to scholar's mode…is homologous to the opposition between aristocracy and democracy, eventually between demagogic oligarchy and authentic rational democracy. Masters and slaves: the overlord reaches with a leap and through feeling what is immediately given him; the people work, elaborate, conceive. (Derrida, *Apocalyptic Tone*, p. 34)

Of course it will be pointed out (with some justice) that this passage —like so much else in the essay—exploits a kind of ventriloquist effect, an instance of *oratio obliqua* (or free indirect style) that cannot reliably be taken as expressing Derrida's thoughts on the matter, any more than is the case with Kierkegaard's pseudonymous writings. Which is also to say, in Habermasian terms, that this discourse mixes up the genres of philosophy and literature, that it exploits the so-called "apocalyptic tone" as a pretext for not responsibly meaning what it says or saying what it means. Here again Kant's polemic prefigures the issue between Habermas and Derrida. What he finds so irksome in the mystagogues is their habit of constantly "raising the tone" to a pitch of quasi-sublime inspirational address where it becomes impossible to determine who is speaking, or how far the utterance takes rise from a realm of cryptic intertextual citations. For nothing is more elusive—and more resistant to philosophical treatment— than this question of the tonal nuances and differences that inhabit every discourse beyond a certain point of rhetorical complexity.

On the standard view such problems can safely be assigned to the margins of philosophy, or to those (maybe in departments of rhetoric, comparative literature, or the history of ideas) who are simply not up to the serious business of first-order philosophic argument. This was clearly Kant's attitude and it is one that lives on among a good few subscribers to the current analytic line. "Through what is called neutrality of tone, philosophical discourse must also guarantee the neutrality or at least the imperturbable serenity that should accompany the relation to the true and the universal." (Derrida, *Apocalyptic Tone*, p. 29) Which means that philosophy should have no truck with those tonal perturbations—those voices of unassignable origin —that might otherwise call its authority into doubt. For one would then have to raise quite a number of difficult questions concerning (for instance) the operative difference between citation, paraphrase and satire in Derrida's treatment of Kant, or the problem of ascertaining where Kant himself passes over from a rehearsal of the "apocalyptic tone" to a satire on its lordly pretensions. What if Kant were less in control of this parodic performance—along with all its tonal ambiguities—than he and the mainstream exegetes would have us believe? What if it should turn out that those "partisans of intellectual intuition", before and after Kant, were not so much lacking or ignoring the lesson of his critical philosophy as perceiving an unresolved issue at its very heart, the issue that Kant himself attempted to cordon off in his treatment of the aesthetic sublime as a modality of somehow (paradoxically) "judging without concepts"? And again: what if the "apocalyptic tone" were just an extreme (hyperbolic) instance of the problem that philosophy has always confronted in accounting for its own authoritative voice, its privileged relation to truth?

From Plato to Habermas, these questions have been posed most often in relation to a certain idea of literature (or poetry) as that which speaks in an alien voice, which threatens to disrupt the composure of philosophical discourse, and must therefore be kept off bounds for the purposes of genuine truth-seeking thought. But their insistence on the point—like Kant's anxiety to discredit the apocalyptic tone—is evidence enough that this insecurity is not so easily laid to rest. Will it always be possible, Derrida asks, "to listen to or detect the tone of a philosopher, or rather (this precision is important) the so-called or would-be philosopher?" (Derrida, *Apocalyptic Tone*, p. 29) The usual response—spelled out most explicitly in John Searle's rejoinder to Derrida—is to assert "yes indeed", and back up the claim by invoking criteria of good-faith utterance, serious intent, speech-act felicity, philosophic competence, etc.[64] These criteria are then taken as adequate grounds for excluding certain parties (e. g. Derrida) from the forum of qualified professional debate. And they are also tacitly invoked when it comes to deciding—in the case of (say) Wittgenstein or Austin—which passages should be read as "seriously" meant, as expressing the author's considered or principled views, and which as examples of language "going on holiday" (in Wittgenstein's phrase), or of its tendency in Austin to generate puzzles which speech-act theory should supposedly resolve.

This is not the place for a detailed exposition of Derrida's exchange with Searle. Sufficient to say that it creates real problems—and problems that Austin was himself quick to recognize—with any direct appeal to context, utterer's meaning or authorial intent as criteria for settling such issues.[65] Other commentators (Shoshana Felman on Austin and Henry Staten on Wittgenstein) have shown to what extent the texts of so-called "ordinary language" philosophy are capable of a reading markedly at odds with the mainstream interpretive view.[66] Nor are such readings—as Searle would have it—mere instances of the bad habit, among literary theorists, of ignoring the plain sense of things and cultivating puzzles and perplexities just for the hell of it. On the contrary: they play the orthodox interpreters clean off the field not only by virtue of their greater attentiveness to "literary" nuances of style, metaphor, irony, oblique narrative voice, intertextual allusion and so forth, but also on account of their raising questions—eminently philosophical questions—with regard to the conditions of possibility for a worked-out theory of speech-act implicature. And among those questions perhaps the most crucial is that of Austin's (or Wittgenstein's) tonal range, their adoption of numerous—so to speak —ventriloquist devices by way of conducting an unmarked dialogue between the various viewpoints on offer.

Of course there is no genuine problem here for those who assuredly know in advance what Austin has to say about the criteria for good-faith performative utterance, or what Wittgenstein thought on the topic of private languages. But in each case there is enough disagreement—both among the commentators and between discrepant passages of the original text —to suggest that this assurance is somewhat misplaced. Moreover, it is precisely in the matter of tone (or of knowing what should count as "serious", good-faith utterance) that their writings solicit such diverse interpretations. For, as Derrida remarks, "a tone can be mimicked, feigned, faked...I shall go as far as to say *synthesized*". And again:

> a tone can be taken, and taken from the other. To change voice or mimick the intonation of the other, one must be able to confuse or induce a confusion between two voices, two voices of the other and, necessarily, of the other within oneself. (Derrida, *Apocalyptic Tone*, p. 34)

Such was Plato's charge against the poets: that they feigned all manner of authoritative utterance (knowledge by acquaintance, by reason, or sheer unaided intuition) while offering not the least show of proof that they actually knew what they were talking about. And for Kant likewise the "apocalyptic tone" was just the kind of shifty rhetorical ruse—along with metaphor and other such figural diversions—that permitted philosophers (or pseudo-philosophers) to evade the requirements of good-faith rational debate. These charlatans "play the overlord" and "give themselves airs" by thus setting up, in oracular style, to pronounce upon matters that exceed the competence of even the best, most competent philosophical minds. For according to Kant in his essay *The Conflict of the Faculties*, philosophy has its place in the parliament of reason as belonging to the "lower" faculty, the tribunal concerned strictly with issues of theoretical truth and falsehood.[67] It is thereby distinguished from those other disciplines (theology preeminent among them, but also medicine and law) which occupy the "higher" faculty, and whose role it is to adjudicate on questions "most serious for existence".

Of course it may be argued that Kant is just pretending here; that he means us to read between the lines (as it were) and make allowance for the pressures of renewed political and religious censorship that were coming into force at the time when he wrote this essay. Indeed, it is almost impossible to read such utterances straight if one considers how far Kant's critical philosophy extends beyond the limits of "theoretical" enquiry in this restrictive sense of the term. In which case the text should perhaps be read as a satire on those in authority (the politicians, theologians, and censors) who might be so simple-minded as to take its pronouncements at face value. But then there is the problem—familiar from Austin—of maintaining any firm or principled distinction between constative and performative modes of discourse. For on Kant's submission it is the privilege of those in the "higher" faculty to "represent the power whose official instrument they are", and thus to promulgate edicts or laws in the name of that authorizing power. That is to say, they possess the performative warrant to enforce or legitimize such sovereign commands. Philosophy, on the other hand, "has the right to inspect everything touching on the truth of theoretical (constative) propositions but no power to give orders". (Derrida, *Apocalyptic Tone*, p. 35) In the parliament of reason it "occupies the bench on the left", by which Kant means—in a usage dating from the French revolutionary epoch and still current today—the role of those who criticize government in a freely dissenting but non-executive capacity. Where the mystagogues give most offence is therefore by "hoist[ing] themselves above their colleagues or comrades", and "wrong[ing] them in their inalienable right to freedom and equality regarding everything touching on reason alone" (Derrida, *Apocalyptic Tone*, p. 35). For such presumption not only deprives philosophy of its proper (critical or dissident) voice vis-à-vis the dictates of established authority and power; it also runs the risk that philosophy will be subject to further—more repressive or arbitrary—forms of censorship on account of its straying across this line between the constative and performative domains.

As I say, there is good reason to suppose that Kant is not entirely in earnest when he counsels philosophers to accept this rather shuffling and evasive *modus vivendi*. All the same it is an attitude not without parallel in the present-day context of government concern to dissuade intellectuals from confusing their proper vocation (their scholarly, academic or specialized business) with matters of a wider socio-political import. Hence—among other things—the revived fashion for those "end-of-ideology" arguments which first broke surface in the late-50s climate of intensified Cold-War propaganda, and which have lately been deployed to much the same effect by ideologues of a "New World Order" premised on the global triumph of capitalist liberal democracy.[69] Such writings display what can only be described as an inverse relation between the pressures of ideological recruitment that bring them into being and the overt protestations of neutrality, disinterest, scholarly objectivity etc, that make up their rhetorical stock-in-trade. In other words they exemplify—in almost pathological form— that confusion between the constative and performative modes that Kant thinks so harmful to philosophy. And yet there is a sense in which Kant's own writings prefigure this current sleight of hand by advising (with whatever ironic or duplicitous intent) that philosophers stick to their appointed sphere and not allow their thinking to be compromised by linkage with any such extraneous interests. For those interests can all the more easily be smuggled in under cover of a rhetoric that professes the virtues of critical detachment or a strictly non-partisan devotion to reason and truth. Which is also to say that the exercise of power in its linguistic (performative) aspect is never more subtly efficacious than when joined to a philosophy—or an ideology—that admits of no dealing with such practical affairs.

V

Derrida has made this point in a number of essays examining the kinship between Kant's doctrine of the faculties—especially his idea of aesthetic disinterest as a touchstone of reason in its "pure" or politically disengaged form—and the way that this doctrine persists in the modern division of intellectual labour (university departments or research-programmes) into so-called "pure" and "applied" disciplines.[69] For it is always the case that this distinction can be seen to break down when set against the sheer multiplicity of interests—government funding, research grants, peer-group review, incentives or disincentives of various kinds—which motivate scholars even in the humanities (and even, as Derrida remarks at one point, in fields like linguistics, semiotics, or literary theory). To put it simply: why would —for instance—the US Navy invest in such a range of unlikely research projects if not with a view to certain "deferred profits" or the possibility (however remote) of long-term practical yield? In short, there is a good deal of mystification about Kant's doctrine of the faculties, whether construed in terms of his critical philosophy as a teaching with regard to the well-regulated uses of reason, or again—with reference to his other, more exoteric works—as addressing philosophy's public role and its relation to the modern (faculty-based) system of school or university education. Derrida's essays are very much concerned with these wider pedagogical issues, especially in the context of French government moves to reduce the amount of philosophy teaching at *lycée* or secondary-school level. For this question of the "right to philosophy"—who is qualified to teach it, to study it (and from what "proper" age), or to pronounce with authority in its name—is always within reach of the Kantian claim for philosophy's imperative (but duly circumscribed) entitlement to speak on matters of public concern.

It is also bound up with the "apocalyptic tone" and Kant's abhorrence of that tone when it intrudes upon the discourse of philosophic reason. What provokes his indignation—as we have seen—is the fact that these charlatans bring philosophy into disrepute by thus laying claim to powers and prerogatives that don't rightfully belong to them. Moreover, they invite an ever-ready suspicion among those in power (a suspicion voiced preemptively by Plato, Kant and Habermas) that such arrogant liberties of tone or style go along with a will to subvert all forms of orderly civic existence. "This leap toward the imminence of a vision without concept, this impatience turned toward the most crypted secret sets free a poetico-metaphorical overabundance." And again:

> Not only do they [the adepts of this tone] confuse the voice of the oracle with that of reason. They do not distinguish either between pure speculative reason and pure practical reason; they believe they *know* what is solely *thinkable* and reach through

feeling alone the universal laws of practical reason. (Derrida, *Apocalyptic Tone*, p. 37)

Here again we are very close to Habermas's insistence on the bad consequences—philosophical, ethical and socio-political—that must flow from any attempt (like Derrida's, as Habermas construes it) to dissolve the generic boundary-distinction between philosophy and literature. Nor are such anxieties altogether unfounded, as Derrida would himself be quick to concede. For we should be wrong to think that this issue of the apocalyptic tone is one that philosophers have blown up out all proportion, or that it is only of pressing concern to those—like Kant and Habermas—who take a highly compartmentalized view of philosophy's proper scope and remit. On the contrary: what sets Derrida apart from Jean-François Lyotard and other celebrants of the postmodern sublime is his refusal to issue apocalyptic statements about the "end of modernity", the demise of enlightenment reason, or other such modish *idées reçues*.

This refusal was already quite explicit in his essay "The Ends of Man" (1968), where Derrida took issue with the then emergent strain of antihumanist or counter-enlightenment rhetoric.[70] But it should be evident to any careful reader of his work that he insists always on *thinking through* the antinomies of philosophic discourse, and not—like the current postmodernists—treating them as so many welcome pretexts for dancing on modernity's grave. Nor is this position abandoned when Derrida takes stock of the "apocalyptic tone", its various performative or speech-act modalities, and its challenge to the more questionable certitudes of Kantian thought. Thus: "[w]e cannot and we must not— this is a law and a destiny—forego the *Aufklärung*, in other words, what imposes itself as the enigmatic desire for vigilance, for the lucid vigil, for elucidation, for critique, and truth". (Derrida, *Apocalyptic Tone*, p. 51) And this principle holds even if such truth can be shown, as the sentence continues, to "keep within itself some apocalyptic desire, this time as desire for clarity and revelation". On the one hand there is no conceiving of enlightenment—of the access to truth through reason or critique—without at the same time conceiving that truth as somehow revealed to the knower's mind in a state of receptive grace, or through some form of intellectual intuition. But it is equally the case—as Kant argues—that such appeals must always be suspect, issuing as they do from a source of self-authorized inward conviction which respects none of the established procedures for assessing their validity-claims.

Hence the well-known problems with Plato's epistemology, his idea of knowledge as arrived at both through *anamnesis* (the "unforgetting" of truths once known to the soul before its fall into mortal ignorance) and also as determined through a process of reasoned dialectical exchange. These are not the kinds of problem that can be made to disappear by any sorting-out of logical grammar or Wittgensteinian recourse to "ordinary language" as a happy deliverance from all our self-induced puzzles and perplexities. They are installed at the heart of philosophical enquiry despite all the various attempts to resolve them from one or another perspective. What Derrida brings out is the impossibility of maintaining a firm, categorical distinction between these orders of discourse, as Kant wished to do and as other philosophers—from Plato to Habermas—have likewise strenuously argued. Their metaphorical kinship is enough to suggest that terms like "enlightenment" and "revelation" (or "clarity" and "vision") cannot be rigorously held apart through any such act of a priori stipulative judgment, And this applies just as much to the present-day issue between those (like Habermas) who would seek to defend the "philosophic discourse of modernity" and those whom they regard—wrongly in Derrida's case—as betrayers of that same tradition. Thus, in Derrida's words,

> Kant speaks of modernity, and of the mystagogues of his time, but...it could be demonstrated that today every slightly organized discourse is found or claims to be found on both sides, alternately or simultaneously...Each of us is the mystagogue and the *Aufklärer* of another. (Derrida, *Apocalyptic Tone*, p. 45).

And he further suggests that his audience will surely perceive, "without [my] having to designate explicitly, name, or draw out all the threads, how many transpositions we could indulge in on the side of *our* so-called modernity". (Derrida, *Apocalyptic Tone*, p. 45). His aim here is not (or not only) to turn the tables on those—like Habermas—who would play the *Aufklärer* to his (Derrida's) typecast role as heir to the "mystagogues" or perverters of reason. Rather, it is to show how every such appeal to enlightenment as a source of countervailing truth- and validity-claims will always at some point have recourse to a language that (metaphorically or implicitly) invokes the "apocalyptic tone".

No doubt it is naive to suppose—as some have understood Derrida to argue —that *just because* many philosophical concepts can be shown to derive from forgotten or sublimated metaphors (including the very terms "concept" and "metaphor"), *therefore* philosophy is metaphorical through and through, or just a "kind of writing" that chooses to forget its own mythologico-poetic origins. For these figures of thought can always be taken up into other, more specialized (philosophical or scientific) registers where they perhaps retain something of their original sense but acquire along with it a genuine cognitive, conceptual or explanatory force. Besides, as Derrida points out, any discussion of metaphor— including such claims for its omnipresence within philosophy—will necessarily draw upon *concepts* of metaphor that have been elaborated by philosophers from Aristotle down, or else by rhetoricians and literary theorists whose thinking is still a part of that same tradition.[71] So we get Derrida wrong if we take him to be arguing simply that "all concepts are metaphors", all philosophy a species of literature, all truth-claims merely a form of rhetorical or fictive imposition, etc. And the same applies to those kindred pairs of quasi-antithetical terms—enlightenment/revelation, constative/performative, reason/intuition and their various cognates—whose structural genealogy Derrida traces in Kant's riposte to the mystagogues. For here also it is not so much a question of collapsing the difference between them as of perceiving the *internal* fault-lines that exist on both sides of this dispute. Hence what he calls the "old solidarity of these antagonists or protagonists", the way that each draws upon the other's metaphorical and conceptual resources while continuing to denounce its imperious truth-claims.

We have seen this already in Derrida's reading of Husserl, more specifically, in his demonstration of the problems that arise when Husserl strives to justify his *de iure* distinction between "expressive" and "indicative" signs.[72] What prevents him from so doing—on the *de facto* evidence supplied by certain crucial passages in his own text—is the impossibility of drawing that distinction with the degree of conceptual or philosophic rigour that Husserl himself explicitly requires. The point will perhaps bear repeating here since it clarifies much of what Derrida has to say about the "apocalyptic tone" and its relation to the discourse of Kantian enlightened critique. If the expressive dimension of language must in some sense be thought of as surpassing the indicative (structural) aspect, and thus as exceeding all the bounds of conceptual accountability, then it is also the case—conversely—that this indicative dimension is the *condition of possibility* for language in general, expressive signs included. But one cannot make sense of this latter requirement without once again encountering the limits of any such structuralist project, the moment when critical reflection discovers the "absolute, principled and rigorous impossibility of closing a structural phenomenology". For it is only in so far as utterer's meaning transcends those pregiven structures of sense that language can communicate anything beyond the banalities of routine (indicative) exchange.

In which case, Derrida asks, "wouldn't the apocalyptic be a transcendental condition of all discourse, of all experience even, of every mark or every trace? And the genre of writings called 'apocalyptic' in the strict sense, then, would be only an example, an exemplary revelation of this transcendental structure" (Derrida, *Apocalyptic Tone*, p. 57). For what the discourse of apocalypse gives us to think is the way that *all* language—every instance of expressive utterance—means something more than could ever be grasped through a structural or a rigorously theorized phenomenological account of its signifying forms and modalities. Moreover, this follows necessarily from the kind of transcendental deduction that Kant (and Husserl after him) regarded as a precondition for establishing the validity of any such enterprise. That it turns out to generate certain unresolvable aporias in the project of phenomenological enquiry is not to say that this project is misguided, or that they might be laid to rest by some further effort of conceptual clarification. Rather, these problems will always reemerge when philosophy reflects on the strictly aporetic relation between language conceived as a realm of open-ended expressive possibility and language as a domain of pre-constituted signifying structures. The apocalyptic genre, as Derrida describes it, is therefore a striking (if exorbitant) case of this "exemplary revelation" which disconcerts the more self-assured projects of structural linguistics, speech-act theory, or transcendental phenomenology.

One likely objection at this point is that Derrida is playing fast and loose with the term 'transcendental'. Thus he seems to be using it both in the technical, Kantian sense ("predicable of all categories", or "presupposed by any act of judgment") and also in the sense more familiar to mystics and adepts of a spiritual wisdom "transcending" the powers of plain-prose reason. So it is—the objector might claim—that Derrida can pass off his otherwise patently absurd line of argument concerning the affinity (or deep-laid collusion) between the "lucid vigil" of enlightenment thought and the visionary transports of apocalypse. It would amount to nothing more than a species of metaphorical free association, or a deconstructive variant of the age-old fallacy (the so-called "proof by etymology") that thinks to uncover deep philosophical truths by delving back into the remote pre-history of this or that privileged lexical item. To accuse Derrida of promoting this mystified jargon of authenticity is to ignore—among other things—his express reservations with regard to such thinking in the essay "White Mythology", and his various criticisms of Heidegger on precisely that account.[73] What he does seek to show is the way that certain (seemingly antithetical) topoi—like the two meanings of "transcendence" or the "end of philosophy" as it figures in the discourse of apocalypse but also, just as insistently, in Kantian thought—are in fact more closely related than appears on the standard (doxographic) account. Thus:

> [i]f Kant denounces those who proclaim that philosophy has been at an end for two thousand years, he has himself, in marking a limit, indeed the end of a certain type of metaphysics, freed another wave of eschatological discourses in philosophy. His progressivism, his belief in the future of a certain philosophy, indeed of another metaphysics, is not contradictory to this proclamation of ends and of the end. (Derrida, *Apocalyptic Tone*, p. 48)

For it is possible to demonstrate, on Derrida's submission, that for every prominent item in the discourse of Kantian enlightenment critique there is not only an analogous metaphor but a corresponding strategy of argument deployed by those who lay claim to a knowledge that transcends all the limits of reason. And this applies no less to the "transcendental" turn which stands as one of

Kant's most distinctive contributions to philosophic thought. Here also, what is revealed—in Kant as in Husserl—is the strict impossibility that reason alone should provide the ultimate self-justifying ground for its own legislative truth-claims.[74]

Of course it is the case—as Derrida would not deny—that Kant's entire project in the three *Critiques* (and also in polemical writings like his essay "Of an Apocalyptic Tone") was aimed toward establishing lines of demarcation between the faculties of pure reason, theoretical understanding, practical reason, and aesthetic judgment, each assigned to its own legitimate domain. And this in turn means the end of a certain mode of philosophizing: namely, that of speculative metaphysics in its pre-critical or conceptually overweening form.[75] But there is—one might think—all the difference in the world between talk of closure that promises a new (more constructive) beginning and that which proclaims an end to every notion of enlightened, truth-seeking thought. Again, Derrida acknowledges the point and doesn't for one moment ask us to view them as minor variations on the same underlying theme. Enlightenment is not an option in the sense that one could choose—reasonably or responsibly choose —to reject all its critical imperatives and bid farewell to the philosophic discourse of modernity. "No doubt", Derrida writes, "one can think—I do—that this demystification must be led as far as possible, and the task is not modest." Indeed, "it is interminable, because no one can exhaust the overdeterminations and the indeterminations of the apocalyptic stratagems". (Derrida, *Apocalyptic Tone*, p. 59) Critique is always necessary since without it—if thinking is persuaded to suspend its "lucid vigil"—then the claimants to revealed truth can impose all manner of dogmatic falsehood (or morally repugnant doctrine) in the name of some god-given superior wisdom. But it will underestimate the adversary discourse (and also risk falling into its own kind of dogmatism) if it fails to acknowledge these "stratagems" and "overdeterminations" that complicate the issue between them.

Such, as I have argued, is the case with Kierkegaard's *Fear and Trembling*, a text whose humanly appalling implications are to some extent qualified—if not countermanded—by the presence of a doubting or reflective narrator. But the problem is more acute with those varieties of postmodern thought which raise the quasi-Kantian sublime into a principle of absolute heterogeneity between various language games, speech-act genres, ethical codes, etc.[76] For the upshot of this ultra-relativist stance is to leave moral judgement suspended over the void of an ultimate undecidability, a situation where nothing could possibly count as a valid reason for or against any given ethical commitment. Lyotard provides a set-piece example when questioned by his interlocutor (Jean-Loup Thébaud) as to whether he condoned the action of the Baader-Meinhof group in murdering a West German industrialist on account of his complicity (as they saw it) with the military-industrial complex and the agencies of state-sponsored violence.[77] Or again: did he think it wrong that the resources of a German computer network should be placed at the disposal of US surveillance and intelligence-gathering operations? "Yes, absolutely", Lyotard responds. "I can say that this is my opinion. I feel committed in this respect."[78] But when Thébaud (very reasonably) presses the issue a bit further—requesting that Lyotard support his "opinion" with at least some show of argued or principled justification—then the dialogue runs up against a sheer brick wall. "If you ask me why I am on that side, I think that I would answer that I do not have an answer to the question "why" and that this is of the order of...transcendence."[79] Not of course in any religious or quasi-mystical sense of the word, he hastens to assure us, but in the sense that—with a glance toward the Kantian sublime—"[w]hen I say 'transcendence' it means: I do not know who is sending me the prescription in question".[80] True to his own postmodernist lights Lyotard insists on the absolute incommensurability of "language games" and the mistake—indeed, the manifest injustice—of supposing that any one such game (e.g. the cognitivist discourse of factual warrant or liberal-enlightenment talk of "reasons" or "principles") could rightly set up as judge of any other. For in so doing we suppress the "differend" or the point at issue between them, and thus inflict a wrong upon one or other (or indeed upon both) parties.

Hence Lyotard's triple nominalist-pragmatic-postmodern injunction: first, that we should "save the honour of the name" (refuse to abstract from the particulars of localized context-specific utterance); second, that we should seek to multiply the range of "first-order natural pragmatic narratives"; and third, that we should "wage war on totality" in the form of those prescriptive ("meta-narrative") schemas that claim access to some ultimate truth at the end of enquiry.[81] Clearly the issues are presented in such a way as to close all exits for the well-intentioned reader save that marked "postmodernism". As so often in these debates it is a straw-man position that Lyotard is attacking, a compound made up in roughly equal parts of Hegelian historicism, enlightenment doctrine in its most uncritical (pre-Kantian) guise, and a crypto-theological notion of truth as arrived at through intuitive access or inward revelation. All the more ironic—though entirely predictable, for reasons I have touched on above—is the way that Lyotard himself has recourse to a rhetoric of "transcendence" (a language with markedly Kierkegaardian overtones) in order to contest what he wrongly perceives as the "totalizing" truth-claims of enlightenment critique. For there is, quite simply, no other way that his argument can go once it has thrown out the idea that ethical judgments might be capable of reasoned and principled discussion on the basis of informed factual understanding. Such is the position that Lyotard arrives at by grafting a "radical" (post-structuralist) variant of Wittgenstein's language-games doctrine onto an inflationary reading of the

Kantian sublime as that which creates an insuperable gulf between cognitive and evaluative orders of discourse. Up to a point this idea might be thought to find warrant in Kant's writings. No doubt the sublime in its aesthetic modality serves as a useful *analogical* means whereby to suggest the crucial distinction between determinate (cognitive or phenomenal) judgments and those of a non-determinate (ethical, reflective or speculative) character. But to treat it as a touchstone of absolute "heterogeneity"—a standing rebuke to any talk of ethical reasons, principles, or justifications—is the kind of (surely wilful) misconstrual that provokes real doubt as to Lyotard's competence as a reader of Kant. For as I have argued elsewhere—in company with other commentators—nothing could be more alien to Kant's thinking than this species of irrationalist dogma raised into a pretext for totally divorcing ethics from the realm of shared (intersubjectively validated) arguments and truth-claims.[82]

On the face of it Derrida is driving toward conclusions very similar to those of Lyotard. Thus he remarks that Kant has difficulty in distinguishing between the "voice" of practical reason—of the moral law within us—and those other kinds of voice that the mystagogues hear in their self-induced states of delusive visionary trance. "What condition does Kant lay down for those who, like himself, declare their concern to speak the truth, to reveal without emasculating the *logos*?" (Derrida, *Apocalyptic Tone*, p, 46). Most importantly, they must follow Kant's strict precept in refusing that voice any form of sensuous or quasi-phenomenal embodiment, any recourse to images—idolatrous representations—that would compromise its absolute purity. The *Aufklärer* then has this much in common with the mystagogue: that both have to strive against a constant tendency to devalue moral law by lessening its remoteness from the realm of mere desire or physical inclination. So it is that "Kant first asks them to get rid of the veiled goddess before which they both tend to kneel". (Derrida, *Apocalyptic Tone*, p. 46) If there is room for some kind of negotiated "truce"—as Derrida puts it, again paraphrasing Kant—then its terms will have to do with this shared liability and the need on both sides to resist its more seductive blandishments. Thus Kant very reasonably asks them

> no longer to personify the moral law or the voice that incarnates it. No longer, he says, should we personify the law that speaks in us, above all, not in the "aesthetic", sensible, and beautiful form of this veiled Isis. Such will be the condition for understanding/hearing the moral law itself, the unconditioned...In other words, and this is a trenchant motif for thought of the law or of the ethical today, Kant calls for placing the law above and beyond, not the person, but personification and the body, above and beyond as it were the sensible voice that speaks in us, the singular voice that speaks to us in private, the voice that could be said in his language to be "pathological" as opposed to the voice of reason. (Derrida, *Apocalyptic Tone*, p. 46)

This passage would bear a good deal of explication, not least—as the metaphors clearly imply—in terms of its bearing on recent debate about the Kantian ("formalist") tradition of ethical thought and the way that it privileges "masculine" ideals of pure, disembodied rationality over "feminine" qualities of nurturing, empathy, intuitive insight and the like.[83] What is thus excluded or driven out of mind in Kant's uneasy truce with the mystagogues is "precisely the body of a veiled Isis, the universal principle of femininity, murderess of Osiris all of whose pieces she later recovers except for the phallus". (Derrida, *Apocalyptic Tone*, p. 46) Of course such a reading will carry little weight with those who maintain a contemporary ("analytic") version of Kant's strict refusal to allow mere metaphors—or sensuous analogues of whatever kind—to play any role in the conduct of genuine philosophical argument. All the same, Derrida asks, "grant me at least this: that the truce proposed between the two declared defenders of a non-emasculated *logos* supposes some exclusion. It supposes some *inadmissible*. There is an excluded middle and that will be enough for me". (Derrida, *Apocalyptic Tone*, p. 46)

One possible reading of Derrida's essay would construe this passage—along with many others—as rhetorically asserting the claims of that "excluded middle" against all the strictures of Kantian philosophy and its various lineal descendants. The point would then be to subvert all the truth-claims vested in a discourse of logocentric (or "phallogocentric") reason whose effect is to silence any voice from outside its privileged domain. And should the question be raised as to whence this voice might issue—with what authority, reasonable warrant, ethical justification, etc.—then his response might appear to place Derrida in the company of those, like Lyotard, who reject such demands and treat ethics as belonging to "the order of transcendence". Then his essay would align itself on one side only (the distaff side, so to speak) of the axis that runs between all those binary distinctions: constative/performative, reason/rhetoric, concept/ metaphor, logic/intuition, masculine/feminine, etc. On this account Derrida rejects the terms of any "truce" or provisional concordat that might claim to reconcile the parties by discovering a measure of common ground in their agreement to maintain the law of the excluded middle. It casts him, in effect, as protagonist of an ethics that would raise the "apocalyptic tone"—or language in its performative/revelatory aspect—to a point of radical incommensurability with every last ground-rule, every precept or criterion for the conduct of "serious" philosophical debate. And one could then go on to claim (as some feminists have) that deconstruction thus conceived is a needful corrective to that whole male-dominated discourse of reason and truth which has sought to monopolize the conversation from Socrates to Kant and beyond.

But this is to ignore the countervailing argument that runs through Derrida's essay, an argument none the less compelling for the fact that it is here rehearsed or played off against the apocalyptic tone. For there is, *contra* Lyotard, no question of simply turning the page on enlightenment or abandoning those critical resources—those interests of reason or reflective judgment—that characterize the philosophic discourse of modernity.

> Several times [Derrida writes] I have been asked why (with a view to what, to what ends, and so on) I had *taken on* an apocalyptic tone and put forward apocalyptic themes. That is how they have often been qualified, sometimes with suspicion, and above all, I have noticed, in the United States where people are always more sensitive to phenomena of prophetism, messianism, eschatology, and apocalypse-here-now. That I have multiplied the distinctions between closure and end, that I was aware of speaking of discourses *on* the end rather than announcing the end, that I intended to analyse a genre rather than practise it, and even when I would practise it, to do so with that ironic genre clause I tried to show never belonged to the genre itself; nevertheless, for the reason I gave a few minutes ago, all language on apocalypse is also apocalyptic and cannot be excluded from its object. (Derrida, *Apocalyptic Tone*, pp. 60-1)

At this point one can well imagine an exasperated reader—Habermas perhaps—who simply loses patience with Derrida's ventriloquist strategy and asks "Well, which is it to be?" For he does rather appear to be having it both ways, running with the hare and the hounds, or maintaining the need for analysis, critique and the "lucid vigil" of enlightenment thought while denying that these values can ever be detached from the residual presence of a certain "apocalyptic tone". Thus on the one hand—in company not only with the mystagogues but also with postmodernists like Lyotard—he rejects the idea that any discourse "on" or "of" apocalypse could attain the level of meta-linguistic grasp required to analyse such phenomena without falling prey to their own language of revelation, unconcealment, "transcendence", and the like. On the other he requires us not to be such simple-minded readers—or so much in thrall to the myth of authorial presence—as to take his rehearsals of the apocalyptic tone (that is to say, his citations, performative enactments, parodies, intertextual allusions etc.) for evidence that Derrida is "practising" that genre, rather than seeking to analyze its effects. "No doubt one can think—I do—that this demystification must be led as far as possible, and the task is not modest." Indeed, it is a strictly interminable task, and this because—as Derrida believes—"no one can exhaust the overdeterminations and the indeterminations of the apocalyptic stratagems". (Derrida, *Apocalyptic Tone*, p. 59)

All the same we should be wrong to count this just a piece of ingenious "textualist" chicanery, a pretence of even-handedness adopted in order to head off his earnest-minded philosophical detractors while continuing to practise those same stratagems. For it is—or it should be—quite clear to the attentive reader of Derrida's text that there is more going on at the level of analysis and critique than could possibly be accounted for on these terms. To read him as endorsing (or uncritically practising) the genre of "apocalypse-here-now" is equivalent to the claim that his essay is performative through and through, that its rhetoric—in Rorty's neo-pragmatist parlance—goes "all the way down", and therefore that we miss the whole point if we assess it according to standards which Derrida is avowedly out to subvert. What this amounts to is a failure to remark the difference between deconstruction and postmodernism, at least when the latter is construed—on Lyotard's submission—as a discourse that renounces all ideas of reason, truth or critique, and which takes as its governing maxim the strictly nonsensical notion of judging somehow "without criteria". For the upshot, as we have seen, is Lyotard's quasi-Kierkegaardian leap of faith, his refusal to offer any justification of ethical or political commitments save by remarking that they "belong to the order of transcendence", and are therefore beyond all reach of argued or principled debate. Whatever its appeal for the latterday mystagogues —postmodernists and adepts of the pseudo-Kantian sublime—this notion is quite without warrant either in Kant or in Derrida's reading of Kant. No doubt there is a genuine puzzle—familiar at least since Hume—as to how we pass from an "is" to an "ought", or—in Kantian terms—how principles translate into lower-level maxims of practical reason, and then again, how these latter apply to the exercise of judgment in particular instances where circumstantial knowledge (along with the appeal to precedent) plays a necessary role. Still it is the case, as neither would deny, that we can and do negotiate this two-way passage whenever moral judgment is brought to bear upon some issue of real-world responsibility or choice. Any theory —like Lyotard's—which erects Hume's puzzle into a sheer rule that we cannot or should not is thereby committed to an ethics of transcendence with very marked apocalyptic overtones.

So it is important that we not misinterpret Derrida when he asks (rhetorically, no doubt): "wouldn't the apocalyptic be a transcendental condition of all discourse, of all experience even", so that "the genre of writings called "apocalyptic" in the strict sense would then be only an example, an *exemplary* revelation of this transcendental structure"? (Derrida, *Apocalyptic Tone*, p. 60) Such a passage might well be taken as further confirmation that critics like Habermas are right when they charge Derrida with having simply collapsed the "genre-distinction" between philosophy and literature, or—what amounts to much the same thing—with promoting a rhetoric (an "apocalyptic tone") that summarily revokes the philosophic discourse of modernity. It would then be a matter of patiently remarking his various (more or less wilful) confusions: of showing, for instance, how the term "transcendental" has a quite different sense when Kant deploys it in the context of an argument directed *against* the fake illuminati and their overweening claim to have privileged access to a knowledge "transcending" the limits of critical reason. Or again, it might entail taking issue with his notion that merely to demonstrate the presence of metaphorical (or rhetorical) elements in a philosophic text is somehow to subvert that text's generic identity and prove that philosophy is just a "kind of writing" or a sub-set of the genre "literature". However these are readings so utterly at odds with the range, depth and philosophical acuity of Derrida's work that they need not detain us here. More relevant to ask what exactly is at issue when he speaks of "another limit of demystification", a limit "perhaps more essential", and one that would "distinguish a deconstruction from a simple progressive demystification in the style of the Enlightenment" (Derrida, *Apocalyptic Tone,* p. 60).

For it is here that Derrida most explicitly measures his distance from that potent strain of irrationalist thought—apocalyptic, revelatory, performative, rhetorical, postmodernist etc.—which adopts, as with Kierkegaard or Lyotard, a stance of *absolute and principled indifference* to the claims of mere reason or humane ethical judgment. And yet, as he remarks, there is a sense in which "each of us is the mystagogue and the *Aufklärer* of another", so that Kant—even Kant—is driven to evoke the "moral law" in a language heavy with apocalyptic images and motifs. Thus:

> The veiled goddess for whom we of both parties bend our knees is the moral law within us, in its inviolable majesty. We do indeed perceive her voice and understand very well her commands. But when we are listening we are in doubt whether it comes from man, from the perfected power of his own reason, or whether it comes from another, whose nature is unknown to us and speaks to man through this, his own reason. (cited in Derrida, *Apocalyptic Tone,* p. 47)

For some—Lyotard among them—this uncertainty can only be resolved in favour of an ethics that would have us judge always "without criteria", that is to say, by harkening to the dictates of an inner voice whose "inviolable majesty" Kant contravened when he held it subject to the precepts and maxims of practical reason. Hence his (Lyotard's) constant invocation of the Kantian sublime as that which somehow "presents the unpresentable", and which thus lies beyond the furthest limits of judgment in its determinate (epistemic) or reflective (moral and political) modes. At this point the mystagogue has clearly won out over the *Aufklärer*, or the adept of "apocalypse-here-now" over anyone who would still deludedly cling to the notion of an ethics whose claims might yet be redeemed in the Kantian "parliament" of intersubjective reason, dialogue, and truth. For Derrida, conversely, there is no question of endorsing this Kierkegaardian leap to a standpoint of unconditional faith—or quasi-sublime revelation —which counts such ideas a world well lost in its rush to abandon the exposed high ground of enlightenment critique. Nor can his reflections be taken lightly at a time when oracular truth-claims of various sorts (including a rhetoric of national destiny with marked religious and apocalyptic overtones) are once again playing a prominent role in the discourse of ethics and politics.

NOTES

1. For an informative survey, see Beiser, *The Fate of Reason.*

2. See for instance Kant, "On a Newly Raised Superior Tone".

3. For a representative sampling, see "Reflections on the Derrida Affair", *The Cambridge Review* 113, October 1992.

4. See especially Derrida, "Of an Apocalyptic Tone Recently Adopted in Philosophy".

5. Rorty, "Philosophy as a Kind of Writing".

6. Habermas, *The Philosophical Discourse of Modernity.*

7. See Austin, *How to Do Things with Words*; Derrida, "Signature Event Context"; Searle, "Reiterating the Differences"; Derrida, "Limited Inc".

8. Kant, "On a Newly Raised Superior Tone".

9. See especially Derrida, *Margins of Philosophy.*

10. See for instance Norris, *Derrida* and "Limited Think".

11. Derrida, *Of Grammatology*, p. 158.

12. In addition to the above–cited works of Derrida see particularly *Speech and Phenomena, Writing and Difference*, "Plato's Pharmacy", and, on Kant, "Parergon".

13. See Derrida, "White Mythology"; also *Speech and Phenomena* and *Of Grammatology.*

14. Murdoch, *The Fire and the Sun.*

15. Derrida, "Plato's Pharmacy".

16. See Habermas, *The Philosophical Discourse of Modernity* and Searle, "Reiterating the Differences", also Murdoch, *Metaphysics as a Guide to Morals.*

17. Habermas, *The Philosophical Discourse of Modernity*, p. 184.

18. Habermas, *The Philosophical Discourse of Modernity*, p. 209.

19. Habermas, *The Philosophical Discourse of Modernity*, p. 207.

20. Habermas, *The Philosophical Discourse of Modernity*, p. 207.

21. See especially Derrida, "Afterword".

22. See Searle, *Speech Acts* and *Expression and Meaning.*

23. Habermas, *The Philosophical Discourse of Modernity*, p. 2O4.

24. Habermas, *The Philosophical Discourse of Modernity*, pp. 179–81.

25. Kierkegaard, *The Point of View.*

26. Kierkegaard, *Either/Or.*

27. See Schlegel, *"Lucinde" and the Fragments*, and *Dialogue on Poetry*; also Kierkegaard, *The Concept of Irony.*

28. Kierkegaard, *Fear and Trembling.*

29. Kierkegaard, *The Point of View*, p. 20.

30. Adorno, "On Kierkegaard's Doctrine of Love".

31. Kierkegaard, *The Concept of Irony.*

32. See especially Fish, "Short People".

33. Adorno "Kierkegaard's Doctrine of Love", p. 193.

34. Kierkegaard, *The Last Years*, p. 200.

35. Kierkegaard, *The Last Years*, p. 201.

36. Kierkegaard, *The Point of View*, p. 18.

37. Fishburn, "Søren Kierkegaard, Exegete", p. 264.

38. On this aspect of the Gospels, see Kermode, *The Genesis of Secrecy.*

39. I explore these possible alternative readings in Norris, "Fictions of Authority".

40. Empson, *Milton's God.*

41. de Man, "Excuses (Confessions)".

42. de Man, "Excuses (Confessions)", p. 285.

43 de Man, "Excuses (Confessions)", p. 293.

44. de Man, "Excuses (Confessions)", p. 295.

45. For further discussion see Norris, "De Man Unfair to Kierkegaard?.

46. See Booth, *A Rhetoric of Irony.*

47. Derrida, "Cogito and the History of Madness", p. 60.

48. Derrida, "'Genesis and Structure' and Phenomenology", p. 159.

49. See for instance de Bolla, *The Discourse of the Sublime,* Lyotard, *The Differend,* Zizek, *The Sublime Object of Ideology.*

50. See Chomsky, *Cartesian Linguistics, Language and Mind,* and *Language and Problems of Knowledge.*

51. See for instance Chomsky, *Problems of Knowledge and Freedom, Reflections on Language, Language and Responsibility.*

52. See especially Derrida, "Force and Signification" and "'Genesis and Structure' and Phenomenology".

53. See for instance the essays collected in Merleau-Ponty, *Sense and Non-Sense, Signs,* and *Themes from the Lectures at the Collège de France.*

54. Derrida, "Force and Signification", p. 5.

55. Derrida, "Force and Signification", p. 4.

56. Derrida "'Genesis and Structure' and Phenomenology", p. 160.

57. See Derrida, *Speech and Phenomena.*

58. Derrida, "'Genesis and Structure' and Phenomenology", p. 158.

59. Kant, "Von einem neuerdings erhobenen vornehmen Ton", p. 406. (The English translation of this work is Kant, "On a Newly Raised Superior Tone".)

60. Derrida, "Apocalyptic Tone".

61. Habermas, *The Philosophical Discourse of Modernity.*

62. See Beiser, *The Fate of Reason,* for a detailed account of these chapters in the history of enlightenment (and counter-enlightenment) thought.

63. See Derrida, "Afterword"; also Norris, "Deconstruction, Postmodernism and Philosophy: Habermas on Derrida".

64. Searle, "Reiterating the Differences".

65. Derrida, "Signature Event Context" and "Limited Inc".

66. Staten, *Wittgenstein and Derrida,* Felman, *The Literary Speech-Act.*

67. Kant, *The Conflict of the Faculties*
68. See for instance Bell, *The End of Ideology* and—for a postmodern update on the same theme—Fukuyama, *The End of History*.
69. See especially Derrida, "The Principle of Reason", "Mochlos", "No Apocalypse, Not Now", "The Age of Hegel". Some of these are collected—along with other texts—in Derrida, *Du Droit à la Philosophie*.
70. Derrida, "The Ends of Man".
71. See Derrida, "White Mythology".
72. Derrida, *Speech and Phenomena*.
73. Derrida's many statements of indebtedness to Heidegger have led some commentators to deny or play down the extent of these differences between deconstruction and the project of "fundamental ontology". See for instance Derrida, "The Ends of Man", *Spurs, Of Spirit*; also—from a different but related standpoint—Derrida, "*Geschlecht*: Sexual Difference, Ontological Difference".
74. See also Derrida, "The Principle of Reason".
75. Kant, *Critique of Pure Reason*.
76. See especially Lyotard, *The Differend*.
77. Lyotard and Thébaud, *Just Gaming*.
78. Lyotard and Thébaud, *Just Gaming*, p. 69.
79. Lyotard and Thébaud, *Just Gaming*, p. 69.
80. Lyotard and Thébaud, *Just Gaming*, p. 69.
81. See Lyotard, *The Postmodern Condition*.
82. See the chapter "Kant Disfigured" in Norris, *The Truth About Postmodernism*.
83. See for instance Nye, *Feminist Theory and the Philosophies of Man* , Irigaray, *Speculum of the Other Woman*, Lloyd, *The Man of Reason,* Le Doeuff, *The Philosophical Imaginary*.

REFERENCES

T. W. Adorno, "On Kierkegaard's Doctrine of Love", in Kepos (ed.), *Nineteenth-Century Literature Criticism*, pp. 192–9.

J. L. Austin, *How to Do Things with Words*, London: Oxford University Press 1963.

Frederick C. Beiser, *The Fate of Reason: German Philosophy from Kant to Fichte*, Cambridge, Mass.: Harvard University Press 1987.

Daniel Bell, *The End of Ideology*, Glencoe, Ill.: University of Illinois Press 1960.

Peter de Bolla, *The Discourse of the Sublime: Readings in History, Aesthetics and the Subject*, Oxford: Blackwell 1989.

Wayne Booth, *A Rhetoric of Irony*, Chicago: University of Chicago Press 1974.

Noam Chomsky, *Cartesian Linguistics*, New York: Harper & Row 1966.

Noam Chomsky, *Language and Mind*, New York: Harcourt 1972.

——, *Language and Problems of Knowledge*, Cambridge, Mass.: M.I.T. 1988.

——, *Language and Responsibility*, New York: Pantheon 1979.

——, *Problems of Knowledge and Freedom*, New York: Pantheon 1971.

——, *Reflections on Language*, New York: Pantheon 1975.

Harold Coward and Toby Foshay (eds.), *Derrida and Negative Theology*, Albany, NY: State University of New York Press 1992.

Jacques Derrida, "Afterword: Towards an Ethics of Conversation", in Derrida, *Limited Inc*, 2nd ed., pp. 111–54.

——, "The Age of Hegel", tr. Susan Winnett, *Glyph Textual Studies* New Series I, 3–35

——, "Of an Apocalyptic Tone Recently Adopted in Philosophy", tr. John P. Leavey, in Coward and Foshay (eds.), *Derrida and Negative Theology*, pp. 25–71.

——, "*Cogito* and the History of Madness", in Derrida, *Writing and Difference*, pp. 31–63

——, *Dissemination*, tr. Barbara Johnson, Chicago, Ill.: University of Chicago Press 1981.

——, *Du Droit à la Philosophie*, Paris: Minuit 1990.

——, "The Ends of Man", in Derrida, *Margins of Philosophy*, pp. 109-36.

——, "Force and Signification" in Derrida, *Writing and Difference*, pp. 3-30

——, "'Genesis and Structure' and Phenomenology", in Derrida, *Writing and Difference*, pp. 154–68

——, "*Geschlecht*: Sexual Difference, Ontological Difference", tr. Ruben Berezdivin, *Research in Phenomenology* VIII (1983), 65–83.

——, *Of Grammatology*, tr. Gayatri C. Spivak, Baltimore: Johns Hopkins University Press 1977.

——, "Limited Inc abc", *Glyph* II (1977), 162–254.

——, *Limited Inc*, 2nd ed., Evanston Ill.: Northwestern University Press 1989.

——, *Margins of Philosophy*, tr. Alan Bass, Chicago, Ill,: University of Chicago Press 1982.

——, "Mochlos, ou le conflit des facultés", *Philosophie* 2 (1984), 21–53

——, "No Apocalypse, Not Now (Full Speed Ahead, Seven Missives, Seven Missiles)", *Diacritics* XIV (1984), 20–31

——, "Parergon", in Derrida, *The Truth in Painting*, pp. 15–147.

——, "Plato's Pharmacy", in Derrida, *Dissemination*, pp. 61–171

——, "The Principle of Reason: The University in the Eyes of its Pupils", *Diacritics* XIII (1983), 3–20.

——, "Signature Event Context", *Glyph* I (1977), 172–97

Jacques Derrida, *"Speech and Phenomena" and Other Essays on Husserl's Theory of Signs*, tr. Richard P. Leavey, Evanston, Ill.: Northwestern University Press 1972.

——, *Of Spirit: Heidegger and the Question*, tr. Geoff Bennington and Rachel Bowlby, Chicago: University of Chicago Press 1989.

——, *Spurs: Nietzsche's styles*, tr. Barbara Harlow, Chicago, Ill.: University of Chicago Press 1979.

——, *The Truth in Painting*, tr. Geoff Bennington and Ian McLeod, Chicago Ill.: University of Chicago Press 1987.

——, "White Mythology: Metaphor in the Text of Philosophy", in Derrida, *Margins of Philosophy*, pp. 207–71

——, *Writing and Difference*, tr. Alan Bass, London: Routledge and Kegan Paul 1978.

Michèle Le Doeuff, *The Philosophical Imaginary*, tr. Hugh Tomlinson, London: Athlone 1991.

William Empson, *Milton's God*, London: Chatto and Windus 1961.

Shoshana Felman, *The Literary Speech-Act: Don Juan with Austin, or Seduction in Two Languages*, tr. Catherine Porter, Ithaca, NY: Cornell University Press 1983.

Peter Fenves (ed.), *On the Rise of Tone in Philosophy: Kant and Derrida*, Baltimore: Johns Hopkins University Press 1992.

Francis Fukuyama, *The End of History and the Last Man*, London: Secker & Warburg 1992.

Stanley Fish, *Doing What Comes Naturally: Change, Rhetoric. and the Practice of Theory in Literary and Legal Studies*, Oxford: Clarendon 1989.

——, "Short People Got No Reason to Live: Reading Irony", in Fish, *Doing What Comes Naturally*, pp. 180–96.

Janet Forsythe Fishburn, "Søren Kierkegaard, Exegete", in Kepos (ed.), *Nineteenth-Century Literature Criticism*, pp. 259–66.

Jürgen Habermas, *The Philosophical Discourse of Modernity: Twelve Lectures*, tr. Frederick Lawrence, Cambridge: Polity Press 1987.

Luce Irigaray, *Speculum of the Other Woman*, tr. Gillian C. Gill, Ithaca, NY: Cornell University Press 1985.

Immanuel Kant, *The Conflict of the Faculties*, tr. Mary J. Gregor, New York: Abaris 1979.

——, *Critique of Pure Reason*, tr. N. Kemp Smith, London: Macmillan 1933.

——, "On a Newly Raised Superior Tone in Philosophy", tr. Peter Fenves, in Fenves (ed.) *On the Rise of Tone in Philosophy*.

——, "Von einem neuerdings erhobenen vornehmen Ton in der Philosophie", in Kant, *Gesammelte Schriften* VIII, Berlin: de Gruyter 1923.

Paula Kepos (ed.), *Nineteenth-Century Literature Criticism*, Detroit: Gale Research Inc., 1992.

Frank Kermode, *The Genesis of Secrecy*, Cambridge, Mass.: Harvard University Press 1979.

Søren Kierkegaard, *The Concept of Irony*, tr. Lee M. Capel, Bloomington, Ind: Indiana University Press 1968.

——, *Either/Or*, tr. David F. and Lillian M. Swenson, Princeton NJ: Princeton University Press 1971.

——, *Fear and Trembling*, tr. Walter Lowrie, New York: Anchor Books 1954.

——, *The Last Years: Journals 1853–5*, ed. and tr. Ronald Gregor Smith, London: Fontana 1958.

——, *The Point of View for My Work as an Author*, tr. Walter Lowrie, London: Oxford University Press 1939.

Genevieve Lloyd, *The Man of Reason: "Male" and "Female" in Western Philosophy*, Minneapolis: University of Minnesota Press 1984.

Jean-François Lyotard, *The Differend: Phrases in Dispute*, tr. Georges van den Abbeele, Minneapolis: University of Minnesota Press 1987.

——, *The Postmodern Condition: A Report on Knowledge*, tr. Geoff Bennington and Brian Massumi, Minneapolis: University of Minnesota Press 1984.

Jean-François Lyotard and Jean-Loup Thébaud, *Just Gaming*, tr. Wlad Godzich, Minneapolis: University of Minnesota Press 1986.

Paul de Man, *Allegories of Reading: Figural Language in Rousseau, Nietzsche, Rilke, and Proust*, New Haven: Yale University Press 1979.

——, "Excuses (Confessions)", in de Man, *Allegories of Reading*, pp. 278–301.

Maurice Merleau-Ponty, *Sense and Non-Sense*, tr. H. L. and P. A. Dreyfus, Evanston, Ill.: Northwestern University Press 1964.

——, *Signs*, tr. R. C. McCleary, Evanston, Ill.: Northwestern University Press 1964.

——, *Themes from the Lectures at the Collège de France*, tr. J. O'Neill, Evanston, Ill.: Northwestern University Press, 1970)

Iris Murdoch, *The Fire and the Sun: Why Plato Banished the Poets*, London: Oxford University Press 1977.

——, *Metaphysics as a Guide to Morals*, London: Chatto and Windus 1992.

Christopher Norris, *Deconstruction and the Interests of Theory*, London: Pinter 1988, pp. 156–86.

——, "Deconstruction, Postmodernism and Philosophy: Habermas on Derrida", in Norris, *What's Wrong with Postmodernism*, pp. 49–76.

——, *The Deconstructive Turn: Essays in the Rhetoric of Philosophy*, London: Methuen 1983.

——, *Derrida*, London: Fontana 1987.

Christopher Norris, "Fictions of Authority: Narrative and Viewpoint in Kierkegaard's Writing", in Norris, *The Deconstructive Turn,* pp. 85-106.

——, "Limited Think: How *Not* to Read Derrida", in Norris, *What's Wrong with Postmodernism?* pp. 134–63.

——, "De Man Unfair to Kierkegaard? An Allegory of (Non)-Reading", in Norris, *Deconstruction and the Interests of Theory*, pp. 156–86.

——, *The Truth About Postmodernism*, Oxford: Blackwell, 1993.

——, *What's Wrong with Postmodernism?*, Hemel Hempstead: Harvester-Wheatsheaf 1990.

Andrea Nye, *Feminist Theory and the Philosophies of Man*, London: Routledge 1989.

Richard Rorty, *Consequences of Pragmatism*, Minneapolis: University of Minnesota Press 1982.

——, "Philosophy as a Kind of Writing", in Rorty, *Consequences of Pragmatism*, pp. 89–109.

Friedrich Schlegel, *Dialogue on Poetry and Literary Aphorisms*, tr. Ernst Behler and Roman Struc, University Park & London: University of Pennsylvania Press 1968.

——, *"Lucinde" and the Fragments*, tr. Peter Firchow, Minneapolis: University of Minnesota Press 1971.

John R. Searle, *Expression and Meaning: Studies in the Theory of Speech Acts,* Cambridge: Cambridge University Press 1979.

——, "Reiterating the Differences", *Glyph* I (1977), 198–208.

——, *Speech Acts: An Essay in the Philosophy of Language*, Cambridge: Cambridge University Press 1969.

Henry Staten, *Wittgenstein and Derrida*, Lincoln, Nebr.: University of Nebraska Press 1984.

Slavoj Zizek, *The Sublime Object of Ideology*, London: Verso 1989.

DEFERRING TO DERRIDA'S DIFFERENCE

In speaking of Jacques Derrida as a philosopher, one cannot fail to be aware of two very large charges against his name and standing: the first, that, whatever skill he has and has shown, Derrida is certainly not a philosopher; the second, that a great deal of academic mischief has been created by wrongly supposing that he is a philosopher and that his methods are professionally acceptable.[1] I take a moderate stand on these matters, by not insisting on the crisis in American education and by not linking Derrida's "methods" to that crisis (whatever it may be said to be), and by supporting Derrida's credentials as a philosopher on the basis of his published work but without insisting on its high originality or ultimate importance. I believe Derrida has brought to light certain deep sources of philosophical and educational disagreement that others have papered over, and the force of saying so bears on the possibility of validating Derrida's principal work. But I do not say his contribution in this regard signifies his importance as a philosopher. I also do not mean to discount the professional significance of what he has done. Derrida *has* shown great skill and ingenuity in unearthing philosophical questions of the first rank, but he has not usually turned his hand to redeeming matters, thereby made pertinent, in a sufficiently articulated and positive way. He has perhaps been divided in his own mind about this: partly opposing the complicitous strategies of analysis in the philosophical academy, partly being committed to an educational program that requires more affirmative analyses than he himself has favored.

In any case, I should like to set aside these headier disputes and say something about Derrida's work as a philosopher and about what we should understand by "deconstruction".

I

First of all, I am convinced that deconstruction, rightly construed, is not a philosophical program or method. Those who accuse Derrida of not advancing a method are, I think, right in so saying. But they may misspeak themselves nevertheless. When, therefore, Dallas Willard says that "'deconstruction' is not a *method* of thought",[2] I should say he was right; but then, I don't happen to think that philosophy *has* a method, and the presumption of a method (in a certain familiar sense of 'method') is utterly uncompelling. The last great effort at formulating a method was made by the positivists: philosophy is surely better off for their method's having been exposed for the great muddle it was.

Husserl had a "method", no doubt. In fact, his method kept evolving with his philosophy. But it was precisely Husserl's method, or at least parts of it, as well as parts of the structuralist method, that Derrida thought to deconstruct. If, therefore, Derrida has succeeded in deconstructing Husserl or Saussure (or Lévi-Strauss), or if he has raised pertinent and well-formed objections to the method of either (which are not to be ignored, philosophically), then, one may reasonably say, Derrida *has* a method (or a method in his madness). And, of course, that *is* what Derrida takes himself to have been up to in his early and middle work.

Willard is explicit here: "you will not find [he says] a *sound argument*, or even anything put forward as such, for Derrida's earth-shaking conclusion". He is referring to the claim, in *Speech and Phenomena*, "that nonpresence and otherness are internal to presence", which Christopher Norris has termed "one of the finest achievements of modern analytical philosophy."[3] Now, if Derrida's "argument" is reasonably telling, against Willard's denial, then, I suppose—on Willard's own view—Derrida *does* have a "method."

My own suggestion is a little more complicated. I should say that Derrida lacks a method—on Husserlian grounds; for his critique of Husserl (caught in the remark taken from *Speech and Phenomena*) is an attack on *Husserl's* method, which, as it happens, Willard endorses. Furthermore, Derrida's *argument* is not a deconstruction of Husserl's method or claim, if, as I say, deconstruction is not itself a philosophical program or method, or, therefore, given to argument. I do think Derrida *deconstructs* Husserl, in *Speech and Phenomena*, and that he effectively challenges Husserl *by argument*, in his analysis of Husserl's *Origin of Geometry*.[4] That is, I think Derrida means to cover overlapping ground in the two books and in two quite different ways; but I insist that he was *not* functioning as a deconstructionist in the second, and he was *not* a Husserlian in either.

The point is of some importance, because the parasitic (or "viral") nature of deconstruction has made it appear to some that Derrida must have been a Husserlian in spite of criticizing Husserl. There is a legitimate question of accuracy regarding Husserl's texts that bears on the admissibility of would-be criticisms of Husserl, whether deconstructive or not; but there is also a question of Derrida's intention in reviewing and citing Husserl's views that bears on whether the force of his arguments, or deconstructions, is compelling, even if they are textually faulty or simply rhetorically cavalier in taking off from Husserl's texts in an altogether idiosyncratic direction.[5] I shall return to the matter shortly. For the moment, I merely wish to offer a sense of what Derrida is up to.

Willard's original charge concerns a perceived decline in the American university system: "its institutional structures and processes", he says, "are no longer organized around knowledge." He does not fault Derrida for this; he does not even fault Derrida for the deepening of the disorder as a result of the rise of

American deconstruction. At best, "American deconstruction" has been opportunistic, he believes, somewhat in the same spirit (but not in the same technical regard) in which, say, Richard Rorty has endorsed the disruptive function of Derridean deconstruction.[6] I put all this aside, therefore, in speaking of Derrida's deconstructive and philosophical work. Willard says that "Derrida has stepped into a pre-existing situation in the American academy", and I accept that finding.[7]

What Willard has in mind, however, is something closer to my purpose. He argues that a "refusal to accept servitude to painful method" accounts for "the most dismal aspects of university life in America", and that Derrida opposes "method" in that he abandons "logic as an objective discipline"—which, then, has been mercilessly exploited by the American deconstructors of the academy. He claims that logic is "a field of exact knowledge"; and he asks: "How could one even know what knowledge is without an understanding of logic?" He therefore means to charge that Derrida's critical practice does not subscribe to that strenuous view of "method" that admits logic as a distinctive "field of exact knowledge". For instance, he opposes "the talk of many logics that...has the effect of making logic seem arbitrary...and of inviting people to find or invent one of their own." I believe this deforms in a very serious way the full significance of what Derrida is attempting to do—and that Willard is aware that it does. (Also, Willard's opposition to there being "many" logics—perhaps "many-valued" logics—puts his insistence on "painful method" and "exact knowledge" in some doubt.) For Derrida, as I say, is bent on attacking Husserl's method, by deconstruction and by argument, precisely with regard to what Husserl supposes constitutes "exact knowledge" of the philosophical sort—which, therefore, fixes what we should mean by 'method'. It is impossible to agree *a priori* with Willard's assumption about logic (however informally advanced) when we know that Derrida's purpose was to dismantle that very presumption. We must step back to understand how much is at stake. We cannot judge whether Derrida has a method if the requisite evidence entails subscribing to Husserl's method (or something of the sort), when the essential thrust of Derrida's "method" is to cast the gravest doubts on the tenability of Husserl's. The point is, there is some danger that the champions of "method" and "exact knowledge" have themselves misled the American academy.

I say deconstruction is not a method. It is a dependent and parasitic practice that cannot stand alone, and it is pursued, by Derrida, in the service of a philosophical method, or program. Furthermore, that method or program is only barely sketched by Derrida himself, who has (in my opinion) spent an inordinate amount of time and effort on the deconstructive side of his endeavor.

II

Let me start again, therefore. I take the following to be a fair summary of Derrida's critical practice:

1. he works as a deconstructionist: which is to say, not by philosophical argument but by the use of a completely parasitic idiom, drawn from his own "victims" and turned against itself, by which he exposes, by negative strategies usually fastened on the marginal features of given texts, their own internal *aporiai*, paradoxes, or other self-defeating tendencies—thereby calling into profound doubt certain large and typical philosophical claims;

2. he is committed to a "Kantian-like" philosophical thesis, *"il n'y a pas de hors-texte,"*[8] within which alone deconstruction is pursued, except that his own doctrine is itself entirely holist, lacks determinate detail, is committed to a symbiosis of "languaged" world and "worlded" language that could never admit (in Kant's way) any invariant structures regarding the nature of the world or the categories of understanding, and is not skeptically or anarchically opposed to the usual claims and ways of proceeding favored in normal discursive inquiry;

3. he tends to work, whether deconstructively or by argument, in such a way as to expose the untenability of so-called "logocentric" claims, that is, philosophical pretensions regarding the "originary", the "apodictic", the "totalized", and similar forms of privilege, which he finds paradigmatically entrenched, in much the same way, in Husserl and Saussure and Lévi-Strauss.

This complex practice is original with Derrida. It is clearly influenced by Husserl, by Saussure, by Heidegger, and by Emmanuel Levinas; but it is original (as a method or program) and it is entirely different from the programs of any of the others—particularly Heidegger's, which it has been accused of being an imitation or extension of. I shall try to show, in passing, that this is due to an obvious misunderstanding. There *is* a clear sense in which Derrida accepts both Husserl's and Saussure's central doctrines; but that holds only in Derrida's deconstructive mode—that is, when he is *not* advancing philosophical claims of his own, when he functions primarily in the "viral" way that deconstruction favors. I offer the following addendum, therefore, as a more controversial characterization of Derrida's practice:

4. what Derrida does deconstructively (1), he also pursues in a positive philosophical manner (2-3) as a comparison of *Speech and Phenomena* and his*Introduction* to Husserl's *Origin of Geometry* shows; but deconstruction

cannot equal the argumentative resources of his (or any) philosophical program.

So, for example, when friendly commentators like Christopher Norris and Rodolphe Gasché insist on treating the *deconstructionist* Derrida as a rather standard philosopher, I am quite sure they go wrong. Still, they cannot be altogether wrong, in the sense in which theorists like Rorty and Geoffrey Hartman insist—or insinuate, as does Willard—that there are no arguments in Derrida. My tally (1-4) is intended to steer a better way between these extremes; but I must postpone the supporting argument. Norris offers the strongest and most explicit philosophical reading:

> If writing is the very *condition* of knowledge [on Derrida's view]—if, that is to say, it can be shown to precede and articulate all our working notions of science, history, tradition etc.—then how can writing be just one object of knowledge among others? What Derrida is using here is the form of "transcendental" reasoning which Kant first brought to bear upon the central problems of philosophy. In fact I shall go on to argue that deconstruction is a Kantian enterprise in ways that few of his commentators have so far been inclined to acknowledge... Derrida's version of the Kantian argument makes writing (or "arche-writing") the precondition of all possible knowledge. And this not merely by virtue of the fact—the self-evident fact—that writing is the form in which ideas are passed down, preserved in a constantly expanding archive, and thus made available to subsequent debate. His claim is *a priori* in the radically Kantian sense that we cannot *think* the possibility of culture, history or knowledge in general without also thinking the prior necessity of writing.[9]

I think Norris is more wrong than right in what he affirms about the philosophical nature of deconstruction, and more right than wrong in what he denies in opposing the philosophical discounting of deconstruction. What I have cited deserves close reading. For although it is true that both Husserl and Saussure (in very different ways) speculate about the function of writing, Derrida speaks of "writing" (or *arche-écriture*) in a way that does not depend primarily on any inscriptional or notational device, which *is* the central concern of both Husserl and Saussure. On the contrary, Derrida is quite explicit in insisting on the priority of "writing" in attacking Lévi-Strauss's discussion of the Nambikwara, the preliterate people of the Brazilian Amazon whom Lévi-Strauss sought to study in order, precisely, to understand (in a Rousseauesque spirit) the supposed origins of language.[10]

I say that Norris must be wrong, because Derrida offers no Kantian transcendental arguments of any kind, because he could not do so consistently, because Kantian arguments are meant to yield synthetic *a priori* truths, because Kant's practice is paradigmatically "logocentric" for Derrida, and because (perhaps most important) Derrida never commits his own inquiries to yielding determinate findings about the invariant conceptual structure of human understanding. Derrida does play fast and loose with Husserl's and Saussure's views on writing—but he telegraphs the fact.

It is true, by item (2) of my tally, that Derrida takes the world to be indissolubly "texted", "textual", suffused with the significative structures of the categories of human understanding. That *is* "Kantian", I don't deny. But Derrida simply *subscribes* to (2). He does not make establishing it the focus of his philosophical practice. He does not derive (and, on the best evidence, does not believe it is possible to derive) any determinate invariant categories of understanding. *That* is not Kantian. This is what I had in mind in saying (2) was a holist thesis, utterly vacuous in any distributed sense, meant both to orient the work of deconstruction (1) and the work of philosophical arguments directed against the forms of logocentrism (3). The irony is that the champions and the detractors of Derrida concur in the oddest possible way: Willard insists that Derrida has no philosophical arguments or method because he is not "logocentric" in Husserl's way; and Norris insists that he has arguments, in at least Kant's way. Rorty smiles all the while like a Cheshire cat, reminding us pleasantly that philosophy is not a matter of argument at all.[11]

III

I don't deny that, for Derrida, *l'arche-écriture* is a kind of "transcendental" condition of thought and speech. But simply saying that encourages all the mistakes I have been hinting at—but have not yet made fully explicit. The key passage in Derrida is perhaps the following, from *Of Grammatology*:

> writing is not only an auxiliary means in the service of science—and possibly its object—but first, as Husserl in particular pointed out in *The Origin of Geometry*, the condition of the possibility of ideal objects and therefore of scientific objectivity. Before being its object, writing is the condition of the *epistémè*.[12]

Let me offer several charges and mollifications which, I believe, will orient us correctly to Derrida's purpose. First of all, Derrida "misreads" Husserl's purpose, in urging that writing is the condition of ideal objects and scientific objectivity, but he plainly does so deliberately and productively. The evidence for this must rest with a comparison between Derrida's *Edmund Husserl's Origin of Geometry* and *Speech and Phenomena*. But it is also the kind of remark that has led commentators to suppose that Derrida is a phenomenologist rather than one who speaks in the manner of the phenomenologists when it suits him in order to deconstruct Husserl or to argue against his theses.[13]

Secondly, Derrida does construe "arche-writing" as a condition of thought and speech and science, but *not* as a constitutive or regulative condition in any Kantian sense, or in any extension of the Kantian sense. This, I am sorry to say, cannot but be the mark of Norris's error, the mistake of the passage from his *Derrida* I cited earlier.[14] *Derrida's* purpose in using the idiom of the "transcendental" is to escape both sheer objectivism (the presumed adequacy of first-order discourse) and transcendentalism (both the Kantian and the Husserlian varieties). He says very plainly that the concept (sc. "arche-writing") "belongs to the history of metaphysics and [hence] we [that is, he] can only use it under erasure [*sous rature*]". He goes on at once to say, in offering his critique of Louis Hjelmslev's glossematics, which he regards as "plagued by a scientific objectivism", an "unconfessed metaphysics":

> It is to escape falling back into this naive objectivism that I refer here to a transcendentality that I elsewhere put into question. It is because I believe that there is a short-of and beyond of transcendental criticism. To see to it that the beyond does not return to the within is to recognize in the contortion the necessity of a pathway [*parcours*]. That pathway must leave a track in the text. Without the track, abandoned to the simple content of its conclusions, the ultra-transcendental text will so closely resemble the precritical text as to be indistinguishable from it...the value of the transcendental arche [*archie*] must make its necessity felt before letting itself be erased.[15]

Derrida explicitly says that the *arche* "cannot, as the condition of all linguistic systems, form a part of the linguistic system itself and be situated as an object in its field". Should one misunderstand, he adds a parenthesis: "Which does not mean it has a real field *elsewhere, another* assignable *site*".[16] The implication is perfectly clear. Derrida is not practising as a radical Kantian. He is explaining philosophically what he is doing deconstructively. In doing that, "*arche-écriture*" is made to appear as a concept—hence, as the fruit of a transcendental argument. But it is not a concept, it is only that "mark" or inscription of Derrida's that, thus transfigured (not transformed), *appears* as a sign and invites the mistaken finding, that Derrida anticipates—namely, that he is a Kantian after all.

In this sense, the trace or track of the *arche* is detected only when one views the work of deconstruction as a form of standard philosophical analysis. That, I say, is what Norris and Gasché have missed. That is what the closed system of a Hjelmslevian glossematics (or a Saussurean linguistics) cannot accommodate.[17] Derrida links "arche-writing" with the "movement of differ*a*nce," which is to say, with the use of that mysterious mark of his that "is literally neither a word nor a concept".[18] He obviously means what he says here. It is true enough, after the fact, that '*différance*' becomes a term. But Derrida has anticipated the event and explained the sense in which he is a "transcendentalist": there is no legible sense, he explains, in which the *term* "différance" functions, transcendentally, *within* a discourse, while at the same time functioning deconstructively.My sense is that "*différance*", "*arche-trace*", and what "*supplémen-*

tation" draws its supplement from, are merely "positive" counters (masquerading as terms: that is, negations) of the negativity that answers to the distributed deconstructions or arguments meant to subvert "logocentrism". (See item 3) Detached from that condition, they appear as full-fledged terms. Derrida thereupon appears as a Kantian, a Husserlian, a Heideggeran, even a Saussurean, sometimes a Hegelian, possibly a pragmatist, whereas he is nothing of the kind. I confess I am a little fatigued by Derrida's extravagances, but I nevertheless rise to his defense as a philosophical contributor of a bold and original sort.

The essential point is that what Derrida designates as the (*arche-*)condition of thought and speech, language and knowledge, is not discernible in any way. It is a "condition" in that nothing determinate *can* be offered as the transcendental condition *of* thought and speech. It is that radical absence (as Derrida says) that is not admitted in Aristotle, Kant, Husserl, Saussure, or Heidegger. They are all "logocentrists", therefore, no matter how unlikely that may seem; they are all ripe for deconstruction, or for the more explicit philosophical arguments that, by the use of potentially misleading devices—for instance, the adoption of the idiom of the transcendental—subvert their respective claims. If I understand him rightly, Derrida "holds" that there *is* no originary point at which thought or meaning and utterance or sound (or "sign", read in a representational way) were ever first joined or from which they could now be recovered. That is why Derrida speaks of *différance* "*sous rature*":

> Now if *différance* ✖ (and I also cross out the "✖") what makes possible the presentation of the being-present, it is never presented as such. It is never offered to the present. Or to anyone...the detours, locutions, and syntax in which I will often have to take recourse will resemble those of negative theology, occasionally even to the point of being indistinguishable from negative theology. Already we have had to delineate *that différance is not*, does not exist, is not a present-being (*on*) in any form; and we will be led to delineate also everything *that it is not*, that is, *everything*; and consequently that it has neither existence nor essence. It derives from no category, whether present or absent.[19]

It is the *presence* of the "originary"—which his deconstructible opponents presuppose—that he deconstructs. Doing that, Derrida is obliged to use the language of "presence"; but, in deconstructing that as well as the texts of his opponents, he draws our attention to the incompletable task the logocentric presumption takes to be manageable.

I regard the practice of deconstruction as a huge (and serious) joke: not a joke about what it accomplishes, but a joke about the extravagant means by which it does its work. It matches the "seriousness" of the logocentrists by employing their idiom. It puts that seriousness into doubt by erasing its own logocentric burlesque. Even more seriously, it insinuates in its "viral" way that there is no originary beginning that the logocentrists could ever have built their systems on—by affirming *différance* or *arche-trace*, or that to which *supplé-mentation* applies, as the true origin of their systems. There is no such origin. That's the joke. Still, it's a better candidate than the presumption of the logo-centrists. Deconstructive insinuation is the negative shadow cast by positive argument directed against the forms of "presence," the targets of item (3) of my earlier tally. It is also a shortcut assurance that such arguments must surely suc-ceed.

The matter has suddenly become very strenuous. I shall return to it in a moment. But what I wish to make clear is that Derrida's deconstruction is utter-ly unlike Heidegger's "*Destruktion*", in spite of the fact that, as everyone admits, Derrida was clearly influenced by Heidegger and even used Heidegger's term originally for his own notion. If, however, you take seriously what I have just attempted to explain, you must see that Heidegger was intent on an alto-gether different objective—and that, in virtue of his own *destrucktive* efforts, Heidegger became a deconstructive target. Theorists like Manfred Frank and Claude Evans are not at all clear about the difference. Indeed, Evans substitutes *Derrida's* term in modifying the standard translation of Heidegger's pertinent passages. He obviously believes their projects are sufficiently similar. Thus, explaining Heidegger's famous "task of the de-struction (*Destruktion*) of the history of ontology", Evans permits himself the luxury of citing Heidegger's account of the hermeneutic nature of understanding:

> It is for this reason [says Heidegger] that there necessarily belongs to the conceptual interpretation of being and its structures...a *destruction*, that is, a critical decon-struction [*sic*] (*Abbau*) of the traditional concepts, which at first must necessarily be employed, down to the sources from which they were drawn."[20]

Evans remarks that Derrida is rather oblique, in *Speech and Phenomena*, about "the sense of deconstruction"; fortunately, he hints, Heidegger affords us a "prehistory" of *Derrida's* term.[21]

Well, not quite. For his part, Manfred Frank says quite straightforwardly:

> Heidegger's critique of the confusion of Being and beings is omnipresent in Derrida's writings; and the artificial expression *différance*, which stood for a time in the centre of his deconstructive reflections, is an undisguised allusion to Heidegger.

He worries whether it yields, in Derrida, "an explicit and comprehensible reflection".[22] But he obviously thinks Derrida is less than original.

I am afraid this line of argument is quite mistaken. Frank realizes of course (quoting Heidegger) that "Being is [on Heidegger's view] the real and only theme of philosophy...philosophy is not the science of beings (*Seienden*) but of Being (*Sein*)".[23] The important factor is that Heidegger believed that our relation to Being *could* actually be reclaimed—against the tradition of metaphysics: if so, then the concept of *Seiendes* may similarly be reclaimed in terms of its special dependence on the concept of *Sein*. So there is an ordinary linkage that Heidegger believes may be recovered. Derrida's entire effort is to dispute that thesis, in all its forms: that is what deconstruction is about. Evans speaks directly of "the originary experience of Being to be retrieved".[24] Derrida, of course, takes that to be the heart of the logocentric mistake. Derrida's purpose is not a radicalization of this part of Heidegger's program: it is a deconstruction of it, a deconstruction of Heidegger's project of *Destruktion*!

Derrida is not a Kantian and not a Heideggerean—and for the same reason: in his eyes, both Kant and Heidegger are logocentrists. He is right, of course.

IV

The most difficult step still lies before us. It concerns the deconstruction of Husserl. But I cannot put the matter merely thus. For, in the *Introduction to Edmund Husserl's Origin of Geometry*, Derrida is not yet a deconstructionist and, in *Speech and Phenomena* (where he surely is), the deconstructive maneuvers are closely informed by the earlier more straightforward philosophical arguments. Furthermore, Derrida's reflections on Saussure do not enter into the argument of the *Introduction*, but they are already linked, in *Speech and Phenomena*, with Derrida's thoughts on *différance* and *arche-écriture*. There is also an earlier essay of Derrida's on Husserl, "'Genesis and Structure' and Phenomenology", first published in 1959, that, in the apparently somewhat altered form from which the English translation is taken, inserts the term *différance*.[25] Furthermore, in an interview published in *Positions*, Derrida names *Speech and Phenomena* as "perhaps the essay which I like best" and which may "be read as the other side (top or bottom, as you wish) of another essay, published in 1962, as the introduction to Husserl's *The Origin of Geometry*." He associates *Speech and Phenomena* with *Of Grammatology* as well, and says of the former:

> In this essay the problematic of writing was already in place as such, bound to the irreducible structure of 'deferral' in its relationships to consciousness, presence, science, history and the history of science, the disappearance or delay of the origin, etc.[26]

I take this to confirm the reasonableness of treating the deconstructive and the argumentative work as different in a formal sense and also as convergent, reciprocally effective, and overlapping strategies in their intended philosophical upshot. *Of Grammatology* is, of the three, the most explicitly deconstructive in style.

John Leavey's Preface to the *Introduction*, is, I'm afraid, a muddle. First of all, Leavey treats the work as a deconstruction; secondly, he inserts (without explanation) the expressions '*deconstruction*' and '*differance*' in introducing the text; and thirdly, he treats Derrida's entire account as if it were a transcendental exercise, pretty much in Heidegger's sense. He misreads passages like those already cited: for instance, "Texts [he says] occur for Derrida only in writing, a writing understood not in the ordinary sense, but as the place of *rature*— the always incomplete erasure of scratching out Western metaphysics", citing the passage from *Of Grammatology* which we have cited above (p. 201). He then goes on to say that, for Derrida,

> Difference is transcendental—transcendental being the primordial Difference of a Different Origin. Thus transcendental is equivalent to differ*a*nt (with an *a*). Consciousness of Difference, that without which nothing would appear, is transcendental consciousness, i.e., differant consciousness. So we could say that consciousness is differance with an *a*).[27]

But this makes it appear as if Derrida was committed to a transcendental program of analysis that could be favorably compared with Husserl's, Heidegger's, Kant's (or even Saussure's), whereas the truth is that Derrida introduces these distinctions in the process of subverting them. Leavey simply misses the joke. Hence he saddles Derrida with some serious versions of the doctrine of the Transcendental Ego, whereas Derrida means to deconstruct them all by insinuating into the transcendental slot what is "radically other"—namely, Nothing (which must then, of course, be dutifully erased as well).

We are at a rather critical point, but it may not be entirely evident. Derrida introduces the "mark"—*différance*—in Chapter 6 of *Speech and Phenomena*, which he plainly identifies with "all the incidences of primordial nonpresence whose emergence we have already noted on several occasions". The use of the expressions "incidences" and "emergence" mark the deliberately paradoxical usage Derrida favors (deconstructively) that, in the double sense already indicated, occurs *sous rature*. He brings the matter to bear on Husserl's account of signs ("signifiers") and "the origin of sense and presence"; and he expressly says,

> This movement of differance is not something that happens to a transcendental subject; it produces a subject. Auto-affection [the "exercise of the voice," which generates the deconstructive puzzle by assuming that original meaning and experience *are* straightforwardly recovered] is not a modality of experience that characterizes a being that would already be itself (*autos*). It produces sameness as self-relation within self-difference; it produces sameness as the nonidentical.[28]

I leave this baffling remark for the moment, and add the opening line of
Chapter 7, which cannot fail to orient us correctly to the novelty of Derrida's
undertaking:

> what is supplementary is in reality *differance*, the operation of differing which at
> one and the same time both fissures and retards presence, submitting it simultane-
> ously to primordial division and delay. *Differance* is to be conceived prior to the
> separation between deferring as delay and differing as the active work of difference.
> Of course this is inconceivable if one begins on the basis of consciousness, that is,
> presence, or on the basis of its simple contrary, absence or nonconsciousness...The
> supplementary difference vicariously stands in for presence due to its primordial
> self-deficiency. Going *through* the First Investigation [of Husserl's *Logical Invest-
> igations*], we must try to ascertain how far these concepts respect the relations
> between signs in general (indicative as well as expressive) and presence in general.
> When we say *through* Husserl's text, we mean a reading that can be neither simply
> commentary nor simply interpretation.[29]

I read this single passage as confirming everything I've said about the
deconstructive strategy. You cannot read it correctly without featuring the point
of Derrida's mentioning that the "operation" of supplementarity or différance is
"inconceivable if..." and that going "through" Husserl is neither "simple commentary nor simple interpretation".

Derrida's objective is deconstruction, and deconstruction entails reading
everything in Husserl in that way that forms the logocentrism which Derrida
finds in the *Investigations* and which he means to deconstruct. This means that
he does not read Husserl "fairly": he does not first set our Husserl's doctrine
and then offer counterarguments. He does not argue, he deconstructs; and he
sees no reason to do full justice to those doctrines of Husserl's that either constitute the logocentric fault or depend upon it. He is impatient in this regard.
Husserlians will be annoyed: they have a right to be. But Derrida is also within
his rights: he is as explicit as he could tactfully be. The only serious question of
accuracy and inaccuracy (that matters) concerns whether Husserl *is* logocentric
in the way Derrida insinuates he is. For, if he is, that fact alone may excuse
Derrida's rather arch practice.

This is a vexed matter, one in which the deconstructive and argumentative
strategies come together. For the moment, it will have to serve to mark the
space of Derrida's deconstructive intent. Two further provisos will help us,
however: first, the question, or charge, of interpretive error regarding the
Investigations, on Derrida's part in *Speech and Phenomena,* is not irrelevant
merely because Derrida is functioning deconstructively; but it *does* remain to be
asked whether what Derrida is pursuing deconstructively is or is not adversely
affected by the errors that do obtain (if indeed textual errors do obtain). Second,
the discussion of Husserl in the *Introduction is* thoroughly argumentative, not

deconstructive, and touches on the *Investigations* (notably the First, mentioned in the passage cited) all the while it pursues the *Origin of Geometry*, which bears on thesis (4) of my original tally.

The Husserlian critics take Derrida to have misinterpreted Husserl in a serious way. Perhaps. I am inclined to doubt it—in the sense suggested. But they cannot be said to succeed if they do not show just how the supposed interpretive errors actually affect the deconstructive work. Evans, for instance, offers the most sustained objections. But the single reference in which he brings the *Introduction* to bear on *Speech and Phenomena* is reasonably open to question: because the supposed error he finds in Derrida may not be decisive for Derrida's deconstructive purpose, because it may be open to a not unfavorable concession, and because it may even correspond to a point of contest Husserl was prepared to admit.[30]

La voix et le phénomène and *De la grammatologie* appeared in the same year, 1967. *Of Grammatology* begins by introducing the notion of "logocentrism", and, in an early footnote, Derrida says that he will, in *Speech and Phenomena*, bring the logocentric issue to bear on those particularly troublesome themes that, in effect, may be found in Husserl's work.[31] He says he means, by "logocentrism", "the metaphysics of phonetic writing", which he then begins to explain in the following way, speaking of "the privilege of the *phonè*":

> The system of "hearing (understanding)-oneself-speak" through the phonic substance—which *presents itself* as the nonexterior, nonmundane, therefore nonempirical or noncontingent signifier—has necessarily dominated the history of the world during an entire epoch.[32]

What Derrida means is that, in conceiving the written word as the "signifier" of the ("prior") spoken word, which (then) is (taken to be) the signifier of some original and privileged meaning indissolubly linked to itself, we cannot fail to confront the riskiness of the notion of language as a system of fixed signifiers of this sort. In short, Derrida "deconstructs" Husserl and Saussure as exemplars of two strong lines of theorizing that converge on this presumption as well as on its inexplicit betrayal. That is perhaps the central thread by which his entire deconstructive and argumentative efforts are joined. Frankly: Derrida is entirely right in essentials, and rather clever to have put his thesis in this way.

V

Derrida has a very simple plan of analysis, but he pursues it in an extraordinarily complicated and quarrelsome way: first, because his enormous literary and philosophical appetite encourages him to suppose he can include pertinently, among his running allusions, just about as much as anyone has ever attempted; second, because, alert at all times to the logocentric traps his opponents have fallen into, he prefers (however annoyingly) to remain supremely playful; third, because he is persuaded that the logocentric problem is ubiquitous, dangerous, overriding, and unavoidable, even where, among the texts he reviews, it does not explicitly surface in the form he favors; and fourth, because he believes (or appears to believe) that a deconstructive reading *is* faithful to a text if it exposes an author's failure to have brought the text to bear in a perspicuous way on some version or other of the logocentric problem. Textual "misreadings", therefore, are more like strategies of rhetoric than errors, meant to bring us back to neglected issues. The result is an indefatigably gymnastic style that, to my mind, is at its most impressive in "Plato's Pharmacy" and begins to fall off the cliff in *Glas*.[33]

I see no reason to make a close philosophical analysis of the deconstructive texts as if they were straightforward philosophy, but I also think a spare argumentive counterpart can (and should) be supplied. In any case, the middle ground yields to the following informal survey:

1. we may ask whether language functions to convey ("present," "represent," "mimic," "refer to") the truth about the world—not whether this or that utterance is true or false but whether it is within the competence of language to disclose the unmediated truth in virtue of its supposed "originary" connection with reality;

2. we may ask whether language functions to convey, in the same sense, the meaning of a speaker's or author's utterance, in virtue of its "originary" connection with "self-present" intention and experience;

3. it may be confirmed that the entire Western tradition—from, say, Plato's *Phaedrus* to Saussure's and Husserl's reflections on language—have indeed favored affirmative answers to these queries, surprisingly similar ones in fact, that "privilege" the "presence" of reality and meaning;

4. on close inspection, we find that each champion of the "logocentric" acknowledges, within his own account, some clue or other, some evidentiary lacuna, that betrays his own profound doubts about vindicating the affirmative thesis;

5. we must admit that "written" signs can rightly claim to function thus only if, at some point in a chain of such signs, what *they* signify—ulteriorly the "spoken" or "natural" sign or signifier—succeeds in its turn in signifying the originary, and only if the "written" sign can be counted on not to lose or deform that linkage; but

6. we are everywhere forced to admit that there is no way of ensuring "writing's" so functioning: the would-be self-presence of speech, of uttered meaning, reportable experience, is encumbered in precisely the same way everywhere.

Hence, summarizing the whole effort—whether deconstructive or argumentative—we may now say that every would-be sign or signifier, whether spoken or written, presupposes an ability to recover the originary truth or meaning queried in (1) and (2). Confident that that is not possible, Derrida playfully insists that there *is* a kind of ultimate "writing" (*arche-écriture, différance*: something that looks like a sign if only you treat the deconstruction as a transcendental inquiry) that is "always other", always receding in the stepwise strategy to convince ourselves that our signs *are* successfully anchored in the true origin. Argumentatively, there *is* no recoverable such origin; deconstructively, every logocentric utterance betrays the need to find one—or (in effect) posits what Derrida calls *différance*, the *arche-trace*.

Derrida himself does not affirm différance: to read him as if he did is to transform him into another transcendental thinker. *Différance*, I venture to say, is Derrida's joking way of exposing, by imitation, the transcendentalist's own strategy; or, according to the deconstructive diagnosis, it is the suppressed premiss all such thinkers share.

Every sign, therefore, is *deferred* in its recuperative function until its linkage is established—if indeed that is necessary; and every familiar sign is *different* from the originary until it can be shown to be the same—if indeed that must be done. This is the plain meaning of the puzzling remark I cited a moment earlier: speaking "produces sameness as self-relation within self-difference; it produces sameness as the nonidentical". The wording is deliberately tricky; but I cannot see that it amounts to much more than the familiar idea that anything that persists changes in some respect or other, and that to claim that a boy and a man are the same individual is to produce the (sense of) sameness (think of David Hume) that overrides, and yet respects, the difference. Derrida's account is primarily centered on the nature of truth and meaning, which makes the idiom of identity and difference initially inapt. But, you must remember, that is meant to be part of its charm.

Saussure and Husserl are Derrida's two great specimens. They have almost nothing in common in their explicit theories. Argumentative comparisons are futile, therefore. What they share is suppressed, incompatible with the official doctrine of each, subversive of each if unearthed: a perfect field for deconstructive play—always, of course, at the price of opposed textual and deconstructive accuracies.

In a way, Saussure is the easier to dismantle, except that, by his deliberately labile tricks, Derrida would have us believe that the fatal disorder of Saussure's account is also Husserl's. In acknowledging this, I am conceding that the question of accuracy to Husserl's and Saussure's texts is not entirely straightforward. But I also cannot see that Derrida is ultimately wrong—deconstructively—about either Saussure or Husserl. That is, I cannot see that any textual correction, save one, could recover Saussure's or Husserl's doctrine: to the extent that it *is* logocentric, each fails; and, to the extent that either may be vindicated, it will prove not to have been logocentric in the first place.

The attack on Saussure exposes two supposed weaknesses: one, regarding the differential nature of language or any system of signs; the other, regarding the analysis of a meaningful sign as such. I confess I find Derrida's account rather creaky and interminable, but not mistaken. He sums up his judgments against Saussure in an opaque way that, on analysis, proves entirely transparent as well as valid: "Presence [he says] is a determination and effect within a system which is no longer that of presence but that of differance, it no more allows the opposition between activity and passivity than that between cause and effect or in-determination and determination, etc."[34] What Derrida means is that there is a profound *aporia* (perhaps not a formal contradiction) between Saussure's insistence that a speaking or signifying subject becomes such only by conforming with the prescriptions of that system, distinct from speech, that is language and Saussure's insistence that, even in thought, consciousness, interior monologue, there is no separation between sound and meaning, signifier and signified.

There is evidence that Derrida deforms Saussure's account so as to read him as if he were coming to terms with Husserl's inquiry regarding the interior 'now' of consciousness.[35] But, of course, Saussure is not discussing Husserl. Nevertheless, that is the point of Derrida's remark, in "Différance":

> What does 'consciouness' mean? Most often in the very form of meaning [*vouloir-dire*], consciousness in all of its modifications is conceivable only as self-presence, a self-perception of presence. And what holds for consciousness also holds here for what is called subjective existence in general...The privilege accorded to consciousness thus means a privilege accorded to the present; and even if the transcendental temporality of consciousness is described in depth, as Husserl described it, the power of synthesis and of the incessant gathering-up of traces is always accorded to the "living present".[36]

In context, this means that Derrida deconstructs a Husserlianized Saussure (just as, in other contexts, he deconstructs a Saussureanized Husserl). Saussure insists on the indissolubility of signifier and signified within the sign, whether the sign functions in public discourse or in interior thought. Derrida is aware of that; but the mention of the *vouloir-dire* is meant to remind us of the problem of the logocentric recovery of meaning and truth about meaning.

Saussure's entire argument opposes the divisibility of signifier and signified: "[language] is to act as intermediary between thought and sound, in such a way that the combination of both necessarily produces a mutually complementary delimitation of units."[37] That is, firstly, language is a differential system, there *are* no atomic elements from which the relationship between signifier and signified is composed: they are only *relata*, differentially specified within a system of differences. Secondly, this is as true of interior thought as of public discourse. Read this way, Derrida merely reiterates what Saussure finally says, but he deforms it to yield the logocentric puzzle he finds explicitly in Husserl (and believes he finds evidence of in Saussure—at least vestigially). Derrida insists on

> the absence of the referent or the transcendental signified. There is nothing outside of the text [there is no outside-text; *il n'y a pas de hors-texte*]... Although it is not commentary, our reading [of a text] must be intrinsic and remain within the text. That is why, in spite of certain appearances, the locating of the word *supplement* is here not at all psychoanalytical, if by that we understand an interpretation that takes us outside of the writing toward a psychobiographical signified, or even toward a general psychological structure that could rightly be separated from the signifier.
>
> [Nevertheless, although it is] in principle impossible to separate, through interpretation or commentary, the signified from the signifier...we...believe that this impossibility is historically articulated [as in psychoanalysis and phenomenology]."[38]

But this is pure Saussure, except that Saussure does not satisfy us on the matter of the subject—that is, the subject's *vouloir-dire*. The deconstruction risks ordinary textual validity in order to feature this deconstructively valid "textual" reading. Saussure blocks the idea that there could be a pre-linguistic correspondence between an external signifier and an internal signified that is the privilege of some "subject" aware of what he wants to say (*vouloir-dire*: mean). Today, we might rather say the self or subject is a cultural emergent, an artifact of having internalized natural-language practices. But, of course, what Derrida means to extract, deconstructively, is the failure of logocentrism to draw support from Saussure's system. *If* Saussure's own texts can be worried enough to locate the logocentric question among them as well, then the Derridean machinery will whir efficiently enough. (Derrida finds the telltale evidence in Lévi-Strauss.) But if it cannot be found there in any argumentative way, then, deconstructively again, the texts fail to address a question that they cannot ignore—which, if they had only addressed, they could not but have failed to treat satisfactorily.

Why is that? The answer, I think, concerns the matter of consciousness already cited: of *vouloir-dire*, in Derrida's pregnant phrasing. Once you agree that there is a subject that *veut-dire* something, anything, for which language is the external indication—signifier—you generate the hopeless logocentric puzzle. Did Saussure over mean to do that? The evidence is that he resists it, at least as far as contrasting public speech and interior thought is concerned. But in a way it doesn't matter—*if,* that is, you concede the license that deconstruction claims for itself.

The most temperate reading of Derrida's reading of Saussure requires the following concession: "writing" is meant, deconstructively, in a figurative way that disallows the usual oppositional use of written and spoken signs. The reason for insisting on this usage is that it enables us to grasp the ubiquity of the logocentric question; doing that enables us to expose the fact, both deconstructive and argumentative, that Saussure betrays his own awareness of the urgency and ineliminability of the question while, at the same time, he fails to address or resolve it. I think Derrida is right in this, but the noise produced ('noise' in the informational sense) in gaining his objective is deafening. His own noisiest critics, however, largely settle for textual corrections rather than direct answers to the logocentric question.

I offer one further citation from *Of Grammatology*, which, of all his books, most successfully harmonizes Derrida's deconstructive and argumentative objectives. Derrida himself signals the nature of the usual "zeal" with which he attacks Saussure: "my quarry [he says] is not primarily Ferdinand de Saussure's intention or motivation [in making the detailed distinctions he does], but rather the entire uncritical tradition which he inherits". That permits us, Derrida insists, to move effectively to "the assured means of broaching the deconstruction of *the greatest totality*—the concept of the *epistémè* and logocentric metaphysics—within which are produced, without ever posing the radical question of writing, all the Western methods of analysis, explication, reading, or interpretation".[39]

This plainly (even barefacedly) concedes the exploitative intention of the deconstructive mode. Nevertheless, in the same passage, titled "The Outside *is* the Inside," which confirms that "phonic" signs are also "written" signs (read deconstructively), the following more explicitly argumentative charge appears:

> Only those relationships between specific signifiers and signifieds in Saussure's account are regulated by arbitrariness. Within the "natural" relationship between phonic signifiers and their signifieds *in general*, the relationship between each determined signifier and its determined signified would be "arbitrary"…We must then conclude that only the signs called *natural*, those that Hegel and Saussure call "symbols," escape semiology as grammatology. But they fall a fortiori outside the field of linguistics as the region of general semiology.[40]

It is an extraordinary fact that, here, Derrida has raised a troubling question about the two obviously important concepts in Saussure's *Cours* that Saussure barely mentions: 'symbol', and 'natural'. As far as I can see, Saussure's pertinent discussion is pretty well restricted to the following single comment: "it is characteristic of symbols [Saussure says 'symbol' often designates "linguistic sign, or more exactly...signal"] that they are never entirely arbitrary. They are not empty configurations. They show at least a vestige of natural connection between the signal and its signification."[41]

Now, if this is conceded to be a sufficient basis for the deconstruction, then, I suggest, Derrida's philosophical question may be put quite straightforwardly. 'Writing' must be doubly equivocal in Derrida's argument: firstly, it signifies what is graphic as opposed to phonic—or, in Derrida's usage, indifferently graphic or phonic, that is, "inscribed," culturally instituted, as opposed to "natural". Secondly, 'writing', read in terms of the first distinction, may be applied either distributively or aggregatively—where, as Derrida concedes in the textual sense, Saussure's preoccupation is with the first sort of application and his own queries about Saussure's system is with the second (or "totalizing") option. If he has succeeded in this, then, with whatever extravagance, he *has* recovered the logocentric issue at Saussure's expense.

V

The procedure is reversed for Husserl. Nevertheless, in his clever way, Derrida implicates Saussure even where he does not mention him. He puts before us (but does not yet answer) the question, "*What* is the sign in general?"

> May we not think [he continues]—Husserl no doubt did—that if one considers the sign as the structure of an intentional movement [*bedeuten, vouloir-dire*], it does not fall under the category of a thing in general (*Sache*), it is not a "being" whose own being would be questioned?...In affirming that "logical meaning" (*Bedeutung*) is an expression, that there is theoretical truth only in a statement, in resolutely concerning himself with linguistic expression as the possibility of truth and in not presupposing the essential unity of the sign, Husserl might seem to reverse the traditional procedure and, in the activity of signification, attend to what—although it has no truth in itself—conditions the movement and concept of truth. Along a whole itinerary which ends in *The Origin of Geometry*, Husserl will accord a growing attention to that which, in signification, in language, and in inscription, deposits [*consigne*] ideal objectivity, *produces* truth or ideality, rather than simply *records* it."[42]

Derrida therefore insinuates that, for Husserl, there must be a disjunction between signifier and signified; raises the question—ultimately, the logocentric question—of what we should mean by truth, particularly truth with respect to *vouloir-dire*; and hints at the special problems the Husserlian subject imposes on the question of logocentric truth ("producing" rather than "recording" truth). (I take the phrasing, "what is the sign in general?" to anticipate the phrasing of the passage regarding the "symbol" cited from Saussure.)

Difficulties arise at once. I will not be able to do full justice to them, however, if I do not draw a particular lesson from the Saussurean material. I have tried to show that, although Derrida is often highhanded in his reading of Saussure, possibly even inaccurate in certain details, possibly even unwilling to be confined to "small" accuracies, he is not simply wrong in his deconstructive play. Characteristically, he returns somewhere in his own text to give evidence both that he *is* accurate about textual details when it suits him, and telegraphically "inaccurate" when the would-be argument might otherwise be discounted on that score. What we find is that, admitting the logocentric question to be a bona fide philosophical concern, Derrida worries the actual Saussurean text so that it becomes a natural space for forms of the logocentric issue. Once that ground is gained, Derrida becomes increasingly exuberant and content with the viral play of freewheeling deconstruction.

The maneuver by which '*vouloir-dire*', for instance, is made to signify consciousness—in Saussure, and then in Husserl—is apt enough, in Derrida's view, to range over both communicative intent (the standard sense), and a certain reflexive awareness or thought, without specific communicative intent. You may not care for the verbal economy; you may even think it misleading. But what Derrida is insisting on (not demonstrating) is that thinking is primarily or paradigmatically linguistic or lingually informed. That, in fact, is very close to Saussure's own intention: it is the very meaning of the relational nature of signifier and signified viewed as the inseparable function of an integral sign, suitable as much for thought as for public speech. Saussure also indicates (very briefly), in his remarks about values and the arbitrary, that *langue* has a social structure and is socially inculcated.[43]

Derrida often, though not always, favors some inadvertence or marginal concession in the texts he deconstructs, which he then makes disproportionately important ("natural" symbols, for instance); he often construes substantive distinctions, where unwanted or not fully relevant, in a figurative way so as to weaken their resistance ("graphic" and "phonic"); and, where he finds an author to have endorsed some palpable form of logocentrism (Saussure or Husserl, obviously) or to have neglected its threat, Derrida tends to ride roughshod over other would-be details of textual accuracy. But, as I say, he nearly always advertises the fact. So it is not quite enough to defeat him to remind us of the mere "inaccuracies". The counterargument must also show that the logocentric charge either does not hold at all or is successfully met when applied to arguments informed by its would-be deconstruction.

The question of the fairness of Derrida's strategy cannot be avoided in Husserl's case. It is, for instance, essential to Claude Evans's careful examination of Derrida's "arguments" against Husserl in the light of Husserl's texts. There can be no doubt that the same uneasiness about textual accuracy appears in spades in following Derrida on Husserl. But I am not convinced that Derrida does not squeak by—even more than squeak by.

Consider this: it is one of Evans's principal concerns. Derrida explicitly translates Husserl's key term *'bedeuten'* as *'vouloir-dire'*. We have already seen how, in "Différance", Derrida brings Saussure and Husserl together in terms of *'vouloir-dire'* construed as self-presence or consciousness. Doing that obliges us to address the logocentric issue at once. Is Derrida fair, in a textual way? Evans objects, championing Husserl against Derrida. *"Vouloir-dire"*, he says, captures "communicative intent." "But Husserl [he goes on] is not really interested in giving a Gricean-style analysis at this point [in the *Logical Investigations*], though he has many of the elements required. He is concerned with formal logic, not with the pragmatics of communication."[44]

This is an extremely complex charge—one, I feel, that cannot be quite right or altogether successfully defended. For one thing, Husserl explicitly says

> Expressions [*Ausdrücke*] were originally framed to fulfil a communicative function...The articulate sound-complex, the written sign etc., first becomes a spoken word or communicative bit of speech, when a speaker produces it with the intention of "expressing himself about something" through its means; he must endow it with a sense in certain acts of mind, a sense he desires to share with his auditors...If one surveys these interconnections [in public discourse], one sees at once that all expressions in *communicative* speech function as *indications* [*Anzeichen*]."[45]

Surely, *'vouloir-dire' is* the right translation. Furthermore, just prior to this passage, Husserl indicates that he wishes to use the term "expression" to range over "each instance or part of *speech*, as also each sign that is essentially of the same sort...whether or not such speech is actually uttered, or addressed with communicative intent to any persons or not"—always excluding "facial expressions" and the like that "are not phenomenally one with the experiences made manifest in them in the consciousness of the man who manifests them, as is the case with speech." Husserl expressly notes that this verbal extension, though needed, does "violence to usage."[46] Husserl plainly means to cover inner thought, that is, languaged thought. If anything is true, therefore, Derrida follows Husserl's usage rather than opposes it, just as he follows Saussure's about signs rather than opposes it. So far, so good.

Now, what is even more interesting is that *Evans's* demurrer in Husserl's behalf—regarding logic and inner thought—hangs in the balance: because, on Derrida's view, Husserl's view cannot but be logocentric. Evans claims that

Derrida misreads Husserl's *Ideas* §124, where Husserl introduces a perspicuous distinction between the usual use of *Bedeutung* and *Sinn* ("in its more embracing breadth of application"). The point of Husserl's reflection is evidently meant to accommodate the extension of "meaning" to (noetic) "acts" that are not "interwoven" [*verflochten*] with language (or "expressions"):

> We restrict our glance exclusively to "meaning" [says Husserl], and "meaning something" (*Bedeuten*). Originally these words relate only to the sphere of speech, that of "expression." But it is almost inevitable, and at the same time an important step for knowledge, to extend the meaning of these words, and to modify them suitably so that they may be applied in a certain way to the whole noetico-noematic sphere, to all acts, therefore, whether these are interwoven with expressive acts or not.[47]

Husserl offers as an example of what he means, "the plain perceptual grasp of a thing" (something that, without the "interweaving" of language, might capture the "sense" of what was perceived, say, "following some such scheme as 'This is white'"), where

> the process makes no call whatsoever on "expression", neither on expression in the sense of verbal sound nor on the like as verbal meaning...But if we have "*thought*" or *stated* 'This is white', a new stratum is there with the rest, and unites with the "meant as such" in its pure perceptual form..Whatever is "meant as such", every meaning (*Meinung*) in the noematic sense (and indeed as noematic nucleus) of any act whatsoever *can be expressed conceptually (durch "Bedeutungen")*.[48]

Evans is certainly right to hold that, for Husserl, although "some judgments may be dependent on linguistic expression for pragmatic reasons...this by no means indicates that thought *essentially* moves in the medium of language."[49] But, of course, *Derrida* knows this, opposes it *deconstructively*—which, then, on *his* practice, takes precedence over mere "accuracy", already sufficiently conceded. Furthermore, when *Husserl* states:

> All theoretical research, though by no means solely conducted in acts of verbal expression or complete statement, none the less terminates in such statement. Only in this form can truth, and in particular the truth of theory, become an abiding possession of science, a documented, ever available treasure for knowledge and advancing research. Whatever the connection of thought with speech may be, whether or not the appearance of our final judgments in the form of verbal pronouncements has a necessary grounding in essence, it is at least plain that judgments stemming from higher intellectual regions, and in particular from the regions of science, could barely arise without verbal expression[50]

Evans is obliged to say (which he somehow supposes counts against Derrida) that *Husserl* is not "willing" to go beyond the point of acknowledging a "pragmatic" or instrumental connection between language and thought: "the

phenomenology of linguistic forms cannot replace the phenomenology of mean-
ing-experiences, the phenomenology of thought".[51] He will say no more. Fair
enough. But what *is* the connection between thought and language? That, after
all, is Derrida's question. If one considers, for instance along Wittgensteinian or
Peircean lines, that predicables are inseparable from actual linguistic practices,
then the depth of Husserl's logocentric presumption becomes entirely clear.
Derrida, I say, is quite right to raise the question—and to refuse to allow lesser
questions of "accuracy" to deflect him from insisting on an answer. As far as I
can see, there is no way to prise language and thought apart (which is not to say
there is no sense in speaking of thought that is not linguistic: such thought is
parasitically posited on the strength of the linguistic exemplars).[52] Frankly,
Derrida seems to me to win hands down. Or, at the very least, he has forced a
question on us that has never been satisfactorily answered in the logocentric
manner.

But, as I say, the matter is more complex. My sense of the deeper issue,
which I have yet to put before you, depends on a conjecture I find reasonable
but cannot hope to confirm. Husserl, as we have seen, distinguishes between
two sorts of signs; at the very start of the *First Investigation*, he offers the following well-known remark:

> Every sign is a sign for something, but not every sign has "meaning," a "sense" that
> the sign "expresses"...For signs in the sense of indications (notes, marks etc.) *do
> not express* anything, unless they happen to fulfill a significant as well as an indica-
> tive function...To mean is *not a particular way of being a sign in the sense of indi-
> cating something.*[53]

My conjecture is this. In opposing Husserl's account of signs, Derrida construes the connection between indicative and expressive signs—loosely, then,
but not exactly, the functional roles of indicative and expressive signs as well—
in accord with the precise sense in which he construes the connection between
the signifier and signified taken as *relata* within Saussure's integral sign; and
then he reads the "connection" (the deconstruction of Husserl's "*verflochten*")
implicitly in a way more or less analogous to the point of the Wittgensteinian
argument against private languages.[54]

The question has been raised about whether '*verflochten*' should be read as
(contingently) 'interwoven' (hence separable: Evans's reading) or as (essentially) 'entangled' (Derrida's). The answer may appease no one. For Husserl, the
two functions—the same sign may function indicatively and expressively—are
essentially "entangled" in communicative contexts, but are only "intertwined"
in "isolated" thought: "*Expressions* function meaningfully even in *isolated mental life, where they no longer serve to indicate anything.* The two notions of sign
do not therefore really stand in the relation of more extensive genus to narrower

species": "all expressions in *communicative* speech function as *indicating*."[55] Derrida admits the point, though he overrides it, deconstructively, in favoring the "entangled" to the "interwoven" sense of "*verflochten*". Clearly, on textual grounds, the two functions of signs Husserl admits are not isomorphic with the two functions Saussure admits: Derrida nowhere insists that they are.

What he features rather (if I read him right) is this: textually, the Husserlian "connection" obtains in communication but not in thought; deconstructively, it is not convincingly shown by *Husserl* that the "indicative" function, or something analogous to it (putatively confined to "isolated mental life"), is not necessary or essential to the expressive function, in Husserl's own account. In that sense, Saussure's and Husserl's difficulties are, logocentrically, the same. What Derrida shows, therefore, is:

1. that Saussure, having extended the indissolubly relational account of signifier and signified to thought as well as speech, betrays a worry about "natural" symbols, the nonconventional sense in which language captures the "presence" of reality or intended meaning; and

2. that Husserl, having separated the functions of indicative and expressive signs in thought as opposed to communicative speech, neglects to explain how that is possible (reading "indicative" of course generously enough to cover not only communicative intent but also the possibility of intelligibly communicating what may be thought "in isolated mental life").

This is the ultimate difficulty of Husserl's account. Husserl worries the point in §8 of the *First Investigation*. Perhaps the following remark will convince you of the reasonableness of Derrida's insistence and the distinctly lame quality of Husserl's explicit text (I can afford no more evidence):

> But expressions also play a great part in uncommunicated, interior mental life... Expressions continue to have meanings as they had before in communicative contexts, and the same meanings as in dialogue. A word only ceases to be a word when our interest stops at its sensory contour, when it becomes a mere sound-pattern. But when we live in the understanding of a word, it expresses something and the same thing, whether we address it to anyone or not.
>
> It seems clear, therefore, that an expression's meaning, and whatever else pertains to it essentially, cannot coincide with its feats of intimation [which "consists simply in the fact that the hearer *intuitively* takes the speaker to be a person who is expressing this or that"]. Shall one say that in soliloquy one speaks to oneself, and employs words as signs, i.e. as indicators, of one's own inner experiences? I cannot think such a view acceptable...In a monologue words can perform no function of indicating the existence of mental acts, since such indication would there be quite purposeless. For the acts in question are themselves experienced by us at that very moment.[56]

Apparently, *meanings* in thought and speech can remain the same; meanings "intended" in "isolated mental life" can be the same as those "indicated" by words in communicative contexts; and this "ideal" identity does not depend in any "essential" way on the "intimating" function of words even with respect to interior thought. How this is possible, Husserl does not satisfactorily explain. The rest of the passage is noticeably murky; reference is made to "imagined verbal sound" and "imagined printed word": "in imagination a spoken or printed word floats before us, though in reality it has no existence".[57] Derrida's "inaccuracy" about indicative and expressive signs is a deliberate deconstructive semaphor for that unresolved difficulty in Husserl's thesis.

It is extraordinary that one should attempt to disqualify Derrida's deconstructive challenge to Husserl's account of the connection between expressive signs and language ("inaccurately" rendered, for maximal deconstructive effect, as "indications"—assimilating Husserl's distinction to Saussure's) by insisting on the literal sense of Husserl's terms, when it is apparent that *that* usage betrays the force of the very question Derrida raises and when it is also apparent that Derrida gives evidence that he is aware of the usage and *means* to deform it for his own unflattering purpose. I agree it is a somewhat tiresome exercise. But when I am confronted with the counterstrategy, I cannot be sure. Perhaps Derrida understands something important about the nature of academic debate. (It is, you remember, what is at stake in the supposed pedogogic dangers of deconstruction.) What I find disquieting in Derrida is that he should spend so much time on the deconstructive work and leave the argumentative treatment of his substantive question in the lurch.

Having said that, let me hasten to add that Derrida *does* offer arguments against Husserl's thesis, which Husserl's champions have either not fully grasped or not answered. They appear principally, but not exclusively, in the *Introduction to Husserl's Origin of Geometry*, and they bear on the connection between expressive and communicative signs. Unfortunately, they are even more complicated than the puzzles already examined, because they presuppose them and go on. I shall have to make a very brief account of Derrida's principal argument in order to bring the discussion to a reasonable close.

In effect, Derrida (I say) offers Husserl an indigestible dilemma: either the recovery of the "meaning-origin" of geometry depends essentially on the contingent history of geometry, in which case, the separability of expressive and indicative—better: linguistic—signs cannot be sustained and the "ideal objects" of geometry cannot be separated from the "natural objects" of geometry's actual history; or, by "history" is meant the recovery, phenomenologically, "in isolated mental life", only of the "meaning-origin" of just those "ideal objects" (in which case, the question of the "connection" between the "natural" and the "ideal" remains as problematic as before). I take this dilemma to be implied in

the following remark of Derrida's, though it is not explicated thus and though
Derrida is careful not to attribute the first option to Husserl in any serious ("textual") way:

> Since every ideal objectivity is produced by an act of a concrete consciousness (the
> only starting point for a transcendental phenomenology), every ideal objectivity has
> a history which is always already announced in that consciousness, even if we know
> nothing of its determined content.[58]

Derrida goes on to make it clear that Husserl generally distinguishes
between the history of geometry and the science of geometry. So there cannot
be any question of Derrida's misunderstanding (or failing to respect) what
Husserl normally means to *say*. Nevertheless, earlier in his text, Derrida makes
the following important and pregnant observation: "when, in the period of the
Crisis [*The Crisis of European Sciences and Transcendental Phenomenology*],
history itself breaks through into phenomenology, a new space of questioning is
opened, one that will be difficult to maintain in the regional limits which were
so long prescribed for it. While constantly *practised* in the *Crisis* itself, the new
access to history is never *made a problem*."[59]

Rightly read, this does not mean that Husserl reversed himself in the *Crisis*.
He did not. Certainly, in Appendix VI ("The Origin of Geometry"), Husserl
maintains the indicated distinction. At the very start of the essay, for instance,
he plainly says:

> We must focus our gaze not merely upon the ready-made, handed-down geometry
> and upon the manner of being which its meaning had in Galileo's thinking...Rather,
> indeed above all, we must also inquire back into the original meaning of the hand-
> ed-down geometry, which continued to be valid with this very same meaning—
> [hence] our problems and expositions concerning Galilean geometry take on an
> exemplary significance.[60]

A few lines later, Husserl strengthens the thesis:

> geometry must have arisen out of a *first* acquisition, out of first creative activities.
> We understand its persisting manner of being: it is not only a mobile forward pro-
> cess from one set of acquisitions to another but a continuous synthesis in which all
> acquisitions maintain their validity, all make up a totality such that, at every present
> stage, the total acquisition is, so to speak, the total premise for the acquisitions of
> the new level...The same thing is true of every science.[61]

This is certainly an eminently deconstructible thesis.

What Derrida focuses for us here is, once again, the problem of the connection between the two kinds of sign-function, now deepened by the deepened
role of history and the deepened role of expressive signs, even though the phenomenological recovery of the "origin" of geometry is the ideally iterable

recovery ("historical", in a curious but not negligible sense: Derrida's sense of the phenomenological "history") of the "meaning" of the historically (actually, contingently) "handed-down" Galilean geometry. That poses an unanswered problem, Derrida says, and he is right. It is because of the essential relevance of the indicative signs for the recovery of the ideal objectivity of geometry— which, presumably, does not depend upon them, but rather informs them first— through "internal historicity", through which, as Derrida says, "I actively re-produce the primordial evidence", that the "entanglement" of the two sorts of function seems insuperable.[62] "If", asks Derrida, "writing is *both* a factual event and the upsurging of sense, if it is both *Körper* and *Leib*, how would writing preserve its *Leiblichkeit* from corporeal disaster?"[63] How are "internal" and "external" history connected? After all, "the Outside ⇥ the Inside"!

Joseph Margolis

Temple University
Philadelphia, PA 19122

NOTES

1.   In Britain, the issue was focused by a heated public controversy about the proposal at Cambridge University to award Derrida an honorary degree. The matter was decided in Derrida's favor, but not before a rather pointed letter was published in *The Times* (9 May 1992) by Barry Smith and a longish list of well-known philosophers who opposed Derrida's candidacy on the two counts mentioned. See the *Cambridge Review* (October 1992), which contains an interview with Derrida and the text of the letter. I would not have signed the letter if asked. This essay will partly explain why. In the United States, it has been charged in various wild as well as temperate ways that Derrida is a philosophical anarchist and that the favorable reception of Derridean "methods" has somehow made its way into the seeming legitimation of relativism, "multiculturalism", and "political correctness" that threaten the American academy. This latter concern was, for instance, part of the motivation for a recent conference—of high quality and distinct scruple—"European Philosophy and the American Academy", sponsored by The Hegeler Institute as a Monist Colloquium and held at Wingspread in Racine, Wisconsin, from February 11-14, 1993. Three of the participants were signatories of the letter to *The Times*. My own assessment of this event is that neither of the charges mentioned were sustained, though a good deal of criticism of Derrida's work and the opportunistic use of his methods were indeed fairly developed and justified. The linkage between Derrida and "multiculturalism" may be roughly discerned from a recent paper by John R. Searle, "Is There a Crisis in American Higher Education?" *Bulletin: The American Academy of Arts and Sciences* XLVI (January 1993), which mentions deconstruction (but not, I think,

Derrida by name) and associates deconstruction with the attack on "realism" (in the manner of T.S. Kuhn and Richard Rorty).

2. The remark appears in Dallas Willard, "The Unhinging of the American Mind". Willard is a temperate critic, I should say.

3. Derrida, *Speech and Phenomena*, p. 66, and Norris, *What's Wrong with Postmodernism*, p. 150. Both remarks are cited by Willard.

4. Derrida, *Edmund Husserl's Origin of Geometry*.

5. See, for instance, Mulligan, "How Not to Read", which clearly converges with Willard's criticism of Derrida. The article appears in a number (*topos*) of *Topoi* titled "Continental Philosophy Analysed", which Mulligan edited.

6. See Rorty, "Is Derrida a Transcendental Philosopher?", and "Deconstruction and Circumvention".

7. I have taken these bits of Willard's view from the original draft of his paper that circulated in advance of the Monist conference mentioned in Note 1.

8. Derrida, *Of Grammatology*, p. 158.

9. Norris, *Derrida*, pp. 94-95. Compare Derrida, *Of Grammatology*, p. 27, which is cited by Norris. See also Gasché, *The Tain of the Mirror*. For a sense of the opposed reading, see Rorty, "Is Derrida a Transcendental Philosopher?", and Hartman, *Saving the Text*.

10. See Lévi-Strauss, *Tristes Tropiques,* Chapter 28.

11. See Rorty, "Philosophy as a Kind of Writing: An Essay on Derrida".

12. Derrida, *Of Grammatology*, p. 27.

13. See the introduction to Evans, *Strategies of Deconstruction*, particularly the summary of an unpublished paper by John Scanlon.

14. See the whole of Ch. 4 of Norris's *Derrida*.

15. Derrida, *Of Grammatology*, pp. 60–61.

16. Derrida, *Of Grammatology*, p. 60.

17. For an excellent clarification, see Pavel, *The Feud of Language*, pp. 43–73.

18. Derrida, *Of Grammatology*, p. 60, and "Différance", p. 3.

19. Derrida, "Différance", p. 6.

20. Evans, *Strategies of Deconstruction*, p. xix, citing Heidegger, *Being and Time*, pp. 21–23 (translation modified).

21. Evans, *Strategies of Deconstruction*, p. xix.

22. Frank, "Is Self-Consciousness a Case of *présence à soi*?", p. 225.

23. Frank, "Is Self-Consciousness a Case of *présence à soi*?", p. 219. The reference to Heidegger is to *Basic Problems of Phenomenology*, p. 15.

24. Evans, *Strategies of Deconstruction*, p. xix.

25. Derrida, "'Genesis and Structure' and Phenomenology".

26. Derrida, "Implications", pp. 4–5

27. Leavey, Jr., "Undecidables and Old Names", pp. 1, 19.

28. Derrida, *Speech and Phenomena*, p. 82.

29. Derrida, *Speech and Phenomena*, p. 88.

30. See Evans, *Strategies of Deconstruction*, pp. 119–120, 172. Evans draws a harsh conclusion (p. 172). The matter depends on Derrida's having construed a thesis offered

in de Muralt's *The Idea of Phenomenology* one way in the *Introduction* and (apparently) the reverse way in *Speech and Phenomena*. This is not altogether clear, but Evans concludes: "This flip-flopping of position without any attempt to give a reason for the change might be a clue that this piece of writing Chapter 6, presumably, of *Speech and Phenomena* is not to be taken seriously in any straightforward sense" (p. 172). Of course, what Derrida has already said in favor of deconstruction makes the mention of "straightforward sense" a bit suspect.

31. Derrida, *Of Grammatology*, pp. 7–8, 324n2. Gayatri Spivak treats *Of Grammatology* as being somewhat later than *Speech and Phenomena*.

32. Derrida, *Of Grammatology*, pp. 3, 7-8.

33. Derrida, "Plato's Pharmacy" and *Glas*.

34. Derrida, *Speech and Phenomena*, p. 147.

35. This marks the connection between the essay "Différance" and the reference, in *Speech and Phenomena*, to Husserl's *The Phenomenology of Internal Time-Consciousness*. See particularly Ch. 5.

36. Derrida, "Différance", p. 147.

37. de Saussure, *Course in General Linguistics*, p. 110; see also p. 111.

38. Derrida, *Of Grammatology*, pp. 158–159.

39. Derrida, *Of Grammatology*, pp. 46, 47.

40. Derrida, *Of Grammatology*, pp. 44–45.

41. de Saussure, *Course in General Linguistics*, p. 68.

42. Derrida, *Speech and Phenomena*, pp. 24–25.

43. de Saussure, *Course in General Linguistics*, pp. 68, 112–114.

44. Evans, *Strategies of Deconstruction*, p. 29; Derrida, *Speech and Phenomena*, p. 18.

45. Husserl, *Logical Investigations* vol. I, pp. 276–277. Evans mentions the general passage but, unaccountably, does not really acknowledge the aptness of Derrida's reading.

46. Husserl, *Logical Investigations* vol. I, p. 275.

47. Husserl, *Ideas*, §124, p. 319. Derrida discusses the text in *Speech and Phenomena*, Ch. 1; Evans's objections appear in *Strategies of Deconstruction*, Ch. 2. Also, Husserl warns us of the liberty he himself takes in speaking of mental "acts" (Fifth Investigation, p. 563).

48. Husserl, *Ideas*, pp. 319–320.

49. Evans, *Strategies of Deconstruction*, p. 31. See, further, Husserl, *Logical Investigations*, p. 250. Husserl evidently has J.S. Mill's view in mind.

50. Husserl, *Logical Investigations*, p. 250 (mentioned also by Evans).

51. Evans, *Strategies of Deconstruction*, p. 32.

52. See my "The Passing of Peirce's Realism".

53. Husserl, *Logical Investigations*, p. 169.

54. Evans spends quite a lot of time questioning Derrida's translation of Husserl's verb; see *Strategies of Deconstruction*, pp. 32–36. On the private language issue, see Wittgenstein, *Philosophical Investigations*, including (at least) §§243–274.

55. Husserl, *Logical Investigations*, pp. 269, 277.

56. Husserl, *Logical Investigations*, pp. 278–280.
57. Husserl, *Logical Investigations*, p. 279.
58. Derrida, *Edmund Husserl's Origin of Geometry*, p. 42.
59. Derrida, *Edmund Husserl's Origin of Geometry*, p. 29.
60. Edmund Husserl, "The Origin of Geometry", p. 353.
61. Husserl, "The Origin of Geometry", p. 355.
62. This does not quite do justice to Husserl's view of arithmetic, which depends on the fortunate contingencies of having hit on a fruitful notation.
63. Derrida, *Edmund Husserl's Origin of Geometry*, pp. 97, 99, in the context of pp. 94-107.

*

I have benefited from a close reading of this paper by my friend and colleague, Newton Garver.

REFERENCES

Jacques Derrida, "Différance", in Derrida, *Margins of Philosophy.*
——, *Dissemination*, tr. Barbara Johnson, Chicago: University of Chicago Press 1981.
——, " 'Genesis and Structure' and Phenomenology", in Derrida, *Writing and Difference.*
——, *Glas*, tr. John P. Leavey, Jr. and Richard Rand, Lincoln: University of Nebraska Press, 1986.
——, *Of Grammatology*, tr. Gayatri Chakravorty Spivak, Baltimore: Johns Hopkins University Press 1976.
——, *Edmund Husserl's Origin of Geometry: An Introduction*, tr. John P. Leavey, Jr., ed. David B. Allison, Stony Brook: Nicolas Hays 1978.
——, "Implications" (an interview with Henri Ronse), in Derrida, *Positions.*
——, *Margins of Philosophy*, tr. Alan Bass (Chicago: University of Chicago Press 1982.
——, *Positions,* tr. Alan Bass, Chicago: University of Chicago Press 1981.
——, "Plato's Pharmacy", in Derrida, *Dissemination.*
——, *Speech and Phenomena*, tr. David B. Allison, Evanston: Northwestern University Press 1973.
——, *Writing and Difference*, tr. Alan Bass, Chicago: University of Chicago Press 1978.
J. Claude Evans, *Strategies of Deconstruction: Derrida and the Myth of the Voice*, Minneapolis: University of Minnesota Press 1992.

Manfred Frank, "Is Self-Consciousness a Case of *présence à soi*? Towards a Meta-Critique of the Recent French Critique of Metaphysics", in Wood (ed.), *Derrida: A Critical Reader.*

Rodolphe Gasché, *The Tain of the Mirror,* Baltimore: Johns Hopkins University Press 1986.

Geoffrey Hartman, *Saving the Text,* Baltimore: Johns Hopkins University Press 1981.

Martin Heidegger, *Basic Problems of Phenomenology,* tr. Albert Hofstadter, Indianapolis: Indiana University Press 1972, p. 15.

——, *Being and Time,* tr. John Macquarrie and Edward Robinson, New York: Harper and Row 1962.

Edmund Husserl, *The Crisis of European Sciences and Transcendental Phenomenology,* tr. David Carr, Evanston: Northwestern University Press 1970.

——, *Ideas: General Introduction to Pure Phenomenology,* tr. W.R. Boyce GIbson, New York: Collier Books 1962.

——, *Logical Investigations,* tr. J.N. Findlay, London: Routledge and Kegan Paul 1970.

——, "The Origin of Geometry", Appendix VI of Husserl, *The Crisis of European Sciences.*

——, *The Phenomenology of Internal Time-Consciousness,* tr. James S. Churchill, Bloomington: Indiana University Press 1964.

John P. Leavey, Jr., "Undecidables and Old Names", the preface to Derrida, *Edmund Husserl's The Origin of Geometry.*

Claude Lévi-Strauss, *Tristres Tropiques,* tr. John and Doreen Weightman, New York: Atheneum 1974.

Joseph Margolis, "The Passing of Peirce's Realism", *Transactions of the Charles S. Peirce Society* xxix (1993).

Kevin Mulligan, "How Not to Read: Derrida on Husserl", *Topoi* X (1991).

André de Muralt, *The Idea of Phenomenology: Husserlian Exemplarism,* Evanston: Northwestern University Press 1974.

Christopher Norris, *Derrida,* London: Fontana 1987.

——, *What's Wrong with Postmodernism: Critical Theory and the Ends of Philosophy,* Baltimore: Johns Hopkins University Press 1990.

Thomas Pavel, *The Feud of Language: A History of Structuralist Thought,* Oxford: Blackwell 1992.

Richard Rorty, "Deconstruction and Circumvention", *Critical Inquiry* XI (1984).

——, "Is Derrida a Transcendental Philosopher?" *Yale Journal of Criticism* II (1989). Reprinted in Wood (ed.), *Derrida: A Critical Reader.*

——, "Philosophy as a Kind of Writing: An Essay on Derrida", in Rorty, *Consequences of Pragmatism*, Minneapolis: University of Minnesota Press, 1982.

Ferdinand de Saussure, *Course in General Linguistics*, trans. Roy Harris, La Salle: Open Court 1986.

Dallas Willard, "The Unhinging of the American Mind: Derrida as Pretext", this volume.

Ludwig Wittgenstein, *Philosophical Investigations*, tr. G.E.M. Anscombe, New York: Macmillan 1953.

David Wood (ed.), *Derrida: A Critical Reader*, Oxford: Blackwell 1992.